Clintonomics

How Bill Clinton Reengineered the Reagan Revolution

JACK GODWIN

AMACOM

American Management Association

NEW YORK • ATLANTA • BRUSSELS • CHICAGO • MEXICO CITY • SAN FRANCISCO
SHANGHAI • TOKYO • TORONTO • WASHINGTON, D.C.

Special discounts on bulk quantities of AMACOM books are available
to corporations, professional associations, and other organizations. For
details, contact Special Sales Department, AMACOM, a division of
American Management Association, 1601 Broadway, New York,
NY 10019.
Tel: 212-903-8316. Fax: 212-903-8083.
E-mail: specialsls@amanet.org
Website: www.amacombooks.org/go/specialsales
To view all AMACOM titles go to: www.amacombooks.org

This publication is designed to provide accurate and authoritative information
in regard to the subject matter covered. It is sold with the understanding that
the publisher is not engaged in rendering legal, accounting, or other professional
service. If legal advice or other expert assistance is required, the services of a
competent professional person should be sought.

Library of Congress Cataloging-in-Publication Data

Godwin, Jack.
    Clintonomics : how Bill Clinton reengineered the Reagan revolution /
Jack Godwin.—1st ed.
        p.   cm.
    Includes bibliographical references and index.
    ISBN-13: 978-0-8144-1398-2
    ISBN-10: 0-8144-1398-6
        1. United States—Economic policy—1993-2001.   2. Clinton, Bill,
    1946-   I. Title.

    HC106.82.G63   2009
    330.973'0929—dc22

                                                        2008052674

Printing number

10   9   8   7   6   5   4   3   2   1

To my seven magnificent colleagues in the
Office of Global Education:
Eric, Janis, Jennifer, Lori, Mlima, Monica, and Tracey

Contents

Foreword by John Garamendi

My wife Patti keeps a plaque on her desk that says there is no limit to what can be accomplished, if you don't mind who gets the credit. When Patti and I began our careers in public service as Peace Corps volunteers in Ethiopia thirty years ago, she taught me always to work for peace and justice, no matter what the odds. If we roll up our sleeves and just keep rowing our little boat, she said, eventually we'd reach that distant shore.

One hundred years ago, my grandfather, Jose Santorino Garamendi, left the Basque Country of Northern Spain to start a new life in America. When he left his homeland behind, he carried with him little more than a dream; but it was a powerful dream, one he shared with millions of other immigrants who came to America. His dream was not only for his own good fortune but also for his children and grandchildren. After disembarking at Ellis Island, he made his way west to California, learned a new language, worked at many jobs, and overcame many hardships. My grandfather took greatest pride not in his own achievements but those of his two children who each went to college, started families of their own, and pursued dreams of their own.

Now as I look at my own nine grandchildren, I feel the same sense of pride, but I wonder if our generation has done enough to ensure they will have the same opportunities Patti and I and our children have had. I have confidence that future generations will overcome whatever hardships they face, but sometimes I wonder how future generations will judge us. At this moment in our history, I believe we have every reason to be optimistic about the future. There's a reason for my optimism. I have seen the incredible resilience and determination Americans and Californians can muster if we are told the truth, are given rational solutions, and are guided by responsible leadership.

Since 1978, I have devoted myself to environmental issues, beginning with my authorship of California's first tax credit law for conservation, solar, and wind energy systems. In 1995, President Bill Clinton asked me to serve in the US Department of the Interior, the cabinet department in charge of national parks, Native American affairs, conservation of wildlife and natural resources, and management of federally owned land. As Deputy Secretary, which is the number two position in the department, I negotiated the Headwaters Forest Agreement to protect a series of old-growth redwood groves. I conducted the Cal-Fed water negotiations to protect our water supply and to ensure efficient use of water resources for the people of California, our farmers and our economy. I worked with Vice President Al Gore to prepare the American agenda for the Kyoto Climate Change Conference, advanced protection of our national parks system, negotiated the largest habitat conservation plan in the Western States, and put a stop to the practice of dumping nuclear waste in the California desert.

California is one of the world's largest economies and a leader for many years in environmental protection. California often serves as a bellwether for the rest of the nation, in politics, technological innovation, or cultural change. Unfortunately, we are also a leader in causing ecological damage to our environment, ranking ninth in greenhouse gas emissions and ranking second only to the US in gasoline consumption. What impact is this having on our environment? According to the *California Climate Change Center Report* of 2006, we have the worst air quality in the US; and more than 90 percent of the population lives in areas that violate the state's air quality standards.[1]

---

[1] *Economic Growth and Greenhouse Gas Mitigation in California*, David Roland-Holst, California Climate Change Center, University of California, Berkeley, August 16, 2006.

If we continue to consume gasoline and produce greenhouse gasses at the current rate, the risk of large, destructive wildfires in California will almost certainly worsen. Rising temperatures will shrink our annual mountain snow pack in the Sierra Nevada Mountains, drastically reducing the primary source of California's water supply. Rising sea levels and the inland flow of seawater will alter the delicate balance of the Sacramento-San Joaquin Delta as well as other wetlands and ecosystems. Rising temperatures will hurt agricultural production, most likely in critical industries such as wine grape production, other fruits, and the dairy industry. For the sake of national security and future generations, we must increase our investment to discover alternative, renewable sources of energy and develop the infrastructure for efficient delivery to the marketplace. We must reduce our dependence on oil, particularly foreign oil purchased from the most oppressive and politically unstable countries in the world. The solution to these interrelated problems—climate change, resource conservation, economic security, and national security—depends on technological innovation. This brings us to education.

Fortunately, our predecessors saw the wisdom of public education and chartered the University of California in 1868. From the oldest campus in Berkeley (my alma mater) to the newest campus in Merced, the University of California (UC) system has become the greatest public university in the world and a catalyst for economic growth. Researchers everywhere in the UC system are pioneers in science, technology and medicine, and responsible for thousands of jobs and billions of dollars in revenues. The UC system is a key element in California's Master Plan for Higher Education, which also formally established the California State University (CSU) system and the California Community College system. Along with the state's excellent private universities such as Stanford, the California Institute of Technology and the University of Southern California, the Master Plan demonstrates the state's long-term commitment to higher education.

As Lieutenant Governor of California, I serve as a Regent of the University of California and a Trustee of the California State University. One of my top priorities has been to focus on the role our educational system plays in workforce and economic development. The CSU system catapults students whose parents never dreamed of going to college into careers as teachers, nurses, engineers, and business professionals. My goal is to make sure our public colleges and universities are always leading, always producing the most advanced research, and always providing quality education to eligible students.

We must ensure these institutions, as well as our primary and secondary schools, receive ample funding and support. I encourage policymakers at every level to promote the use of technology to enhance course curriculum, pedagogy and assessment of student learning outcomes, and apply the awesome research capabilities of our universities to the complex task of teaching in classrooms with multiple languages and cultures. We cannot waste taxpayer money and certainly cannot waste even one child. As Bill Clinton said, America has the finest system of higher education in the world but until we can say the same thing about our system of elementary and secondary education, we will never live up to our potential.

In 2005, the Public Policy Institute of California issued a report, *California 2025: Taking on the Future*, which warned that California's higher education system may not be able to produce enough college graduates to keep California's economy growing.[2] Although I'm more optimistic about the future, the report's twenty-year timeframe is useful because it forces us to focus on the future.

---

[2] *California 2025: Taking on the Future*, Ellen Hanak and Mark Baldassare (editors), Public Policy Institute of California, June 2005.

Given our chronic budget deficits at the state and federal level, I think Jack Godwin's approach in *Clintonomics* also concentrates our attention on the future and reminds us the purpose of public policy is to optimize the allocation of scarce resources, minimize waste, and maximize the outcome. We should also remember the lesson Bill Clinton learned as an undergraduate about "future preference," the belief that the future can be better than the past and that each of us has a responsibility to plan for it, work for it, and make it so.

This is the point I want to make about *Clintonomics*. It is not a nostalgic look at the nineties, but a governing philosophy for the global era. Reading *Clintonomics* is like going on a journey to rediscover the great ideas and great principles that have guided us for more than two hundred years. Godwin narrates the genealogy of *Clintonomics* from the most primitive impulses of human nature, as he says, to the most complex expressions of human development. Along the way, he explores the principles of our founders, the influence of Ronald Reagan, the forces of globalization, and the new science of complexity.

Godwin acknowledges Reagan's political genius, but ultimately concludes Clinton succeeded where Reagan failed. Godwin's conclusion may seem controversial at first glance but if you read carefully, you see both Clinton and Reagan receive fair treatment and equally high respect. Although Reagan was the great communicator, Clinton was the great policy wonk who repaired the theoretical flaws in Reaganomics, effectively solved problems such as welfare and the budget, and offered a coherent governing philosophy for the global era.

This brings us back to education. Whenever we debate the state or federal budget, we must decide whether we will continue to invest in the future or whether we will abandon our historic commitment. How can we possibly abandon our responsibility to future generations? We can and should have the best system of public education in the world. We can and should increase our investment and at the same time implement serious reforms to improve the quality of public education. I'm not saying that because I have six children and nine grandchildren, but because I believe public education is critical to maintaining economic development and social mobility in the global era.

If you have ever attended a graduation ceremony at the California State University, Sacramento, you know exactly what I mean. At the end of every graduation ceremony, there is a wonderful tradition when the university president asks everyone in the audience who is a first-generation college graduate to stand. Hundreds (sometimes thousands) of people stand up or jump up as the audience bursts into applause. It is a good reminder that behind every dollar we invest in public education, there's a person and a family, and somewhere maybe a proud ancestor like my grandfather Jose, who left the old country to start a new life in America because he too believed the future could be better than the past.

John Garamendi
Lieutenant Governor, State of California
January 2009
Sacramento, California

Acknowledgments

Thanks to everyone who helped me along the way.

Thanks to all my colleagues at California State University, Sacramento.

Thanks to Elizabeth Rindskopf Parker of McGeorge School of Law.

Thanks to Dan Godwin of KDFW, Dallas, Texas.

Thanks to Michael Brennan of the OTF Group.

Thanks to Eric Magnuson of the Magnuson Capital Group.

Thanks to Shirley Daniel of the University of Hawai'i at Manoa.

Thanks to Sylvia and Leon Panetta of the Panetta Institute for Public Policy, California State University, Monterey Bay.

Thanks to David Gergen of the Center for Public Leadership, Harvard University.

Thanks to Andy Ambraziejus, Jim Bessent, Ellen Coleman, Sue Ducharme, Barry Richardson, Stan Wakefield, and everyone at AMACOM Books.

Thanks to Jeffery McGraw and Cricket Freeman of the August Agency.

Most of all, thanks to Emilia and Audrey.

Hope is the pillar of the world.—*African Proverb attributed to the Kanuri Tribe of Nigeria, Niger, and Chad*

Introduction

I wasn't a great communicator, but I communicated great things, and they didn't spring full bloom from my brow, they came from the heart of a great nation—from our experience, our wisdom, and our belief in the principles that have guided us for two centuries. They called it the Reagan revolution.[1]

—RONALD REAGAN, 1989

ON SEPTEMBER 11, 2001, I awoke early at my home in Sacramento. As usual, I made coffee, retrieved the newspaper from the front porch, and turned on the *Music of Your Life*, the station that plays Frank Sinatra, Ella Fitzgerald, and Tony Bennett. It was a picture-perfect September morning, sixty degrees and not a cloud in the sky. I was reading the newspaper when the radio announced a second plane had hit the World Trade Center. I thought for a moment: *a second plane?* Then I put down the paper and turned on the television.

In the days that followed, I supported George W. Bush, particularly when he stood on the rubble of the World Trade Center and put his arm around that retired firefighter. When Bush visited

1

the Islamic Center in Washington and read from the Koran, I thought it put the American commitment to freedom of religion in the best possible light. His speech to Congress at the end of September was not bad. Rescue workers were still digging through the rubble, but we were all beginning to recover from the shock. British Prime Minister Tony Blair was in the gallery, and it moved me when Bush said America had no truer friend than Great Britain.

When the Taliban refused to hand over Osama bin Laden, I supported the invasion of Afghanistan—but then we failed to capture him. When Saddam Hussein continued to defy United Nations Security Council resolutions, I supported the invasion of Iraq, too. Given the savagery of the 9/11 attack, I thought Bush's doctrine of preemptive action made sense. For a while, I thought there might be a plausible explanation why we found no weapons of mass destruction. When news broke in April 2004 about the criminal abuse of Iraqi prisoners at Abu Ghraib prison in Baghdad, however, it wiped out any hopes I had for a positive outcome. I knew a clean break would be impossible. Like a goat who tries to butt a hedge, we got our horns tangled, and the more we struggled, the more tangled we would become.

Then in February 2006, when I read the al-Askari Mosque in the ancient city of Samarra was destroyed, I began to speculate how some of Bush's predecessors—Nixon, Reagan, or Clinton—would have responded to the 9/11 attacks. I started regretting the Twenty-second Amendment (the one that limits presidents from serving more than two terms, which Congress passed in March 1947 and the states ratified in February 1951) and wondered what Bill Clinton might have accomplished during a third or fourth term. People from all over the world line up to hear Clinton speak and pay him huge fees. According to one report, Clinton made more than $40 million on the lecture circuit in the first four years after leaving office, two-thirds of which came from foreign sources.[2] Though not exactly scientific, it is a reliable indicator that Clinton has become the leading voice on political economy in the global era. No one of his generation dominates the political discourse like Clinton does, and no one else makes it look so easy.

In August 1998, about three years before the 9/11 attacks, members of al Qaeda simultaneously bombed two American embassies located in Dar es Salaam and Nairobi, killing more than two hundred fifty people. Clinton was president at the time, and this is what he said:

> The world we are living in and the world we are moving toward will allow us to move around the world more rapidly and more freely than ever before and to move information, ideas and money around the world more rapidly, more freely than ever before. It will be a global society that I am convinced will bring all Americans our nation's best years. But there has never been a time in human history when we have been free of the organized forces of destruction. And the more open the world becomes, the more vulnerable people become to those who are organized and have weapons, information, technology and the ability to move.[3]

Notice the cool appraisal of the not-too-distant future, in which the forces of destruction will have the same mobility and the same access to ideas, information, and technology as the rest of us. Notice the dispassionate analysis, devoid of hysterical rhetoric. Finally, notice Clinton's optimism despite the profound changes taking place as the world moves to a global society, not just a global economy, which will connect us in ways beyond business and economics. As Clinton also said, "The ground is moving under America."[4]

I tried to draw a diagram of Clinton's governing philosophy, but it came out looking like a bathtub full of spaghetti. I discarded the diagram and decided to write a book instead. My ultimate goal is to capture Clinton's ideas on power, strategy, and twenty-first-century statecraft from the perspective of the Oval Office, with all the privileges, responsibilities, and burdens that come with the presidency, and present his governing philosophy as a single, unified idea. This requires understanding Clinton's political ambitions and the importance he placed on being skilled in politics and public policy. It also requires exploring the philosophical origins and intellectual influences of Clintonomics, beginning with the essentials of political economy and later venturing into the new science of complex systems.

When I began my research, my intention was to focus exclusively on Clinton. The more research I did, the more I realized I could not accomplish my goal without studying the extent of Reagan's political influence on Clinton. In public, Clinton positioned his governing philosophy as the antidote to Reaganomics. In fact, Clinton and Reagan are fellow travelers separated more by party affiliation than political ideology. If this assertion seems controversial at the beginning of the book, it will not at the end.

During his eight years in office, Clinton's political opponents were so hell-bent on character assassination it was difficult sometimes to hear what Clinton had to say. One critic disparaged his "ideologically fuzzy pragmatism" as if that were a character flaw.[5] Others complained that he was an opportunist, that he had no core beliefs and would do or say anything just to win an election. One popular metaphor was the jellyfish—that spineless, gelatinous creature that floats passively along with the current. While he was in office, Clinton's critics—so vocal and so vicious—made listening to him difficult. Now that Clinton is long out of office—and now that Hillary Clinton's own presidential ambitions are on hold—perhaps we can hear his views, without any spin from the left or the right and without interruption.

People who enjoyed reading Clinton's best-selling autobiography, *My Life*, but could not keep track of all the names and found the details a little exhausting will find relief in *Clintonomics*. Presidential memoirs are inevitably (and understandably) self-serving. As I was researching and writing *Clintonomics*, I treated *My Life* as an artifact whose authenticity was beyond dispute but whose contents were open to interpretation. The chronological structure of Clinton's autobiography—first this happened, then this and this—does not lend itself to the study of big ideas. In contrast, *Clintonomics* is all about the big ideas.

One of those big ideas was reinventing government, meaning "the fundamental transformation of public systems and organizations to create dramatic increases in their effectiveness, efficiency, adaptability, and capacity to innovate."[6] Clinton first became interested in reinventing government when David Osborne profiled Clinton and several other governors (mostly Democrats) in the mideighties. When Osborne published *Laboratories of Democracy* (1988), Clinton promoted it among his fellow governors in the Democratic Leadership Council (DLC). Clinton wrote a blurb for Osborne's second book, *Reinventing Government* (1992), which described ways various state and local governments around the country were becoming less bureaucratic and more entrepreneurial.

As president, Clinton came to believe reinventing government was the only way to cut the deficit without hurting the public interest, and he hoped to make it a permanent process.[7] In a speech to a group of Democratic governors, Clinton said he was proud to be with people who had experience dealing with "the legacy of the 1980s": people who dealt with real problems; who struggled with healthcare, welfare, jobs, and education; and who did not make excuses or print money. By the time he became president, he believed the people elected him because they wanted a new approach, literally wanted to reinvent government. Clinton said, "We are going to change the culture of the way this federal government works," and then he explained what he meant by his *legacy of the 1980s* reference: "We are going to try to do what our adversaries always talked about, and that is to empower people, not entitle them."[8]

In 1993, management consultants Michael Hammer and James Champy published their landmark book *Reengineering the Corporation*, which also spawned several sequels. According to their formal definition, reengineering is "the fundamental rethinking and radical redesign of business processes to achieve dramatic improvements in critical, contemporary measures of performance, such as cost, quality, service, and speed."[9] Reengineering was to the private sector what reinventing was to the public sector. Both became popular buzzwords, concepts much talked about, much misunderstood, and then much maligned. As of this writing, however, neither reengineering nor reinventing is posted on buzzwhack.com, the Web site where buzzwords receive eternal damnation.

By 1996, reinventing government became part of the Democratic Party platform: "Today's Democratic Party believes in a government that works better and costs less. We know that government workers are good people trapped in bad systems, and we are committed to reinventing government to reform those systems." Though this would seem harmless enough, it required a response from the Republican Party in its 1996 platform: "The Clinton administration's 'Reinventing Government' program to reform the welfare state bureaucracy has failed. In fact, management reforms of the Reagan years were repealed and new labor-management councils that diluted efficient management were added as additional bureaucracy and red tape. We will revoke these Clinton administration policies and oppose the liberal philosophy that bureaucracy can reform welfare."

Nevertheless, we must ignore those who would dismiss reengineering and reinventing as meaningless jargon and remember Reagan's parting words about rediscovering our common values and our common sense. We must maintain the illusion, "the fourth wall," through which the audience observes the action—or in this case reads the text. We must step into the breach between left and right and present Clintonomics as a coherent governing philosophy equal to the twenty-first-century global system.

I HAVE ORGANIZED the book into nine chapters, plus this introduction. *Part One: Political Economy* consists of five chapters and presents the theoretical framework. *Chapter 1: The Purpose of Politics* takes care of the housekeeping, defines terms for politics and economics, and then describes Bill Clinton's own definition of power. It explores his ambition to seek high office as a way to understand his fascination with power and then explains some of what Clinton hoped to accomplish, on a range of issues, as the occupant of the most powerful office in the world's most powerful country.

Chapter 2: The Philosophical Foundation explores the genealogy of Clintonomics, from John Locke to John Kenneth Galbraith, with a little Karl Marx thrown into the mix. This chapter explains the fundamental elements of Clintonomics—such as Jean-Jacques Rousseau's social contract, which inspired Clinton's New Covenant and other concepts—which are the bricks and mortar of political economy. From Adam Smith's metaphor of the invisible hand and Jeremy Bentham's principle of the greatest good to Friedrich Hayek's ideas on limited government and John Kenneth Galbraith's writings on the social balance, this chapter helps place Clintonomics in philosophical and intellectual context.

Chapter 3: The Reagan Legacy continues along a similar line of inquiry as the previous chapter, except with a specific focus on conservative principles such as resistance to radical change, individualism, economic freedom, and limited government. This chapter also explores Ronald Reagan's governing philosophy using the same approach we will take to Clinton's, meaning we will not limit ourselves arbitrarily to fiscal and monetary policy but also consider a range of political, economic, and social issues. Because Clinton deliberately positioned Clintonomics as the antidote to Reaganomics, it is fascinating to compare and contrast the two.

Chapter 4: The Global System presents Clintonomics as a governing philosophy—part social science, part systems science—with a global perspective. This is analogous to the "overview effect," the conversion that takes place in the minds of astronauts when they see Earth from space for the first time. In this chapter, we will venture into the new science of complexity to explain what Clinton called "the inexorable logic of globalization," the political, economic, and technological forces transforming our lives in the global era.

Chapter 5: Reflections on Change explains how to recognize the forces of change in the global economy. First the chapter presents a typology on change, which describes different types (or states) of change and their overlapping characteristics. The typology is a management tool that combines abstract and systems thinking, which will be thought provoking for political junkies, students, business executives, and anyone interested in change management. Then Bill Clinton will offer his authoritative analysis and advice on the need to manage change in order for America to prevail in the twenty-first century, a topic on which he was (and is) a relentless advocate.

Part Two: Public Policy consists of four chapters and describes the role of government and the administration of public policy on a variety of problems and issues. *Chapter 6: The Role of Government (A)* considers other political influences on Clintonomics, beginning with what our founding fathers actually wrote in the *Federalist Papers* about the true principles of American government. This chapter considers more of Reagan's political influence, as well as Newt Gingrich's Contract with America. It also explores Clinton's New Covenant and the signature phrase of Clinton's presidency: The era of big government is over.

Chapter 7: The Role of Government (B) explains the role of government in the twenty-first century. Clinton had some ideas that were not politically pure: not perfectly liberal, not perfectly conservative. For example, he had the idea you could cut the deficit, reform the way the government delivers services, and still have money to invest in things like research, education, and infrastructure. Clinton considered redefining the role of government to be more than an abstract argument. It was all about defining the country's mission in the global economy and post–Cold War world.

Chapter 8: Theory of Constraints is not a theory at all but a management tool to improve the performance of organizations in businesses and government, as well as other systems. Every system has at least one constraint that limits its capacity to realize its goal. Increasing the system's capacity requires identifying the factors that constrain the system and then managing the constraints. In the early years of the twenty-first century, constraining factors include entitlements, healthcare, welfare, diversity, education, immigration, international trade, and national security, among others.

Chapter 9: Bridge to the Future briefly summarizes two arguments that run parallel through most of the book. First, the years 1989 through 2001 were no holiday from history and to suggest otherwise indicates a severe case of tunnel vision: not merely a lack of peripheral vision, but a failure to recognize globalization—not terrorism or any specific act of terrorism—as the central reality of our time. Second, in 1981 Reagan said government is not the solution; government is the problem. In 1996, Clinton said the era of big government is over. What's the difference? The calendar is the difference. When the Cold War ended, the world entered a new era and rendered much of Reaganomics obsolete. Clinton transcended the simplistic debate between liberals who want to expand government and conservatives who want to starve it to death. Thus, Clinton built on Ronald Reagan's legacy and repositioned the American economy for the twenty-first century.

THE DAY CLINTON delivered his farewell address came barely six weeks after the final decision in the 2000 presidential election came down. Throughout much of the country as well as in Washington, people were in a state of disbelief. Although Al Gore won the popular vote by more than half a million ballots, he lost the election on a technicality. Bush's narrow margin of victory in Florida triggered an automatic statewide recount, which resulted in an even narrower margin the second time around. Gore asked Florida for another recount in several counties, but Florida's secretary of state refused to extend the deadline to certify election returns. On December 12, the Supreme Court terminated Florida's selective manual ballot recount, which effectively gave Florida's twenty-five electoral votes—and the presidency—to George W. Bush.

On January 18, 2001, the sky was overcast, and temperatures hovered around the midthirties all day. Clinton began his farewell address from the White House at 8:00 that evening as a light rain began to fall. Clinton's speech contained no stern warnings about the dangers of foreign entanglements or the military-industrial complex. It was uncharacteristically short (1,114 words) and contained "three thoughts about our future" regarding fiscal responsibility, global connectivity, and ethnic diversity, all themes that ran throughout Clinton's presidency. With the Cold War receding into the past and 9/11 beyond the horizon, he referred to the periods of dramatic transformation around the world that were shaping the country. He used one of his favorite phrases, "opportunity for all, responsibility from all," and summed up his eight-year effort "to give America a new kind of Government, smaller, more modern, more effective, full of ideas and policies appropriate to this new time, always putting people first, always focusing on the future."[10] Finally, he said, "My days in this office are nearly through, but my days of service, I hope, are not."

Clinton had less than forty-eight hours remaining in his presidency. He spent his final hours in the Oval Office working on a number of issues, large and small, foreign and domestic, that exemplify the range of presidential duties. He announced the new chief of staff for his postpresidency transition office, for example, made proclamations on land mines and responsible fatherhood, and issued 140 pardons.[11] He wrote two open letters, one to the people of Israel and another to the people of Palestine, reminding them of the moment Yitzhak Rabin and Yasser Arafat shook hands on the White House lawn, urging them not to give up on the peace process. At twelve noon on January 20, 2001, his last day in office, he watched as chief justice William Rehnquist administered the presidential oath of office to George W. Bush.

PART ONE

The Political Economy

CHAPTER 1

The Purpose of Politics

I identify with Babe Ruth. He was a little overweight.
And he struck out a lot, but he hit a lot of home runs.[1]
— BILL CLINTON, 1995

THROUGHOUT HIS PRESIDENCY, Clinton joked about his so-called "laws of politics." Even as Clinton joked, however, he was conveying useful data—raw material we can use to reconstruct his governing philosophy as a basis for our discourse. I have reduced Clinton's laws of politics to ten bullet points, as follows:

- First, do no harm. While we're doing no harm, let's do some good.
- Let's keep the American dream alive for the next generation.
- Let's make educational opportunity available for everyone.
- Let's make public service a noble calling.

- Before every speech, make sure whoever gives the introduction is someone you have appointed to high office.
- Whenever you hear a politician say something is not a "money problem," you can be sure he is talking about somebody else's problem.
- Everyone is for change in general but against it in particular.
- You can have good policy without good politics, but you cannot have good government without both.
- If you don't win, you can't govern.
- When you start to have a good time, it means you should be somewhere else.

Some of these laws made the list because of the number of times Clinton repeated them verbatim. Others are composites of phrases or ideas that summarize elements of his governing philosophy. However, if I had to reduce Clinton's governing philosophy to a single bullet point, I would choose "If you don't win, you can't govern," because that's where his presidential ambitions converge with his political goals.

Clintonomics is an extremely complicated philosophy of governance: part economics, part political science, and part systems science—and that is only the philosophical side. The practical side comes from Clinton's extraordinary ability to see and clearly explain politics and public policy, or, as political scientist Harold Lasswell would say, who gets what, when, and how.[2] That remarkably concise definition reinforces the concept that politics is about power, while pinpointing precisely where politics intersects economics: at the distribution of resources. This is the epicenter of Clintonomics, which of course originates with politics and economics but then transcends the social sciences altogether, radiating into the new science of complex systems.

Clinton's own definition of politics is more lyrical than Lasswell's: Politics is about giving people a chance to live their dreams. He is a Democrat by heritage, instinct, and conviction, he explains, because for most of American history, Democrats were "on the side of ordinary people, on the side of bringing people together, and on the side of the future." This is what Clinton refers to as "the national enterprise" or "the purpose of politics": to help people realize their God-given potential, help them live together in harmony, and help them fulfill their dreams and duties.

At one Democratic Party fund-raiser, Clinton gave a fascinating analysis of American politics throughout its 220-year history. What is politics, he asked? What is its purpose? Politics cannot possibly be as bad as some people say, especially if you consider politics is why American-style democracy has lasted as long as it has. The American constitutional system is the political framework within which we have negotiated, compromised, made decisions, and worked together for more than 220 years. By perpetuating this framework, the American people preserve liberty in their own time and ensure future generations have the resources to meet future challenges. Because every generation inevitably faces its own challenges—sometimes even existential crises—every generation is entitled to debate what the Constitution means to it. Every generation is entitled to ask what the Constitution has to do with decisions it makes on immigration, education, or economic policy. Every generation is entitled to ask what it means to say all of us are created equal by God.[3]

Clinton's vision was appropriately idealistic and optimistic, which we would expect from a sitting president. He highlighted the democratic process: negotiating, compromising, making decisions, and building coalitions. He invoked the Almighty and declared the Constitution a living document open to interpretation. His version embraced past, present, and future generations, which suggested the nation's trajectory was ascendant. When Clinton remarked that every generation is entitled to debate the Constitution, the word *entitled* stood out. What he meant was every generation has a duty, an obligation, to future generations.

As formulaic as Clinton's definition may appear at first glance, it suggests political economy is essential—even timeless—no matter how distasteful the political process may be. Although the burning issues of the day—education, healthcare, welfare reform—provide context for Clinton's governing philosophy, Clintonomics also focuses on things that do not change. The laws of political economy and complexity are not artificial statutes we can rewrite or ignore. Politics is about power. Economics is about resources. Complexity is ubiquitous.

So why run for president? Why seek the most powerful office in the world's most powerful country? The answer is in why Clinton chose not to run in 1988:

> I didn't run for president the first time I had a chance to run, because I didn't think I was ready to run. And I had been governor for quite a long time. In 1988, when the election was open and it looked like we had a good chance to win, and I almost ran. And I realized that no one should run for president who does not have a very clear idea, not only of what the conditions of the country are and the challenges facing it, but of what you would do on the day after the inauguration, across a whole broad range of issues.[4]

This is very revealing. After trouncing Walter Mondale in 1984, Ronald Reagan was termed out. In 1988, Vice President George Bush became the Republican nominee, but the nomination for the Democrats was wide open. Early on, Gary Hart was the front-runner, but he withdrew over allegations of marital infidelity. Michael Dukakis did well in the Super Tuesday races and went on to win the nomination. Although Dukakis was well ahead after the conventions, Bush defeated him in the general election.

At the age of forty-two, Clinton decided he was not ready. By then, Clinton had been governor of Arkansas for a total of eight years. Although Clinton thought he could win, he decided against it, because no one should run who did not have a clear idea what he wanted to accomplish and where he (or she) wanted to lead the country. By inauguration day in January 1993, however, he knew exactly what he wanted to do. "I want us to drive the agenda of this country until the last hour of the last day of my term in January of 2001," he said. "That is what we signed on for; that is what we owe the American people."[5] And for the next eight years, that is exactly what Clinton did.

The Old Dogmas

In Abraham Lincoln's 1862 annual message, he said, "As our case is new, so we must think anew and act anew"—a useful reminder if we are going to find our way in the post–Cold War, post–9/11 era. Of course, Clinton admires the Great Emancipator who won the Civil War, freed the slaves, and gave his life. However, only a true policy wonk like Clinton would revere Lincoln for signing the Homestead Act, which gave land to pioneer families as long as they agreed to live on, cultivate, and develop it and the Morrill Act, which created the system of land-grant colleges to provide educational opportunity to the working class. Clinton considered Lincoln the greatest Republican president; he studied his writings and looked to him for inspiration and guidance on race relations. Of all the unforgettable phrases Lincoln wrote, however, this one makes the most compelling case for Clintonomics: "The dogmas of the quiet past are inadequate to the stormy present."

Another inspirational figure in Clinton's life was Robert Kennedy, who died in 1968, around the time Clinton graduated from college. In 1998, when people were observing the thirtieth anniversary of Robert Kennedy's assassination, Clinton recalled what Kennedy meant to him and compared the task he set for himself to Kennedy's heroic effort to break free from the old dogmas "and dream things that never were." The country was deeply troubled and divided over civil rights and the war in Vietnam. According to Clinton, Kennedy was trying to do for the Democratic Party and the country exactly what Clinton was trying to do, which was to get people to give up the old dogmas and go beyond the false liberal-conservative dichotomy.[6]

Of course, Lincoln, Kennedy, and Clinton—especially Clinton—were not separatists or hermits who withdrew from the world but politicians actively engaged in the political process. When Clinton described what he loves about politics, this was apparent.

> Now, all I've done so far is talk about political activists and politicians. I think it's a high calling. I still want children to want to grow up to be president, to be in the Senate, to be governor, to come to fundraisers, to go to rallies, to pass out cards, to believe in the political system. . . . And the reason most of us belong to our party is that we believe that the real thrill of public service is not partisan triumph or political power, but advancing the lives of people and helping them to make the most of their own lives.[7]

We cannot just read this quotation on the literal level and leave it there; we owe it to ourselves to read the subtext. He mentions children growing up. He talks about the path to power in the American system: political activism, parties, rallies, and fundraisers. He talks about partisan triumph, the thrill of public service—and political power. It is not as if there is anything particularly wrong about children growing up wanting to be president, if all it entailed was attending rallies and fund-raisers and believing in the political system. Why would anybody want to be president of the United States? Power is why. Let us not forget, it is the most powerful office in the most powerful country in the world. Let us also not forget Lord Acton's dictum: Power corrupts.

A month before the 1998 midterm elections, Clinton offered his analysis of the political situation to a room full of donors. It all came down to the Republicans' "cynical theory of history, money, and strategy." First, Republicans believed they had history going for them. Ever since the Civil War, the president's party always lost seats in midterm congressional races, particularly during the president's second term in office. Speaking to a room full of donors and party loyalists, Clinton bravely predicted history wouldn't hold this time around. As it turned out, Clinton was right. Republicans retained control even though they broke even in the Senate and the Democrats won a handful of seats in the House.

Second, Clinton said Republicans believed they had money going for them and would outspend Democrats, perhaps by as much as three to one in some of the closer races. Their financial advantage would certainly be helpful, though not necessarily decisive. In Clinton's experience, "If the other person has more money than you it's devastating, unless you have enough." What's enough? According to Clinton, enough ensured your message would be heard, your voters contacted, and all attacks countered—but even then much depended on the campaign and the candidate. The third spoke in the Republican cynical theory was strategy. Republicans were more likely to turn out on Election Day because they were older, wealthier, and much more ideological than Democrats. Based on this premise, the Republi-

can strategy was to inflame the Republican base and then hope
for low voter turnout among Democrats.

Finally, Clinton merged his two roles as political scientist and
fund-raiser in chief: "So I'm asking you not just to give your
money," he said. "I'm asking you to be part of doing something
that I think is pretty important."

Like every capital city in the history of the world, Washington
is full of intrigue and infighting. Powerful people and office seek-
ers maneuver for position and sometimes forget about the
people, the people who work, raise their families, pay their
taxes—and vote. At the beginning of his final year in office, Clinton observed, "Washington had become a place that was almost
turned in on itself, obsessed with itself, and stuck in the thinking
and the debate of a time that was long gone." He also said,
"Washington is a place where . . . a lot of people profess to be
profoundly religious but actually worship power." In his autobiography, Clinton said power is the narcotic of choice in Washington: "It dulls the senses and clouds the judgment." Based solely
on these quotations, it might seem like Clinton is referring to
somebody else. If we did not know better, it might seem like
Clinton is trying to separate himself from the rest of the power-
hungry heathens. Indeed, there is nothing particularly problematic about children wanting to be president, unless you consider
addictive, controlling, corrupting behavior in children a problem.
Politics may or may not be as high a calling as Clinton claims.

Clinton often says he ran for president because he was tired of
the uncivil tone of our national political dialogue. Unless we
change the divisive, disrespectful, and often dishonest tone—at
both the national and local level—we will be lucky if we ever get
the political results we wish. He wanted to change the country,
overcome gridlock in Washington, and pull the country together.
Clinton expressed his "commitment to opportunity for all Americans; and insistence on responsibility from all Americans; and a

belief that we [are] one community, that we are all in this to-gether." This three-part declaration is brief but carefully struc-tured. First, it appeals to the Democratic principle of equal opportunity and the Republican principle of personal responsi-bility. Finally, there is a call to union. No wonder supporters and critics alike sometimes found it difficult to figure out where he stood.

"I think my job is to do everything I can to help every Ameri-can reach his or her God-given potential," he said, "and to try to bring the American people together to make our country stronger. In other words, even though you often don't read about it in these terms, the real purpose of our political system, when it's working properly, is to get people together and to get things done." He ran because the country was drifting, unable to move forward, coming apart when it should be coming together. What does that mean, to Clinton in particular? His answer is familiar. He said, "I always thought that public life at best was about bring-ing people together and bringing out the best in people, and actu-ally getting things done so that next year you could talk about a new set of problems. You wouldn't have to keep on talking about the same old thing over and over again."[8] Although this state-ment is full of clichés, we should acknowledge that effective polit-ical communication, in order to reach the broadest constituency possible, depends on repetition.

One very important indicator of the importance of political communication is the need to raise increasingly large amounts of money for television advertising. At one event, Clinton made this astute observation: "The fundamental problem in campaigns is the cost of communications has exploded and, therefore, the de-mand to raise funds and to keep communicating for political parties and for candidates has been severe." The drive to reform campaign financing is not simply related to "the cost of com-munications," but specifically to the cost of television advertising. Television airtime is expensive and very persuasive, if viewers see advertisements with sufficient frequency. Cigarette manufacturers, for example, used television advertising to persuade millions of people to consume a product that killed them. This explains why, in the early seventies, the federal government banned all cigarette advertising on television: because it works. Although there is a powerful freedom-of-speech argument against campaign finance reform, there is another powerful argument in favor of campaign finance reform, which recognizes that the concentration of wealth leads to concentration of power and is inherently undemocratic.

IN ALL THE RESEARCH I did, which included reading thousands of pages of documents, Clinton's speeches at Democratic fundraisers were the most interesting. These events were full of people who shared the same party affiliation. Far from "preaching to the choir," Clinton often used these occasions to convert his supporters to his way of thinking. Perhaps it is because of the role money plays in American politics; raising money for political consultants and campaign managers, television advertisements, and other kinds of marketing is essential to modern politics. Clinton made this funny observation about the intersection of activism and fund-raising: "I think that politics only works if you have certain principles and values, you have ideas about how to implement them, and then you have some sense of what the human impact of what you do is. I mean, if this doesn't make any difference to anybody's life, why did you come out here tonight? You could have eaten downstairs for less money."[9]

At another such event, Clinton capped his inspirational message with a not-too-subtle reminder about the economics of political campaigns.

Now, this is what I thought public life was about, and this is what I think the presidency is about and this is what I think the Congress ought to be about, and what I think the American people really care about—how are we going to get together, how are we going to get things done, how are we going to lift up the human potential of the American people? That's why I ran for President, and that's what's going to make this dinner worth your investment tonight—if we do what we're supposed to do.[10]

Some of the themes are familiar, particularly building coalitions and getting things done. The part about lifting up our "human potential" sounds almost too good to be true. If politics is about power, isn't that rhetoric a little syrupy? No, it is not. Clinton has a deceptively simple way of expressing the timeless laws of politics. When he says, for example, the purpose of politics is getting people together to get things done, he is describing the high art of coalition building, assembling an alliance (combining the resources of individuals, organizations, or nations) to accomplish a common goal. Coalition building is essential to one of Clinton's laws of politics: If you don't win, you can't govern. If you don't win, you won't have the power.

Clinton's obsession with politics and policy is the secret of his success. "In Washington," he says, "we have too many people who do policy, but don't do politics. And then we have people who do politics, but don't do policy. And really it only works if you do both. There's nothing wrong with politics; I've always sort of enjoyed it. And I think I've embarrassed a lot of people because I'm not ashamed of it. I love politics, I love the system."[11]

He loves politics. Check. He loves public policy and the system. Double check. He loves campaigning, fund-raising, and attending rallies. Check, check, check. So, why run for president?

He wanted to restore the American *dream* of opportunity and the American *value* of responsibility; he wanted to bring the American people together so we could go into the new century together. Clinton's frequent invocation of the American dream is noteworthy because of the connection he made to his favorite themes, opportunity and responsibility, drawing on Biblical themes of individual initiative and the public interest. With this, the big man outlined the three great tasks for his presidency:

- **Restore the American dream:** Create more economic opportunity, enlarge the middle class, and shrink the underclass.
- **Reassert fundamental values:** Emphasize self-sufficiency and personal responsibility, remind people of their obligations to the public interest, and encourage them to contribute to their community.
- **Reform the government:** Shrink the bureaucracy, make it more cost-effective, more relevant, and more responsive to the competitive pressures of the global economy.

Clinton expressed his desire to grow the middle class and shrink the "underclass," which really meant putting the American dream—he calls it the "economic" dream—within the reach of more people. He wanted to reform the government, make it less bureaucratic, in order to create more economic opportunities, particularly more opportunities for entrepreneurs. He wanted to increase security, but give it a new definition, a global definition, meaning security around the world and on our streets, in our schools, and in our homes. He also wanted to promote education, because he knew how important it is in the hyper-competitive global economy.

Clinton had powerful enemies, comfortable with the status quo, who considered him an interloper. At the 1994 National

Baptist Convention, Clinton told the audience he ran because "we seemed to be going in the wrong direction, where ordinary Americans were ignored, and people with money and organized power were heeded, but somehow the thing was not working."[12] He also talked about taking responsibility for ourselves and for one another. In a bit of overstatement, he called responsibility one of "the fundamental values that made this country great." We could dismiss it as a rhetorical flourish, except he returned to this theme—opportunity for all, responsibility from all—throughout his time in office. The theme underlying all of this is: Let's overcome our differences and work together. Let's overcome the gridlock and get things done.

He frequently raised another issue—the role of government—to distinguish himself from his political adversaries. He observed that people made fun of him from time to time for being a "policy wonk," someone a little too knowledgeable and a little too fascinated by the details of government policy. It is a gently pejorative term, but to this day Clinton wears it like a badge of honor. Clinton's argument, which his immediate successor proved beyond dispute, is that details matter. You can argue all you want about liberal versus conservative, but good government requires more than rhetoric. Eventually, reality makes a difference. According to Clinton:

> I ran for President because I thought that Washington had become a place where there was too much rhetoric and too little reality; where every statement that every person made was automatically pushed to its ultimate extreme. The government can do nothing—you're on your own; or the government can do everything—there's nothing for you to do. But real people and real life want us to come together as a people and figure out how to deal with our problems and seize our opportunities.[13]

The Stormy Present

By June 1997, a few months into his second term, Clinton had a well-rehearsed answer whenever someone asked him why he wanted to be president.

> So the first thing I wanted to do was to change the economic policy of the country. I said, we can't keep on spending all this money we don't have—we're going to bankrupt the country. But we don't want to walk away from the poor or the dispossessed or the future of the country. So we have to find a way to reduce the deficit, for example, and spend more on education, and spend more on preserving the environment because they're our children and our future.[14]

Back in 1992—which may seem like an eternity ago—Clinton's campaign strategist James Carville proclaimed, "It's the economy, stupid" as the theme of Clinton's presidential campaign. Like any good slogan, it was brief, memorable, and mostly true. It revealed something essential about the world we are living in and the world we are moving toward. It is an example of Clinton's ability to frame an issue and articulate what an election is all about. Every election is about something different, and once he knew what an election or any issue was about, Clinton usually positioned himself with a decisive number of voters. "Every election is almost like a different symphony being written by the American people," he said, "and the language is always the same, just like musical notes, but you have to go and listen to the people and hear them—the way they speak, the way they talk, the way they feel about what this is."[15]

In Clinton's first annual message—delivered less than a month after taking office—he said the economy was the single most important challenge facing the country. To launch his presidency, Clinton proposed a comprehensive plan to set a new course for the country. In order to ease the discomfort any members of his audience might feel, he assured them the new course was consistent with "the basic old values that brought us here over the last two centuries." Among these are a commitment to values such as opportunity, individual responsibility, community, work, family, and faith. Using language that infuriated almost everyone in the chamber, Clinton said, "We must now break the habits of both political parties and say [there] can be no more something for nothing."

Clinton attributed the country's less than optimum economic performance to low productivity, low growth, stagnant wages, unemployment, budget deficits, and high healthcare costs, among other things. He said partisanship and special interest groups had caused paralysis in the political system, hindering prompt solutions, permitting our problems to fester. He outlined the essential components of his economic plan: shifting our emphasis from consumption to investment; making public policy friendlier to workers and families; reducing the federal deficit and cutting government waste; reforming the tax code; and, of course, creating jobs.

Clinton spoke in favor of international trade, arguing that economic growth depends on opening new markets overseas. In the aftermath of the Cold War, Clinton advocated removing obsolete export restrictions—relics of the Cold War—that no longer served any national security function and only hindered expansion of world trade. He also pledged his commitment to "fair trade" in all negotiations and in the North American Free Trade Agreement (NAFTA), particularly in terms of labor laws and environmental protection. He announced his intention to cut the budget deficit.

> We have to cut the deficit because the more we spend paying off the debt, the less tax dollars we have to invest in jobs and education and the future of this country. And the more money we take out of the pool of available savings, the harder it is for people in the private sector to borrow money at affordable interest rates for a college loan for their children, for a home mortgage, or to start a new business.[16]

Cutting the deficit, he said, would decrease the percentage of the federal budget that goes toward interest payments, which in turn would lower interest rates and increase the capital available for public and private investment in areas critical to the nation's economic future, such as roads, bridges, railways, transit systems, and information systems. This would lead to long-term economic growth, but only if Congress agreed to cut spending and increase taxes simultaneously.

CLINTON CERTAINLY DESERVES high marks for consistency, except when it comes to conventional ideologies. "I had some ideas that people said were nutty, and they weren't appropriately pure. They were not perfectly liberal, or perfectly conservative."[17] As a governing philosophy, Clintonomics alternately adopted Republican policies and Democratic policies. In general, this approach entailed modernizing the federal government, making it more entrepreneurial, and distributing more authority to state and local governments. This meant making the government smaller, more flexible, less wasteful, and better suited for the global economy. It meant economic policies that are pro-growth, and friendly toward working people, entrepreneurs, and the middle class. It meant overhauling the unemployment system, encouraging the welfare bureaucracy and welfare recipients both to focus on work, and thus to end "welfare as we know it."

As Clinton says, however, politics is about a lot more than economics. When you get the economics right, people figure out for themselves how to build strong communities, raise their children, and lead productive lives. When you get the economics wrong, it usually makes other problems worse. Clinton's experience as governor of Arkansas taught him this lesson and taught him to reach across party lines. His affiliation with the Democratic Leadership Council taught him to believe "that ideas could matter in national politics just like they do in other forms of public endeavor."[18] Unlike in 1988, when Clinton chose not to run, he now had a very good idea what he wanted to accomplish as president.

Indeed, good governance comes from good ideas. But how do you know a good idea from a bad one? How do you know the right questions to ask? How do you know the right answers? Faced with the inexorable logic of globalization, how do you know the difference between good policy and bad? We will begin answering these questions and more as we study the philosophical foundation of Clintonomics in Chapter 2.

CHAPTER 2

The Philosophical Foundation

I warn the reader that this chapter requires careful read-ing, and that I am unable to make myself clear to those who refuse to be attentive. Every free action is produced by the concurrence of two causes; one moral, i.e., the will which determines the act; the other physical, i.e., the power which executes it.[1]

—JEAN-JACQUES ROUSSEAU, 1762

ECONOMICS AND POLITICAL SCIENCE belong to the social sci-ences, meaning they study relationships among people, individu-als, and groups. Economics studies the production, distribution, and consumption of commodities, goods, and services. It as-sumes human wants are unlimited and resources are scarce. For the most part, it assumes that economic growth is more impor-tant than equality and justifies huge gaps in the distribution of wealth across society. Economic activity is "value added," mean-ing it creates resources to satisfy our needs for material well-being.

Political science, on the other hand, studies power relationships among people. Politics is about power, and relationships become politicized when power is introduced. Politics appeals to the most basic emotions in human nature: fear and insecurity. That does not mean politics is amoral. On the contrary, it is unusual when politicians can elevate the dialogue beyond the primitive motives of security and self-interest, so when they use fear and insecurity to unify and motivate people, they may simply be acting on principle. In wartime, this is obvious and necessary, but even in peacetime there are fear and insecurity: crime, economic hardship, and illness.

As societies organize themselves politically to maximize their security, the scope of political activity may range from a mutually beneficial social contract to situations in which social order disintegrates, human rights are severely restricted, and the social contract is suspended. Political behavior also includes the legitimate use of violence by the government, such as military or paramilitary police activity, as well as cases of violent crime, terrorism, and riots. Political activity is "value subtracted," meaning it redistributes power by consent or because of threat, intimidation, or coercion.

If we combine politics and economics, which are relatively simple systems, we get political economy, a social science with great potential for insight and action. To understand political economy, it helps to think about politics the way you think about economics and vice versa. Political economy is analogous to the economy of motion, a concept borrowed from management that refers to the method in which human energy is conserved during the performance of a task. Applied to public policy, the objective is to produce the maximum positive outcome while optimizing allocation of scarce resources and minimizing waste.

Our understanding of political economy has certainly come a long way since the days of John Locke, Jean-Jacques Rousseau, and Adam Smith, though it is hardly a unified discipline. The enormously influential twentieth-century British economist John Maynard Keynes thought the ideas of economists and political economists were much more powerful than most people realized. "Indeed the world is ruled by little else," he said. "Practical men, who believe themselves to be quite exempt from any intellectual influences, are usually the slaves of some defunct economist."[2] We can be sure Keynes was not talking about Bill Clinton, who in many ways epitomizes both the man of ideas and the man of action, combining the skills of philosopher and statesman imagined by the ancient Greeks two thousand years ago. Clintonomics is certainly not exempt from intellectual influences. In fact, we can trace its historic origins to the year 1689, when John Locke published his *Two Treatises of Government*.

John Locke: The Labor Theory of Value

John Locke (1632–1704) was an English philosopher who argued that owning property was a fundamental right because it was the result of a person's labor. While not as famous today as some political economists who followed him, Locke does come highly recommended. Thomas Jefferson, author of the Declaration of Independence, considered Locke one of "the three greatest men that have ever lived." According to Locke, whatever people produce with their labor is their property. They have a fundamental right to their own labor, to sell it or use it for their own personal gain. In American history, we tend to view slavery as a racial, political, or moral issue, but we should also consider the influence of this *economic* rationale. Because slavery entails ownership, involuntary servitude, and forced labor, it is fundamentally incompatible with the labor theory of value.

Furthermore, because this fundamental ownership right precedes any rights the government has, no government can deny one's property rights without due process. The government's power, said Locke, must never encroach on the power of the people and must always be subordinate to the will of the people. "Thus *Labour*, in the Beginning," Locke wrote, "*gave a Right of Property*."[3] Although we can trace the origins of this labor theory of value as far back as Aristotle (384–322 BC), it was Locke who directly linked the labor theory of value to limited government. And although we tend to associate limited government with conservatism, this concept exerted a powerful influence on Bill Clinton, as we shall see.

Jean-Jacques Rousseau: The Social Contract

The ideas of Jean-Jacques Rousseau (1712–1778) were influential (inspirational, one might say) during the 1789 French Revolution. Rousseau argued that individuals would live longer, happier, and more productive lives if they relinquished their "natural rights" and submitted to the sovereign will of the people. The problem, wrote Rousseau, is to find a form of society that will protect and defend individuals and their property such that each individual feels as free as before. "This," he said, "is the fundamental problem of which *The Social Contract* provides the solution."

A contract is any agreement between two or more parties who consent to do (or not to do) certain things. The social contract is the unspoken agreement between members of a society who, first, choose to become or remain a member of the society, and, second, choose to relinquish some of their rights and freedoms to society in exchange for security. In 1991, Clinton introduced his variation of the social contract, which he called the New Covenant, in a three-part lecture series prior to his first presidential campaign. Clinton drew inspiration from a variety of sources, including the mission statements of many African American churches, as well as John Winthrop, one of the Pilgrims who fled religious prosecution in Europe and founded Massachusetts Bay Colony in 1630. One difference between Rousseau and Clinton is that Rousseau's contract is between fellow citizens, while Clinton's covenant updates the social contract and redefines the relationship between individuals and the government for the twenty-first century. Because we consider Clintonomics a unified governing philosophy rather than merely a set of economic policies, we should keep this in mind.[4]

Adam Smith: The Invisible Hand

Adam Smith (1723–1790) was a Scottish philosopher and author of *Wealth of Nations*, a pioneering study of commercial and economic development in Europe during the industrial revolution. The marketplace as a venue for exchanging goods is as old as recorded history. Smith's monumental contribution was to explain, for the first time, the market system as an organizing principle for an entire society. Among other things, he argued that trade and labor, rather than gold or land, were the true source of wealth.

Smith argued that the government's three fundamental duties were defense, justice, and public works. That means protecting society from violence and foreign invasion; maintaining a system of law and public order to protect every member of society from every other member; and building a public infrastructure to facilitate commerce, education, and other services that are useful but not necessarily profitable. Smith's most famous phrase is perhaps the "invisible hand" analogy he used to describe the free market:

> As every individual, therefore, endeavours as much as he
> can both to employ his capital in the support of domestic

industry, and so to direct that industry that its produce may be of the greatest value; every individual necessarily labours to render the annual value of society as great as he can. He generally, indeed, neither intends to promote the public interest, nor knows how much he is promoting it. By preferring the support of domestic to that of foreign industry, he intends only his own security; and by directing that industry in such a manner as its produce may be of the greatest value, he intends only his own gain, and he is in this, as in many other cases, led by an *invisible hand* to promote an end which was no part of his intention. Nor is it always the worse for the society that it was no part of it. By pursuing his own interest he frequently promotes that of society more effectually than when he really intends to promote it.

Smith's argument is that when people, households, and companies in a market economy act in their own self-interest, they also promote the public interest. That's the invisible hand: in a market economy, selfish behavior is socially beneficial, sometimes more beneficial than altruistic behavior. No matter how disorganized the free market may appear, according to Smith, it is the most effective mechanism to regulate the supply and demand for goods, services, labor, and commodities. Too much government regulation of the market not only limits economic growth but also disrupts social development.

The market system removes economic activity from the control of political authority. The market system functions as a system of checks and balances analogous to our constitutional separation of powers. Our Constitution divides the government into three coequal branches with exclusive powers. The legislative branch makes the laws, the judicial branch interprets them, and the executive branch enforces them. Although the legislature may pass a law, the president may veto it; although the legislature may override the veto, the courts may nullify it. Just as the separation of powers works to prevent the concentration of power within government, the invisible hand depoliticizes as many decisions as possible and thus distributes power across society.

Smith's paradigm is essential to understanding Clintonomics. In the early years of the post–Cold War era, Clinton was unequivocal: "We live in a moment of hope. We all know that. The implosion of communism and the explosion of the global economy have brought new freedoms to countries on every continent. Free markets are on the rise. Democracy is ascendant." Despite the longevity of Smith's metaphor, however, we must consider the possibility the invisible hand is no match for the forces of globalization. According to Hammer and Champy, "Reengineering rejects the assumptions inherent in Adam Smith's industrial paradigm—the division of labor, economies of scale, hierarchical control, and all the other appurtenances of an early-stage developing economy. Reengineering is the search for new models of organizing work. Tradition counts for nothing. Reengineering is a new beginning."[5] If this is not clear now, it will be soon enough.

Jeremy Bentham: The Greatest Good

Jeremy Bentham (1748–1832) was a nineteenth-century British political economist. The range of his philosophical writings is wide: law, education, economics, women's rights, animal rights, and religious freedom, among other things, but he is most famous as a proponent of utilitarianism. According to utilitarianism, or the "greatest happiness principle," the best policies produce the best results for the greatest number of people. That is, public policies should maximize the good, and we should measure the success of public policies by the extent to which they help the greatest number of people. As we discussed in Chapter 1, this is what Clinton calls the purpose of politics. At a 1999 campaign rally in Iowa, Clinton said:

> Politics, the purpose of politics, is to allow free people to be more fully alive and to help each other have better lives. That's what we believe. And so I say, let them make fun of us for telling our stories. That is all that matters in the end. There is nothing abstract about America—it's a bunch of people who believe in liberty and who believe in each other and who believe that they can make life better for their children.

According to Clinton, "Power is the instrument through which you do things for people, but the power belongs to them. All of us, every single one of us, we're just hired hands for a fleeting period of time in the broad sweep of our nation's odyssey."[6] Note that power is *not* an end in itself, but an instrument, a means toward an end. Likewise, politics is not an end in itself. It has a purpose, and that purpose is to maximize the public interest, to help people live up to their potential and live together in harmony. Although pursuing the greatest good for the greatest number seems harmless enough—perhaps even meaningless in our modern society—Ronald Reagan warned about the potential for government encroachment on individual freedom, even when our public servants had the best intentions.

David Ricardo: Free Trade

David Ricardo (1772–1823) stands alongside Adam Smith and John Stuart Mill (discussed later) as one of the great political economists in history. His most famous work is *On the Principles of Political Economy and Taxation*. He was also an astute businessman and made a huge fortune in the stock market. The aspect of Ricardo's work that interests us most is another of those invisible laws of political economy, the theory of comparative advantage. According to Ricardo, countries should not try to produce every-thing they need, but trade with other countries to satisfy their other needs:

> Under a system of perfectly free commerce, each country naturally devotes its capital and labour to such employ-ments as are most beneficial to each. This pursuit of indi-vidual advantage is admirably connected with the universal good of the whole. By stimulating industry, by rewarding ingenuity, and by using most efficaciously the peculiar powers bestowed by nature, it distributes labour most effectively and most economically. . . . It is this principle which determines that wine shall be made in France and Portugal, that corn shall be grown in America and Poland, and that hardware and other goods shall be manufactured in England.[7]

Ricardo elevated Smith's invisible hand to a national scale and argued countries should specialize in industries where they have a comparative advantage. Ricardo's work is most influential with respect to Clinton's position against protectionism in support of free trade and his belief that all nations can benefit from free trade. Perhaps most importantly, Ricardo's groundbreaking work supports the idea of economic *interdependence*, which is why it re-mains relevant in an era when rich and poor countries alike are struggling with the powerful forces of globalization.

Friedrich List: Limits of Free Trade

Friedrich List (1789–1846) was a German economist who wrote about national economies (or the "national system"). His major work *The National System of Political Economy* was inspired and influenced by Alexander Hamilton, America's first treasury secretary. List built his theory of national economics on several of Hamilton's ideas, such as promoting economic growth through a national bank, investing in commercial infrastructure, and using tariffs and subsidies to protect domestic industry.

List's writings about national economies and the national system, rather than the global system, drew attention to the failures of free trade. People often speak about free trade with the same reverence as they speak about political or religious freedom, wrote List. "Hence the friends and advocates of freedom feel themselves especially bound to defend freedom in all its forms." According to List, however, free trade between wealthy and poor countries is unequal and thus inherently unfair. Furthermore, List believed advocates of free trade in wealthy economies were self-serving, and he was particularly skeptical when the British advocated free trade only after developing their own economy, their own merchant shipping, and their own manufacturing base:

> Any nation which by means of protective duties and restrictions on navigation has raised her manufacturing power and navigation to such a degree of development that no other nation can sustain free competition with her, can do nothing wiser than to throw away these ladders of her greatness, to preach to other nations the benefits of free trade, and to declare in penitent tones that she hitherto wandered in the paths of error, and has now for the first time succeeded in discovering the truth.[8]

At the dawn of the twenty-first century, skepticism toward free trade and globalization in general is a reasonable attitude, to say the least. From Friedrich List's writings on the national system to Henry Charles Carey's writings on the American system (next page), we begin to understand why Clinton mitigated his support for unlimited free trade with a commitment to fair trade.

Henry Charles Carey: Benefits of Fair Trade

Henry Charles Carey (1793–1879) was Abraham Lincoln's chief economic advisor and a leading nineteenth-century economist of the American School of capitalism. His major work *Harmony of Interests* promoted the "American System" of developmental capitalism through protectionism, tariffs, and government subsidies. He considered government intervention in the economy—in the form of tariffs and subsidies, but also in terms of supervision and management—necessary to promote equitable economic development.

Carey loathed nineteenth-century British dominance, particularly in India and Ireland, where British policies built on cheap labor consistently drove the value of labor down. Carey thought our economic policies should try to increase the value of labor, and thus elevate and equalize living standards for people around the world. "To raise the value of labour throughout the world," he wrote, "we need only to raise the value of our own."[9] Elsewhere he said:

> The policy that produces a necessity for depending on trade with people who are poorer than ourselves tends to reduce the wages of our labour to a level with theirs, and to diminish commerce. That which should give us power to trade with nations who might be richer than ourselves would tend to raise our wages to a level with theirs.[10]

Despite Clinton's differences with Carey regarding specific policy options and the appropriate degree of government intervention in the economy, we can see Carey's influence in Clinton's position on international trade. As stated, Clinton wanted a balance between free trade and fair trade. Although Clinton vigorously supported the North American Free Trade Agreement (NAFTA), for example, he always insisted on enforcement of labor laws and environmental protection.

John Stuart Mill: The National Debt

Jeremy Bentham's student John Stuart Mill (1806–1874) was another great European political economist. He revised and expanded utilitarianism and wrote about political economy in general. Mill also considered the issue of national debt, particularly the question of raising money for government works not through taxation, but through borrowing. Mill had no problem with short-term loans lasting one or two years for what we might call operating expenses. Because future generations frequently benefited from government works, Mill argued we should not force the current generation to make the "great sacrifice," but make sure future beneficiaries paid their share. A certain amount of national debt for public infrastructure is acceptable, he said, and practically indispensable. However, he warned against "the propriety of contracting national debt of a permanent character." Mill considered the national debt "a very great evil; and the worst thing about it is, that there is no getting rid of it."

When we consider Clinton's relentless advocacy of downsizing government, balancing the budget, and reducing the national debt, Mill's influence is self-evident. Clinton advocated deficit reduction because long-term structural deficits reduce the government's flexibility to respond to different economic problems, such as inflation, unemployment, or recession. Early in Clinton's first term, his primary goal was to support economic recovery, and reducing the deficit was a means toward that goal. Whereas Reagan disliked deficit spending because it is inflationary (see Chapter 3), Clinton disliked it because when too much of the federal budget goes toward interest payments, too little goes toward public investment in roads, bridges, railways, transit systems, and information systems. "It is simply not true that all government spending is equal," Clinton said, because there is a difference between investment and consumption.[11]

Karl Marx: The Capitalist System

Karl Marx (1818–1883) was born in Germany and spent much of his life in England. Of course, Marx is most famous for *Manifesto of the Communist Party* (with Frederick Engels) and *Capital: A Critique of Political Economy* (in three massive volumes), which was Marx's criticism of the capitalist system. The ideas of Adam Smith and David Ricardo, particularly their writings on the labor theory of value, influenced Karl Marx, but Marx had a fundamentally different understanding of human nature. He questioned whether labor was simply a commodity to be bought and sold and argued that the pursuit of self-interest was not innate, but a response to the economic system—the capitalist economic system.

Like Smith and Ricardo, Marx studied the laws of political economy invisible to ordinary people. Unlike Smith and Ricardo, Marx had the extraordinary ability to see the whole system and describe the incredibly complex set of interconnections between humans and their political and economic environment across an epoch. Marx believed the cycle of economic growth, depression, unemployment, and regrowth would inevitably lead to a severe economic crisis:

> This much is evident: the cycle of interconnected turn-
> overs embracing a number of years, in which capital is

held fast by its fixed constituent part, furnishes a material
basis for the periodic crises. During this cycle business
undergoes successive periods of depression, medium activity, precipitancy, crisis. True, periods in which capital
is invested differ greatly and far from coincide in time.
But a crisis always forms the starting-point of large new
investments.[12]

Marx analyzed and criticized capitalism as a system whose internal flaws inevitably caused disruption, conflict, even self-
destruction. Although capital is not "held fast by its fixed constituent part," Marx understood that our capitalist modes of production, distribution, and consumption belong to an economic
system that functions in symbiosis with our political system. Perhaps it goes without saying that Marx underestimated the ability
of markets to self-correct, a characteristic that allows all complex
systems to adapt to changes in the environment the same way
living organisms evolve. Nonetheless, Marx insisted that our economic systems, which satisfy our needs for material well-being,
are inseparable from our political systems, which satisfy our
needs for security and stability.

John Maynard Keynes: Deficit Spending

John Maynard Keynes (1883–1946) was renowned as an economic philosopher and policy maker. Early in his career, Keynes
was in the British civil service (posted in India) and later one of
Britain's representatives at the Paris peace talks in 1919. Toward
the end of World War II, Keynes led the British delegation at the
Bretton Woods conference, which led to the creation of the
World Bank and International Monetary Fund.

In 1936, Keynes published his *General Theory of Employment, In-*

terest and Money and advocated increasing government expenditures to stimulate the economy. Keynes's ideas were particularly influential on Franklin Roosevelt and his New Deal program. During the Great Depression there was high unemployment and excess capacity, so Keynes advocated priming the pump—increasing government spending on public works to stimulate consumer demand—even if it entailed incurring a large, permanent deficit. When unemployment is high, so goes the argument, deficit spending (often in the form of public works) increases consumer spending, which creates a multiplier effect and thus increases demand for goods and services. Although Keynes ignored John Stuart Mill's warning about the dangers of permanent national debt, Mill himself might have conceded the Great Depression called for special intervention.

Keynes said, "The outstanding faults of the economic society in which we live are its failure to provide for full employment and its arbitrary and inequitable distribution of wealth and incomes." Keynes advocated government intervention in the economy, using fiscal and monetary policies to influence and mitigate cycles of boom and bust. So sure was Keynes of the advantages of deficit spending, he suggested the government bury money in abandoned coal mines for people to dig up.

> If the Treasury were to fill old bottles with banknotes, bury them at suitable depths in disused coal-mines which are then filled up to the surface with town rubbish, and leave it to private enterprise on well-tried principles of *laissez-faire* to dig the notes up again (the right to do so being obtained, of course, by tendering for leases of the note-bearing territory), there need be no more unemployment and, with the help of the repercussions, the real income of the community, and its capital wealth

also, would probably become a good deal greater than it actually is.[13]

As far as we know, the Clinton administration never buried money in abandoned coal mines. In terms of Clintonomics, the influence of Keynes is similar to the influence of Carey, in that both argued the necessity of government intervention in the economy. Although Clinton and Keynes disagree how much government intervention in the economy is too much, they do agree that two of our economic system's outstanding faults are chronic unemployment and the inequitable distribution of wealth.

Clinton often touted how low the so-called *misery index* was during his presidency. The misery index is the unemployment rate added to the inflation rate. Unemployment is miserable, particularly if you are also without income. Inflation is miserable even if you have a job but live on a fixed income, like a teacher or a state employee. Inflation is also miserable if you are living on social security or on a pension, because your monthly check never seems to keep up with the cost of living, particularly the cost of fuel.

Shakespeare said, "Misery acquaints a man with strange bedfellows" (*The Tempest*, Act II, Scene II). The problem with the misery index—other than the name—is it tells us only half of what we need to measure the success of our economic policies. If public policies should maximize the good and be measured by the extent to which they help the greatest number of people, then we also need to measure economic growth and the distribution of wealth. In nonpolicy-wonk terms, economic growth is an indicator of economic activity, the increase of national income, or the national product. Ideally, when we measure economic growth over time and adjust it for inflation, we will see an increase in our standard of living along with an increase in the production of goods and services. Both parties, Republicans and Democrats alike, love economic growth because it benefits investors and (usually, but not always) expands the middle class.

The other indicator we need to keep track of is the distribution of wealth, a comparison of the allocation of resources across society. American politicians rarely discuss the distribution of wealth in public and seem unable to distinguish it from the *redistribution* of wealth. Others seem uncomfortable discussing it except when condemning their adversaries for giving tax breaks to people in the upper income bracket. Still others raise the issue indirectly, often in reference to another country, Mexico, for example, whose inequitable distribution of wealth contributes to the problem of illegal immigration.

Clinton was one of those who discussed the distribution of wealth in public, but only indirectly.

> I believe no great nation, at any point in human history, has ever, ever, gotten greater without extending opportunity to more and more people and having responsibility for more people to build a strong community. This is the greatest nation in human history because we have built a middle class of people, and average people have had a chance to make it if they have done the right things.[14]

In nonpolicy-wonk terms, our best indicators to measure the success of our economic policies are low unemployment, low inflation, steady economic growth, and a booming middle class.

Joseph Schumpeter: Entrepreneurship

Joseph Schumpeter (1883–1950) was an Austrian economist, finance minister, banker, and one of the Austrian School of economists who rejected the labor theory of value and argued, directly in opposition to Marxism, that value is subjective, driven by market forces such as supply and demand. In Schumpeter's most popular book, *Capitalism, Socialism and Democracy*, he coined the phrase "creative destruction," the catalytic process of change essential to capitalism. "The fundamental impulse that sets and keeps the capitalist engine in motion comes from the new consumers' goods, the new methods of production or transportation, the new markets, the new forms of industrial organization that capitalist enterprise creates." Thus, capitalism never is, and never can be, stationary.

The legendary figure who causes creative destruction is the entrepreneur, who identifies and exploits inefficiencies in the market, disturbs the equilibrium, and challenges the status quo. Schumpeter describes the heroic function of entrepreneurs as follows:

> We have seen that the function of entrepreneurs is to reform or revolutionize the pattern of production by exploiting invention or more generally, an untried technological possibility for producing a new commodity or producing an old one in a new way, by opening up a new source of supply of materials or a new outlet for products, by reorganizing an industry and so on.[15]

The entrepreneurial spirit exists in only a small segment of the population. It thrives on self-motivation, creativity, and risk contrary to routine patterns of behavior and outside of familiar ways of thinking. It withers in bureaucracies and committees and anywhere the forces of equilibrium hinder individual initiative. According to David Osborne and Ted Gaebler, authors of *Reinventing Government*, however, "Any institution, public or private, can be entrepreneurial, just as any institution can be bureaucratic." Even though governments cannot always run like businesses, they can become more entrepreneurial, meaning mission driven, market oriented, and customer friendly.

Clintonomics rests on the hope we can reengineer government beyond two-dimensional thinking, away from bureaucracy and toward a culture of *public entrepreneurship* that makes government more efficient and less expensive. Clinton believed the government could and should follow the example set by innovative state and local governments and other leading private sector companies. "In short, it's time our Government adjusted to the real world, tightened its belt, managed its affairs in the context of an economy that is information based, rapidly changing, and puts a premium on speed and function and service, not rules and regulations."[16]

Friedrich Hayek: Limited Government

Friedrich Hayek (1899–1992) was an Austrian-born political economist who defended liberal democracy and free-market capitalism against socialism. Like John Locke, Hayek believed property rights were fundamental. In *The Fatal Conceit*, Hayek attributed the birth of civilization to private property. Hayek argued Locke's philosophy "was based in the insight that the *justice* that political authority must enforce, if it wants to secure the peaceful cooperation among individuals on which property rests, cannot exist without the recognition of private property: 'Where there is no property there is no justice.'"

Hayek was one of the most important political economists of the twentieth century, exerting an influence on Margaret Thatcher, Ronald Reagan, and others. He argued that the market system was the most efficient mechanism to optimize allocation of resources and was thus opposed to economic planning, not just the kind undertaken in centrally planned socialist economies, but almost all economic planning. He believed the whole idea of central planning was "confused," as if planning was in direct competition with the market. Governments should enforce the rule of law, he said, and intervene in the economy as little as possible. When a government sacrifices freedom for social justice, it risks becoming a welfare state, whose primary (and ultimately arbitrary) method is redistribution of wealth:

> The chief danger today is that, once an aim of govern-
> ment is accepted as legitimate, it is then assumed that
> even means contrary to the principles of freedom may
> be legitimately employed. The unfortunate fact is that, in
> the most effective, certain, and speedy way of reaching a
> given end [is] to direct all available resources toward the
> now visible solution. To the ambitious and impatient re-
> former, filled with indignation at a particular evil, noth-
> ing short of the complete abolition of that evil by the
> quickest and most direct means will seem adequate. If
> every person now suffering from unemployment, ill
> health, or inadequate provision for his old age is at once
> to be relieved of his cares, nothing short of an all-com-
> prehensive and compulsory scheme will suffice.[17]

One amusing anecdote demonstrates the extent of Hayek's in-fluence. In the late seventies, Margaret Thatcher—before she came to power—attended a meeting of the shadow cabinet, the loyal opposition in British Parliament. While she was listening to one of her conservative colleagues present a paper, she took exception to something she heard. She removed one of Friedrich Hayek's books (*The Constitution of Liberty*) from her briefcase and held it up for everyone to see. Then she slammed it on the table and said, "This is what we believe."

In the years before Thatcher became prime minister, Reagan

worried about the United Kingdom drifting further and further toward a welfare state. Reagan considered welfare an addictive drug that ultimately destroyed its intended beneficiaries. Reagan believed the huge increase in the number of welfare recipients was conclusive proof of the system's failure, which is an innovative and ultimately persuasive interpretation of Bentham's utilitarian principle. If public policies should maximize the good and should be measured by the extent to which they help the greatest number of people, then the greatest good comes from how much we *decrease* the need for welfare.

If we dismantle the welfare state, however, who will provide welfare to those unable to provide for themselves through no fault of their own? British sociologist Anthony Giddens, who influenced Tony Blair in his effort to reposition Britain's labor party, replies with some skepticism: "The answer is market-led economic growth. Welfare should be understood not as state benefits, but as maximizing economic progress, and therefore overall wealth, by allowing markets to work their miracles." Bill Clinton launched his campaign *to end welfare as we know it* because he, too, believed millions of people were trapped in the system. Many were women with young children who wanted to be good parents but lived in neighborhoods where there were gangs, guns, and drugs, but no jobs. Most wanted to work but had too little formal education. Their families were struggling, their communities were unsafe, and their options were limited. When Clinton signed welfare reform legislation in 1996, he passed the greatest test of federalism, according to the standard set by Ronald Reagan himself, as we will see in Chapter 7.[18]

John Kenneth Galbraith: The Social Balance

John Kenneth Galbraith (1908–2006) was a Canadian-American political economist who served under several presidents, including as ambassador to India under John Kennedy. In *The Affluent Society*, Galbraith argued that our progress into an age of affluence rendered classical economics obsolete. His concern was that as society became more affluent and the production of consumer goods and services increased, the public sector (schools, libraries, roads, bridges, parks, even entire cities) would suffer from neglect.

In *The New Industrial State*, Galbraith said neglecting the social balance—the balance between the consumer sector and the public sector—would inevitably produce a class of technocrats addicted to planning. He worried about the abuse of power in economic life, particularly the kind of power technocrats and corporations exerted over consumers, politicians, presidents, and the entire government. No matter how loudly the technocrats argue in favor of the market system, no matter how frequently they mimic Hayek's hostility toward planning, they love it, particularly when it comes to defense procurement and defense technology. Planning means long-term contracts that call for major capital investment, full protection against any change in requirements, no risk of price fluctuations, and no change in demand.

The idea that affluence would cause deterioration of the social balance is counterintuitive. Didn't Adam Smith argue that people and companies promote the public interest even when they act in their own self-interest? We should remember Smith acknowledged the government had a fundamental duty to provide defense, law and order, and maintain the public infrastructure. However, if the invisible hand works the way Smith said it works, then the social balance should maintain long-term equilibrium whether we neglect it or not. Is the invisible hand nothing more than a quaint artifact, a relic from an earlier stage of economic development? If so, our affluent society requires a new theory of political economy.[19]

A BRIEF DIGRESSION is in order here. Political economist Robert Reich, who served as labor secretary in the first Clinton administration, wrote, "The official reason given for why America cannot invest more money in infrastructure, education, and training is that we cannot afford it. In his inaugural address, George Bush [the elder] noted regretfully, 'We have more will than wallet'—a frequent lamentation. But only excessive politeness should constrain one from inquiring: Whose will? Whose wallet?"[20] Two things should be apparent: The deteriorating social balance is worse than ever, and market forces alone will not solve it.

Even though I quote Reich, I should disclose he disagreed with the premise of this book—presenting Clintonomics as a single, unified idea. He said there was not one version of Clintonomics, but three. The first was during Clinton's 1992 campaign, which promoted balancing the budget and increasing public investment in areas such as education, job training, infrastructure, research, and development. The second incarnation promoted deficit reduction. The third—once the budget surpluses appeared—focused on saving Social Security and keeping it out of the red for the next seventy-five years. The bottom line according to Reich: There was no Clintonomics.[21] If we limit ourselves strictly to Clinton's economic policies, then I would agree with Reich. However, if we consider Clintonomics as a unified philosophy of government with political and economic elements developed over time, then I would respectfully disagree.

This chapter lays the philosophical foundation of Clintonomics and shows how difficult it is to pinpoint Clinton on the liberal-conservative spectrum. We will explore other perspectives in subsequent chapters, but first we will consider Ronald Reagan's governing philosophy. Although Clinton began his presidency four short years after Reagan finished his, the end of the Cold War and the end of communism create an apples-and-oranges problem for us. Despite this political and economic bifurcation, however, Reagan's political influence on Clinton was considerable, as we will see in Chapter 3.

CHAPTER 3

The Reagan Legacy

We asked the Republicans to discard their hatred of government, and their blind faith that the only thing that would ever matter was having more tax cuts.[1]
—BILL CLINTON, 1999

THIS CHAPTER WILL RECONSTRUCT Ronald Reagan's governing philosophy using the same approach we will take to Clinton's—that is, as a complex governing philosophy with political and economic elements. As we proceed, we will not put every little particle under the microscope but instead focus on basic principles and big ideas. Likewise, we will not arbitrarily limit ourselves to fiscal and monetary policy or economic policy in general. Our field of inquiry is political economy, from the most primitive impulses of human nature to the most complex expressions of human development.

Several scholars affiliated with the Hoover Institution, the public policy research center and conservative think tank adjacent to Stanford University, have produced two anthologies of Reagan's speeches, letters, and other writings from the period before he became president. George Shultz, himself a Hoover fellow, wrote a brief foreword for both volumes. Shultz served as secretary of state under Reagan for almost seven years. He served in the Marine Corps and many other government agencies, including cabinet-level appointments at Labor and Treasury. He earned a PhD in industrial economics from the Massachusetts Institute of Technology, was dean of the business school at the University of Chicago and president of the Bechtel Group, one of the world's largest engineering companies.

According to Shultz, who is probably the most highly qualified American public servant of his generation, the anthologies prove Reagan was a lot smarter than most people thought.[2] Because Reagan wrote so many of these speeches in his own hand, it is hard to argue with Shultz on this point. Reagan was a genius as a communicator, a broadcaster literally and figuratively, but not an original thinker. That is not to say his beliefs were insubstantial, just unoriginal. Reagan became spokesman-in-chief for conservative ideas such as lower taxes, minimal spending for social services, minimal government regulation of the economy, and major increases in military spending, a brief discussion of which will help us reconstruct Reagan's governing philosophy.

So, what is conservatism? Cobbling together more than a dozen different definitions, I came up with this: Conservatism is a belief system (or ideology) respectful toward traditional institutions and resistant to radical change, which generally places a high priority on the following principles:

- **Individualism:** Self-reliance, individual freedom, and individual autonomy supersede social obligations.
- **Economic Freedom:** The right to work, own property, and participate in the free market are fundamental human rights.

- **Limited Government:** Government authority should be decentralized and restricted by law.

According to the Hoover Institution, conservatism seeks to secure and safeguard peace, improve the human condition, and
limit government intrusion into peoples' lives according to the
principles of individual, economic, and political freedom; private
enterprise; and representative government.[3] According to the
Heritage Foundation, another conservative think tank similar to
the Hoover Institution, its mission is "to formulate and promote
conservative public policies based on the principles of free enterprise, limited government, individual freedom, traditional American values, and a strong national defense." Although national
defense is last on the Heritage Foundation's list, it considers it a
top priority. Its definition of freedom is synonymous with having
many choices, particularly in terms of education, healthcare, and
retirement. Its definition of limited government is government
that recognizes its limitations, concentrates on its core functions,
and levies taxes that are "fair, flat, and comprehensible." It considers its mission to promote its ideas aggressively and seek solutions to contemporary problems based on the principles that
motivated the founding fathers.[4]

This emphasis on founding principles (rather than founding
policies) is important. In September 1787, in order to form a
more perfect union, the states unanimously agreed to discard the
Articles of Confederation and establish the Constitution for the
United States of America. Reaching unanimous agreement required acquiescing to the Southern slave states and resulted in
two particularly stomach-churning policies. First, according to
Article I, Section 2, slaves counted as three-fifths (or 60 percent)
of a free person for the purposes of apportioning legislative representation and taxes. Second, according to Article IV, Section 2,
slaves who escaped to a free state "shall be delivered up" to their

rightful owner. When we reflect on the principles of the founding fathers, we should keep these policies in mind.

Due diligence requires considering the ideas of conservative talk radio icon Rush Limbaugh, whose definition of conservatism closely parallels Reagan's. Limbaugh considers conservatism the ultimate realism, because it doesn't idealize or otherwise distort human nature. Limbaugh's version is part of a larger belief system that includes political and economic elements and a strongly pro-American stance, as well as beliefs about religion, race relations, gender relations, human nature, and other topics. The enemies of conservatism, according to Limbaugh, are "the forces of socialism and collectivism, the ever-expanding governmental bureaucracy, the emasculation of our system of law and order, the assault on our nation's value base, the undermining of our spirit of patriotism, and the systematic effort to weaken our nation's economic and military prowess."[5]

Limbaugh believes in the power of the individual and the sanctity of human life. He believes that political freedom is inseparable from economic freedom and that political freedom is America's greatest attribute, because it allows for maximum individual achievement. In general, Limbaugh believes in limited government—enough to ensure law and order and enough to ensure equal opportunity, but not to guarantee equal outcomes. He believes "that compassion is not defined by how many people are on the government dole, but by how many people no longer need governmental assistance," which, as we will discover, is almost identical to Reagan's views on welfare.

Limbaugh also believes that "racial relations will not be enhanced or prejudice eliminated by governmental edict."[6] Although this is consistent with the conservative principle of limited government—one that certainly does not idealize human nature—I mention it to make a point. An edict is a formal proclamation with the force of law, such as the Emancipation Proclamation that Abraham Lincoln issued in January 1863 during the Civil War. That particular edict declared all slaves held in the Confederate states "shall be then, thenceforward, and forever free." One could argue the Emancipation Proclamation did not actually free a single slave, just as one could argue it did nothing to enhance race relations or eliminate prejudice, but there is no denying presidential edicts can be very powerful, with or without the force of law. Also, let's not forget Lincoln was the first member of the Republican Party ever elected president.

For the sake of diversity and inclusiveness in our discussion of conservatism, we should also check in with the Log Cabin Republicans, the party's gay and lesbian wing, dedicated to educating members of the Republican Party about gay and lesbian issues and informing gays and lesbians about Republican principles and values. Their Web site includes a "What We Believe" section, without Margaret Thatcher slamming Friedrich Hayek's *The Constitution of Liberty* on the table:

> We are loyal Republicans. We believe in limited government, strong national defense, free markets, low taxes, personal responsibility, and individual liberty. Log Cabin represents an important part of the American family—taxpaying, hard working people who proudly believe in this nation's greatness. We also believe all Americans have the right to liberty and equality. We believe equality for gay and lesbian people is in the finest tradition of the Republican Party. We educate our Party about why inclusion wins. Opposing gay and lesbian equality is inconsistent with the GOP's core principles of smaller government and personal freedom.[7]

We should also pay our respects to the Iron Lady herself. In her autobiography, Thatcher said, "No theory of government was ever given a fairer test or a more prolonged experiment in a democratic country than democratic socialism received in Britain. It was a miserable failure in every respect." Before she came to power, the ideas of Friedrich Hayek and others gave Thatcher hope and convinced her that socialism would ultimately fail. "That is a vital feeling in politics; it eradicates past defeats and builds future victories." Like Reagan, Thatcher was a long-term optimist who favored political and economic freedom, and she preached the gospel of free enterprise "with very little qualification."[8]

At a state dinner early in Reagan's presidency, Thatcher toasted Reagan and toasted the philosophy of government they shared. Conservatism does not mean maintenance of the status quo, she said, but "maintenance of the old values." Traditional values provide the foundation that permits society to change, to adapt to the technological advances that drive economic growth. Conservatism means harnessing and liberating the resources and fundamental strengths that create prosperity and make people self-reliant. "As a Conservative I want determined and decisive government. But that's something very different from an all-powerful government. You and I, Mr. President, believe in strong governments in areas where only governments can do the job, areas where governments can and must be strong—strong in the defense of the nation, strong in protecting law and order, strong in promoting a sound currency."[9]

The Genealogy of Reaganomics

Based on the previous chapter, we can trace the genealogy of conservatism to John Locke's writings on the labor theory of value, property rights, and limited government. Adam Smith's simple metaphor of the invisible hand continues to be influential, and so is his argument that government has a duty to provide public services that are useful but not necessarily profitable. David Ricardo's work on free trade is still relevant, though his argument with Friedrich List on the limits of free trade is unlikely ever to end.

Among the defunct economists, Friedrich Hayek gets the last word: Based on the principles of conservatism, the government should provide national defense, enforce the rule of law, and intervene in the economy as little as possible. Even then, faithful conservatives may find it necessary to ignore this principle altogether during wartime, peacetime, or election time. Here is Hayek's definition of "conservatism proper":

> [Though] the position I have tried to define is also often described as "conservative," it is very different from that to which this name has been traditionally attached. There is danger in the confused condition which brings the defenders of liberty and true conservatives together in common opposition to developments which threaten their different ideals equally. It is therefore important to distinguish clearly the position taken here from that which has long been known—perhaps more appropriately—as conservatism. Conservatism proper is a legitimate, probably necessary, and certainly widespread attitude of opposition to drastic change.[10]

Conservatism is an attitude of opposition to drastic change, according to Hayek, an attitude that is legitimate (meaning sensible and logical) and *probably* necessary. We briefly discussed the high art of coalition building in Chapter 1. We can see elements of the coalition Reagan came to personify in the quotation above, when Hayek makes the distinction between "defenders of liberty" and "true conservatives."

Not only was Reagan a world-champion defender of liberty and opponent of drastic change, he was also a leading proponent of fiscal conservatism, an idea whose genealogy we can trace to Edmund Burke (1729–1797), an Irish politician and writer who supported the American Revolution but opposed the French Revolution, because he considered it a rebellion against legitimate political authority. One of Burke's most important contributions to conservatism was his resistance to radical change—not all change, but excessive change. In Burke's most influential work, *Reflections on the Revolution in France*, he questioned the idea that the French government was so incapable and so undeserving of reform that it absolutely needed to be destroyed. Leveling is not the same as equalizing, Burke reasoned, and thus no one should dismantle political or economic institutions that have served society to any tolerable degree without infinite caution.[11]

Burke reserved his most forceful arguments for fiscal conservatism, particularly his opposition to public debt. Government services funded through public debt may bring security and stability in the short term, but if the government consistently lives beyond its means and incurs what John Stuart Mill called national debt of a permanent character, somebody has to pay for it. Public debt becomes not simply a budgetary or economic issue, but a political issue. Government creditors—the moneylenders—inevitably acquire undue influence, which exposes the government to bribery, extortion, and other forms of corruption. Burke's prose may be hard to follow, but his contemptuous tone leaps from the page:

> The men who compose this interest look for their security, in the first instance, to the fidelity of government; in the second, to its power. If they find the old governments effete, worn out, and with their springs relaxed, so as not to be of sufficient vigor for their purposes, they may seek

new ones that shall be possessed of more energy; and this energy will be derived, not from an acquisition of resources, but from a contempt of justice.[12]

As a matter of principle, individual autonomy and economic freedom must precede government authority. The freedom to work, the freedom to enjoy the fruits of one's labor, the freedom to own and control one's property, and the freedom to participate in a free market are fundamental rights that precede the government's rights. Because the most fundamental and most personal property right is ownership of one's labor, society owes its "first and original faith" not to the creditor of the state, but to the people. "The claim of the citizen," Burke wrote, "is prior in time, paramount in title [and] superior in equity."[13]

Reagan's opposition to national debt and high taxes comes directly from Burke, while his belief that political freedom is inseparable from economic freedom comes from Milton Friedman (1912–2006), an American economist and Nobel Prize winner who taught for many years at the University of Chicago. Like Reagan, Friedman believed political economy is one indivisible thing, not two separate entities with interchangeable parts. Because political freedom cannot exist in isolation from economic freedom, there are only two fundamental ways to coordinate the economic activities of societies with millions of people. "One is central direction involving the use of coercion—the technique of the army and of the modern totalitarian state," said Friedman. "The other is the voluntary cooperation of individuals—the technique of the marketplace."

In *Capitalism and Freedom*, Friedman worried about the abuse of power in economic life, particularly in relation to defense spending. When the government buys so much of the nation's economic output, it concentrates a dangerous amount of economic power in the hands of a few political authorities and endangers the free market. When it came to John Kennedy's lofty rhetoric, Friedman was a fearless dissenting voice. When Kennedy said in his 1961 inaugural address, "Ask not what your country can do for you—ask what you can do for your country," Milton countered that it would never occur to free people to ask either question. Friedman said truly free people would instead ask what they can accomplish *through government* to achieve their goals; discharge their responsibilities; and, above all, protect their freedom. What's more, free people would ask a follow-up question: "How can we keep the government we create from becoming a Frankenstein that will destroy the very freedom we establish it to protect?" The concentration of power represents the greatest threat to freedom, regardless of the good intentions of the people who wield the power, which is why government must be limited and power must be dispersed.

In *Free to Choose*, Friedman and his wife, Rose, wrote extensively on the interdependence of political and economic freedom, arguing that freedom is one whole, and anything that reduces freedom in one part is likely to reduce it in other parts of our society. This does not eliminate the need for government. On the contrary, said Friedman, the role of government is to establish the rules, arbitrate them, and enforce them. There are things the market cannot do for itself, such as defining property rights; adjudicating disputes; promoting competition; enforcing contracts; providing a monetary framework; and, of course, maintaining a system of law and order. However, he argued forcefully against using fiscal policy (taxes or deficit spending) to reduce unemployment or redistribute wealth.

Friedman thought that the greatest threat to freedom comes from people with good intentions who want to reform the system and that government programs to redistribute the wealth usually do more harm than good. On the other hand, he definitely considered it the appropriate role of government to repair natural imperfections in the market, such as public education, because it treated the source of inequality rather than alleviated the symptom. In 1988, Reagan presented Friedman with the Presidential Medal of Freedom for restoring "common sense to the world of economics," a testament to Friedman's influence.[14]

Reagan believed all governments acquired a momentum of their own, fueled by high taxes that inevitably led to the abuse of power. Paraphrasing chief justice John Marshall's 1819 opinion in *McCulloch v. Maryland*, Reagan said, "The power to tax is the power to destroy. If so, then the power to cut taxes must surely be the power to create—the power to force government to stand back and let the people themselves give expression to the spirit of enterprise—building and imagining; giving to you, our sons and daughters, a nation of ever-greater prosperity and freedom."[15]

Reagan once described himself as "a former New Deal Democrat" and "*something* of a liberal."[16] Indeed, Reagan began his political life as a Democrat, casting his first vote in 1932 for Franklin Roosevelt. The effects of the Great Depression were bad and getting worse. Unemployment was high, particularly in mining and logging. Banks closed their doors; people lost their jobs, their savings, and their homes. Prolonged drought in the agricultural heartland and low prices for agricultural commodities forced hundreds of thousands of people to migrate in search of work. Such were the conditions in which Reagan began his political life, and he embarked on an ideological migration of his own.

The more successful Reagan became during his long career in movies and television, the more offended he became by the government's confiscatory tax policies. In 1962, Reagan switched parties and officially registered as a Republican. In 1964, two years before he ran for governor of California, Reagan gave a televised address on behalf of Barry Goldwater's presidential campaign. This speech launched Reagan's political career. If one of those crime scene investigators we see on television today could take a sample of Reagan's political DNA, this is what it would look like:

> Our natural unalienable rights are now presumed to be a dispensation of government, divisible by a vote of the majority. The greatest good for the greatest number is a high-sounding phrase but contrary to the very basis of our nation, unless it is accompanied by recognition that we have certain rights which cannot be infringed upon, even if the individual stands outvoted by all of his fellow citizens. Without this recognition, majority rule is nothing more than mob rule.[17]

If *the greatest good for the greatest number* sounds familiar, that's because it is Jeremy Bentham's utilitarian principle. When Reagan says *we have certain rights which cannot be infringed upon*, that should also sound familiar, courtesy of John Locke and Edmund Burke. With a running time of twenty-nine minutes, Reagan's televised endorsement speech is long by today's standards, but two fragments encapsulate his governing philosophy. The first is "the maximum of individual freedom consistent with law and order," and the second is "you can't control the economy without controlling people." Together, these fragments explain what it means to believe in individualism, economic freedom, and limited government, the timeless principles of conservatism.

Public Versus Private Ownership

One of Reagan's favorite lines was, "Communism works only in heaven, where they don't need it, and in hell, where they've already got it."[18] His legendary anticommunism affected almost every aspect of his governing philosophy, so it is impossible to discuss Reaganomics without addressing it. He considered communism the ultimate abuse of power, the ultimate violation of individual autonomy, and the ultimate form of unlimited government. Reagan considered communism a form of insanity rather than a political and economic system. He used the terms *socialism* and *communism* interchangeably—and always pejoratively— much the way Clinton ridiculed trickle-down economics. According to Reagan, communism had one fatal flaw: It was contrary to human nature.[19] His observation may be astute, or maybe not, but we need to place it within the context of the laws of political economy: Politics is about power; economics is about resources. Political and economic systems are projections and expressions of one aspect of human nature or another. They are synthetic, human-made artifacts.

It is possible Reagan's observation is accurate: Communism is contrary to human nature and thus destined to fail. More likely, Reagan is making what social scientists call a *unit of analysis error*. We know any governing philosophy is a value system and that some values receive higher ranking than others receive.[20] Furthermore, we know Reagan believed individuals have certain natural, unalienable rights that no government—even democratic government—can take away. The basic entity in Reaganomics, the essential unit of analysis, is the individual. In political economy, the individual is a common unit of analysis, but not the only one. Other units of analysis include families, groups, organizations, corporations, countries, geographic areas, and, of course, the global system as a whole. Although communism may be contrary to human nature, it may not be contrary to family nature, village nature, or any other unit of analysis. However, given Reagan's belief that human rights are natural and the power of the state is arbitrary, his anticommunism is perfectly logical.

In practice, Reagan objected to any system based on public ownership of the economy, including most kinds of government regulation and central planning, but not all kinds of authoritarian rule. His public statements, speeches, and interviews are full of anecdotes that depict the monumental incompetence and corruption in Eastern bloc countries, their obsolete technology and backward economies. In speech after speech, Reagan ridiculed the nepotism in Nicolae Ceausescu's family in Romania, the bombastic Russian general whose indiscreet comments followed the party line, and the wheat shortage in Russia, despite millions of Russians working in the agricultural sector. As far as Reagan was concerned, *nothing* proved the failure of communism more clearly than the Soviet Union's inability to feed its people and simultaneously produce weapons for its military ambitions.[21] Everything about the Soviet system was ridiculous and incompetent—except its military.

His anticommunism led him (for a time) to support some of the world's most brutal dictators, as long as they were anticommunist. For example, Reagan criticized Salvador Allende—who died under suspicious circumstances during the Chilean coup of 1973—for being a Marxist and taking Chile "down the road of socialism." At the same time, he praised Augusto Pinochet's efforts to "restore democratic rule" and "allow elections" in Chile. Although Pinochet outlived Reagan by a couple of years, he died before he could stand trial for numerous charges of murder, torture, kidnapping, illegal detention, and other human rights abuses. Reagan's support for Pinochet and others, such as Ferdinand Marcos of the Philippines, and his military adventures in Central America and the Caribbean, not to mention his blunt rhetoric, demonstrate the depth of his conviction.

In addition to the epic struggle between capitalism and socialism, there was another struggle taking place—on a smaller scale—between taxpayers and tax users. For Reagan, it was a conflict between honest, hardworking people paying unfair taxes on one side and incompetent government bureaucrats and welfare cheats on the other. We know what a taxpayer is, but what is a tax user? Anyone dependent on government retirement or disability programs, recipients of survivor or unemployment benefits, and their dependents. (For more discussion on the politics of entitlement, see Chapter 8.) Of course, there are tax users worthy of our respect and gratitude, such as those serving in the military, along with police and firefighters, and all the others providing services we want and need.

The problem is the army of unworthy tax users, people who receive government benefits, but who are not truly needy. These are the fabled welfare cheats, slackers, and malingerers who, for example, would refuse a good job because it paid less than unemployment insurance, food stamps, and whatever they earned moonlighting.[22] When it came to welfare, foreign aid, or other poverty programs, Reagan's basic philosophy was: Give a hungry man a fish and he will be hungry tomorrow; teach him how to fish and he will never be hungry again. Reagan (like Clinton) believed we had a responsibility to help those unable to provide for themselves and their families through no fault of their own, but our costly and cumbersome bureaucracy encouraged people to accept welfare as a way of life. Should we judge welfare based on whether it raises the standard of living for recipients, or should we also consider what it does to the people who participate? According to Reagan, the increase in the number of welfare recipients proved the present programs were failing. Thus, we should measure our success by how much we decrease the number of welfare recipients and the need for welfare.

In 1981, Reagan raised some difficult questions about welfare and other federal government policies at the NAACP national convention:

> Can the black teenager who faces a staggering unemployment rate feel that government policies are a success?

Can the black wage earner who sees more and more of his take-home pay shrinking because of government taxes feel satisfied? Can black parents say, despite a massive influx of Federal aid, that educational standards in our schools have improved appreciably? Can the woman I saw on television recently—whose family had been on welfare for three generations and who feared that her children might be the fourth—can she believe that current government policies will save her children from such a fate?[23]

In his 1986 annual message, Reagan said,

In the welfare culture, the breakdown of the family, the most basic support system, has reached crisis proportions—in female and child poverty, child abandonment, horrible crimes, and deteriorating schools. After hundreds of billions of dollars in poverty programs, the plight of the poor grows more painful. But the waste in dollars and cents pales before the most tragic loss: the sinful waste of human spirit and potential.[24]

Reagan's most passionate argument for reforming the welfare bureaucracy was based on the problem of welfare fraud. His favorite anecdote was the infamous "Welfare Queen of All Time," whose crimes went far beyond welfare fraud. According to Reagan, the Welfare Queen owned three houses and several luxury cars, used dozens of addresses, Social Security cards, and phone numbers. She received welfare checks under dozens of aliases in various states and raked in thousands of dollars. Reagan told this story many times. According to speaker Thomas P. "Tip" O'Neill, however, this woman never existed, and Reagan knew she never existed, but he kept using the anecdote anyway.[25]

Nonetheless, the alleged criminal genius of the Welfare Queen helped Reagan make his case for welfare reform.

Before we take another step, a few words about Tip O'Neill, who served in Congress thirty-four years (first winning the seat in John Kennedy's old district in 1953) and, more importantly, served as speaker of the house for six of Reagan's eight years as president. On the surface, O'Neill and Reagan had a lot in common: They were both almost the same age, both sports fans, both gregarious Irish descendants who idolized Franklin Roosevelt in the 1930s. Whereas Reagan went into show business, O'Neill went directly into politics and served several years in the Massachusetts State Legislature before serving in Congress. Whereas Reagan left the Democratic Party by the midsixties, O'Neill remained a lifelong Democrat and never lost faith in the New Deal.

O'Neill was a vocal critic of Reagan's economic policies, but he was not the only one. For those who may not recall the 1980 election, presidential candidate George H.W. Bush coined the unflattering nickname "Voodoo economics" to describe Reagan's economic policies. In O'Neill's autobiography, he recalled the first time he sat next to Vice President George Bush during Reagan's February 1981 address before a joint session of Congress. During many of the interruptions for applause, O'Neill would turn toward Bush and whisper "voodoo economics," much to Bush's annoyance. According to Reagan's version of events, however, every time Reagan made a new proposal, he could hear O'Neill whispering to Bush, "Forget it. No way. Fat chance."

O'Neill totally rejected the idea the Reagan revolution was some sort of grand new beginning. "Despite what many people believe, and what the Republicans want us to think, Reagan's victory in 1980 did not represent a revolution in American values. And despite what the media claimed, Reagan was not elected because people were fed up with the huge federal deficit and were clamoring for budget cuts." As the de facto opposition leader,

O'Neill made a convenient target, and Reagan routinely ridiculed him as an unrepentant "tax and spend" Democrat. Despite their numerous and sometimes bitter disagreements over the years, Reagan and O'Neill remained friends—in private and after six o'clock in the evening. At a St. Patrick's Day dinner to honor O'Neill, Reagan downplayed their political rivalry. Besides, said Reagan, "Imagine one Irishman trying to corner another Irishman in the Oval Office." When I first read this anecdote, I didn't get it. Then it dawned on me: The Oval Office has no corners.[26]

Civil Rights and Social Issues

Let's peer through a window into Reagan's mind and look at the path he took toward his position on abortion. Reagan began his political life in his early twenties but gave almost no thought to abortion until he was in his mid-fifties—when he became governor of California in 1967. The California State Legislature introduced a bill to make abortion available on demand. Suddenly, Reagan had to take a position on abortion. He began to study the issue, did some soul searching, and (of course) consulted attorneys and advisors on his staff.

According to Reagan's retelling, the same California legislature that introduced the abortion bill also introduced a bill to make it a capital crime to abuse a pregnant woman and thus cause the death of her unborn child. This inconsistency in the law led Reagan to conclude a fetus had human rights protected by the Constitution. But this did not exclude the mother's rights, particularly in cases of rape or if the mother's health was at stake. During a debate with Walter Mondale in the 1984 presidential campaign, Reagan reiterated his opposition to abortion on constitutional grounds: "With me, abortion is not a problem of religion, it's a problem of the Constitution. I believe that until and unless someone can establish that the unborn child is not a living human being, then that child is already protected by the Constitution, which guarantees life, liberty, and the pursuit of happiness to all of us."[27]

Five years *before* Reagan became president, he said the government had no greater responsibility than to protect even the least among us if that person's right to life, liberty, and the pursuit of happiness was being unjustly denied.[28] Historians and jurists will be quick to remind us the Constitution guarantees no such thing. According to the Fifth and Fourteenth Amendments, the government may not deprive any person of life, liberty, *or property* without due process. The phrase Reagan used does not appear in the Constitution, but in the Declaration of Independence, authored by Thomas Jefferson, who appropriated it from John Locke. Rather than analyze the details, however, we should synthesize the big ideas. Given the potential for governmental overreach and the abuse of power, and given Reagan's belief in the primacy of human rights, his position on abortion is reasonable.

Speaking of the least among us, in 1965 when a reporter asked about his stance on civil rights, Reagan said it was "the responsibility of the government, at the point of a bayonet if necessary" to see that the rights of every individual were protected. In 1982, Reagan signed legislation extending the Voting Rights Act of 1965 for many years. As Reagan said, actions speak louder than words, and his signature proved his unconditional commitment to voting rights. "The principle that guides us and the principle embodied in the law is one of nondiscrimination," he said. His stance on affirmative action was more complicated. In response to a reporter's question implying he ignored the interests and concerns of African Americans, Reagan said:

> I respond to it with the simple answer that it isn't true.
> And I know that there are some leaders in various orga-

nizations . . . who have said things of this kind. But I am for affirmative action; I am against quotas. I have lived long enough to know a time in this country when quotas were used to discriminate, not end discrimination.[29]

One of the things that complicated Reagan's position—or perhaps confused people—was his belief in the principle of federalism, a topic we will cover in Chapter 7. When Reagan announced his decision to run for a second term as president, he listed a few items of unfinished business: "We have more to do in creating jobs, achieving control over government spending, returning more autonomy to the States, keeping peace in a more settled world, and seeing if we can't find room in our schools for God." The two middle goals stand out: getting control over government spending and returning more autonomy to the states. Reagan wanted to stop the power shift toward the federal government that encroached on rights guaranteed by the Constitution, specifically the tenth amendment of the Bill of Rights, which says, "The powers not delegated to the United States by the Constitution, nor prohibited by it to the States, are reserved to the States respectively, or to the people."

Although Reagan believed some government functions were better performed at the state and local levels, this belief did not diminish his dedication "to the principle of civil rights." He recognized it was one of the federal government's primary responsibilities "to assure that not one single citizen in this country can be denied his or her constitutional rights without the Federal Government coming in and guaranteeing those rights." When a reporter asked Reagan if the federal government would retreat on its advocacy of affirmative action, Reagan said, "No, there will be no retreat. This administration is going to be dedicated to equality." All told, Reagan was proud of the progress in civil rights but worried some affirmative action programs were becoming quota systems.[30]

The Conservative Deficit

If Edmund Burke is the godfather of conservatism, Irving Kristol is its architect. In *Reflections of a Neoconservative*, Kristol writes:

> Mr. Reagan, with his massive tax cuts, has put the welfare state in a moderately tight straightjacket for the rest of the decade at least. And he has done this by being bold enough to create a conservative deficit (one resulting from tax cuts) as a counterweight to liberal deficits (resulting from increased government expenditures).[31]

There is nothing wrong with standing on principle against the welfare state. If you cannot dismantle it, then putting it in a straightjacket is the next best thing. Although the tax code may change society, tax cuts alone do not create a deficit. That requires the government to spend more than it takes in during the fiscal year. If there are no funds held in reserve (such as a budget surplus from the previous year), then the government either has to sell assets or borrow the money.

If you read Kristol, he makes it seem as though Reagan's intention was to use the conservative deficit as some sort of imaginary counterweight to the liberal deficit. If you read Reagan himself, however, you see he made little or no distinction between good and bad deficit spending. All deficit spending is bad, because it is inflationary; weakens the currency; and devalues bank accounts, pensions, and the salaries of people living on a fixed income, such as teachers, police officers, and firefighters.

This highlights an important point: A governing philosophy is a value system, and some values will necessarily receive higher priority than others receive. For Reagan, low inflation was one of those values. Remember, Reagan was born in 1911. He was in his teens and twenties during the Great Depression and saw the effects firsthand. The economic failure that frightened Reagan most was not deficits, unemployment, recession, or depression, but hyperinflation, a condition in which prices spiral out of control and money becomes worthless, as was the case in Germany in the early twenties. To this day, Germans share Reagan's aversion to high inflation and gladly suffer double-digit unemployment to keep inflation low.

Reagan believed politicians resorted to deficit spending—literally *used* inflation—to fund social programs they could not fund through tax revenues. He never accused such politicians of conspiracy or knowingly setting out to rob people; their only crime was economic illiteracy.

> We know now that inflation results from all that deficit spending. Government has only two ways of getting money other than raising taxes. It can go into the money market and borrow, competing with its own citizens and driving up interest rates, which it has done, or it can print money, and it's done that. Both methods are inflationary.[32]

Deficit spending not only caused inflation, it also slowed economic growth, and, coupled with confiscatory taxation, drove up interest rates and unemployment. He claimed all we would have to do to prevent inflation would be to end deficit spending. Elsewhere, Reagan claimed, "The cause of inflation is government," and if our government's advisors on economic and fiscal policy believe there is more than one factor causing inflation, then "you and I are in deep trouble." Reagan said it again but phrased it slightly differently: "Inflation is caused by one thing—government spending more than government takes in. It will go away when government stops doing that."[33] Of course, the government never stopped doing that, at least not during his presidency.

Another element of Reaganomics was cutting taxes to stimulate economic growth, which would offset lost revenues and create a multiplier effect. This is commonly known as supply-side economic theory, which according to Reagan means the government "can increase its tax revenues and create the jobs we need *without* inflation by lowering the tax rates for business and individuals." Despite insurmountable evidence to the contrary—in the form of huge budget deficits—Reagan never stopped believing. It would be easy to accuse Reagan of hypocrisy, but then what? Our task is not to pass judgment, but to understand Reaganomics so we can compare and contrast it to Clintonomics. Reaganomics is a complex governing philosophy with political and economic elements, and a value system.

According to Reaganomics, inflation was evidence of a much larger problem and proof positive of Hayek's assertion that the government should intervene in the economy as little as possible, which Reagan explained in a 1976 radio address. The topic of the day was James Callaghan, who was Thatcher's immediate predecessor as British prime minister. Callaghan was a member of the Labour Party and thus not someone Reagan would normally agree with regarding economic policy. In Reagan's radio address, however, he refers to one of Callaghan's speeches at length and praises Callaghan's courage for espousing nominally conservative principles at a recent Labour Party convention.

What is the cause of unemployment? Paraphrasing Callaghan, Reagan said unemployment is caused by paying ourselves more than the value of the goods and services we produce. "We used to think you could just spend your way out of a recession and increase employment by cutting taxes and boosting government spending [but] . . . that option no longer exists and insofar as

it did exist it worked by injecting inflation into the economy."
Furthermore, we will never be economically competitive unless
we make the right kind of investment at the right level and significantly improve our productivity.[34]

On the printed page, the tone of Reagan's commentary is
slightly sarcastic, which is extremely rare for him. Perhaps Reagan
just appreciated the irony of the situation, because what the
speaker wanted to say was not what the audience wanted to hear.
Perhaps Reagan's appropriation of Callaghan's speech signaled a
new model of governance, a third way. Callaghan's prescription
to cut taxes and cut spending (or at least try to get spending
under control) sounds like Reaganomics, but Callaghan's call for
the right kind of investment at the right level sounds awfully
like Clintonomics. Whatever the causes or proximate causes of
inflation and unemployment, there was no doubt in Reagan's
mind that deficit spending was the root (more or less) of all political and economic evil.

Reagan disliked the term *Reaganomics* because he thought it
sounded like an aerobic exercise or fad diet.[35] Originally, Reaganomics was a mildly derogatory term—though not as derogatory
as voodoo economics—to ridicule his economic policies. How
did Reagan define Reaganomics? At one question-and-answer
session, someone asked him how he would summarize Reaganomics. Reagan shared his political and economic philosophy on
many other occasions but rarely, if ever, offered his own un-
scripted definition of Reaganomics. According to Reagan, it is an
economic theory and an economic policy that argues that cycles
of recession result from the government taking too much out of
the private sector. It calls for cuts in government spending and
reduction of the structural deficit. It calls for reducing punitive
taxes on individuals and businesses in order to create incentives
for people and businesses to invest. In its distilled form, Reagan-

omics is an incentive to work, invest, and grow. When taxes are too high, there is no incentive to earn that extra dollar:

> I saw an example of that very often in Hollywood in the old days, when there were income tax rates as high as 90 percent. And you'd be offered a picture, to play a role in a picture, and you already knew that your earnings had pushed you up in that 90-percent tax bracket, so all you'd get was 10 cents on the dollar if you made the picture. So you said, "I'm not going to make the picture." So, it is a combination of reducing government spending and reducing taxes on individuals and punitive taxes that were assessed against business, so that business can afford to expand and modernize.[36]

Reagan often joked he knew the economy was beginning to recover when his opponents stopped referring to Reaganomics. In one speech, Reagan passed around an editorial cartoon that amused him because it parodied all those people who expected instant solutions to problems that took decades to develop. The cartoon shows a television reporter saying, "And so it seems clear to this reporter that Reaganomics has failed, failed to thrive in a climate of optimism, failed to blossom into a viable economic alternative, failed to bear the fruit of prosperity—at least in these first five disappointing minutes."

Debt that took years to accumulate does not disappear overnight. In 1978, when Reagan was an ex-governor and people in California were trying to find ways to replace revenue lost as a result of Proposition 13 (a successful ballot initiative that amended the state constitution limiting real estate taxes), Reagan argued against arbitrarily cutting government payrolls. Prior to Proposition 13, local school districts received most of their funding from property taxes. The state government needed to devise a new financial model to fund school districts, and that meant cutting programs elsewhere. In response to angry demands simply to eliminate 10 to 25 percent of state jobs across the board, Reagan suggested a more compassionate solution. Rather than mass layoffs, he advocated reducing government payrolls through attrition, instituting a hiring freeze on replacement of workers who retired or left government service.[37]

Reagan's attitude toward balancing the federal budget was similar to his attitude toward balancing the California budget after passage of Proposition 13.

> Over the years, growth in government and deficit spending have been built into our system. Now, it'd be nice if we could just cut that out of our system with a single, sharp slice. That, however, can't be done without bringing great hardship down on many of our less fortunate neighbors who are not in a position to provide for themselves. And none of us wants that.[38]

All of this goes toward explaining why Reagan supported the idea of a constitutional amendment requiring a balanced budget. That would entail weighing the entire federal budget against estimated revenues—a nearly impossible task. Nonetheless, Reagan threw his support behind a balanced budget amendment:

> A wise and frugal government which does not take from the mouth of labor the bread it has earned is not economic theory. The integrity to stand for sound money, an end to deficit spending, and eventual retirement of the national debt is not economic theory. Those principles are the very heart of a tried and proven system—our system, the system which created the greatest outpouring of wealth in all history and distributed that wealth more

widely among the people than anywhere else in the world.[39]

This excerpt is brief but interesting, for a number of reasons beyond budgets and deficits. First, look at the way Reagan disparages theory, specifically economic theory, in the first two sentences. Then, notice how he speaks in praise of principles and systems in the third sentence. Finally, notice Reagan's comment about the distribution of wealth, specifically the large middle class the American system of political economy has created.

Another remedy Reagan supported was the line-item veto, the executive power to cancel specific budget appropriations without vetoing the entire spending bill. Reagan asked for line-item veto power in his 1986 annual message:

> Give me a line-item veto this year. Give me the authority to veto waste, and I'll take the responsibility, I'll make the cuts, I'll take the heat. This authority would not give me any monopoly power, but simply prevent spending measures from sneaking through that could not pass on their own merit. And you can sustain or override my veto; that's the way the system should work. Once we've made the hard choices, we should lock in our gains with a balanced budget amendment to the Constitution.[40]

Clinton also asked for it in his 1995 annual message:

> For years, Congress concealed in the budget scores of pet spending projects. Last year was no different. There was $1 million to study stress in plants and $12 million for a tick removal program that didn't work. It's hard to remove ticks. Those of us who have had them know. But

I'll tell you something, if you'll give me line-item veto, I'll
remove some of that unnecessary spending.[41]

For a while, Clinton did have this power, until the courts (including the Supreme Court) declared it an unconstitutional violation of the separation of powers clause.

We should note Clinton opposed rewriting the Constitution to
include a balanced budget amendment because it could cripple
the government during a national security crisis or an economic
crisis. Clinton consistently advocated fiscal discipline in the belief
he could reduce the deficit through executive action, but he cau-
tioned against "fooling with the Constitution." He considered any
attempt to pass a balanced budget amendment nothing but a
gimmick that would lead to huge tax increases; slower economic
growth; and, inevitably, unwise budget cuts to defense, Social Security, Medicare, and other popular entitlement programs.

ON DECEMBER 3, 1989, George H.W. Bush met Mikhail Gorbachev on the island of Malta and declared an end to the Cold War.[42]
Two years later, at midnight on New Year's Eve, 1991, the Soviet
Union officially ceased to exist. In January 1993, Clinton took
the oath of office, promising to reinvent government. He did not
advocate change for its own sake but merely pointed out that the
country's dominant paradigm that guided our foreign and defense policies since 1947 was obsolete. In 1992, the same year as
Clinton's first victorious presidential campaign, Francis Fukuyama published his masterpiece *The End of History and the Last Man*.
According to Fukuyama, the end of the Cold War and disintegration of the Soviet Union signaled the end of history. Fukuyama
did not mean the end of history literally but rather the end of
the international rivalry between competing ideological systems.
Time's arrow points in one direction, toward the system of politi-

cal economy that most effectively maximizes economic growth and minimizes chaos in the global system. Thus, the defeat of communism, fascism, and other authoritarian systems left free market capitalism and multiparty democracy as the last viable system of political economy.[43] This is where Chapter 4: The Global System begins.

CHAPTER 4

The Global System

"Learn a lot, eliminate the doubtful, and speak discreetly about the rest."[1]

—CONFUCIUS, RESPONDING TO A REQUEST
FOR GUIDANCE ON EDUCATION, *Analects 9:29*

CLINTONOMICS IS A GOVERNING philosophy with a global perspective analogous to what astronauts call the "overview effect," the conversion that takes place in the minds of astronauts when they see Earth from space for the first time.[2] It is not the same as looking down at Earth from the window of an airplane. To see Earth when you are standing on the moon, you have to look up into the sky. From this vantage point, you can see—or at least imagine—Earth spinning on its axis, giving us night and day, and orbiting around the sun, giving us winter, spring, summer, and fall. You can see other parts of the solar system, the sun and maybe Venus and Mars. You can see some of the large physical systems humans depend on for their survival: continents, oceans, and weather systems.

Although Reagan made a handful of references to globalization, mostly related to economics, I couldn't find any occasion when he referred to a "global society," even though Reagan believed politics is inseparable from economics, a belief he shared with Karl Marx, Milton Friedman, and Rush Limbaugh, among others. According to my research, Reagan used the phrase "global system" once in public, during a speech in Berlin—not the famous "tear down this wall" speech at the Brandenburg Gate, but in front of the Charlottenburg Palace five years earlier.

Reagan quoted German writer and social critic Thomas Mann, who said, "A man lives not only his personal life as an individual, but also consciously or unconsciously the life of his epoch." Nowhere was this truer, said Reagan, than in Berlin, where people lived every moment of every day against the backdrop of competing global systems. "To be a Berliner is to live the great historic struggle of this age, the latest chapter in man's timeless quest for freedom."[3] If you lived on either side of the Berlin Wall back then, you lived on the front line between two ideological systems and their global competition for power and resources, hearts, and minds.

Then the Berlin Wall fell and the Cold War ended. "Millions threw off the constricting yoke of communism," said Clinton and assumed "the ennobling burdens of democracy." The new era brought new opportunities, but also new threats, such as those from polluters, terrorists, drug runners, and other equal opportunity criminals with no respect for national boundaries. The collapse of the Soviet Union, rise of the global economy, proliferation of weapons of mass destruction, reemergence of China and India, and resurgence of ethnic conflict changed the international order forever and convinced Clinton that globalization was *the central reality of our time.*

> It is tearing down barriers between nations and people; knowledge, contact, and trade across borders within and

between every continent are exploding. And all this globalization is also, as the barriers come down, making us
more vulnerable to one another's problems: to the shock
of economic turmoil, to the spread of conflict, to pollution and, as we have painfully seen, to disease; the terrorists, the drug traffickers, the criminals who can also take
advantage of new technologies and globalization, the
openness of societies and borders.[4]

Globalization is multiplying communication and trade across
borders and across every continent. It is tearing down barriers
between nations and people, sometimes literally, as in the case of
the Berlin Wall, but also in terms of a freer flow of ideas and
information. It is breaking down barriers of all kinds, both those
that protect us from harm and those that constrain our forward
progress. Globalization also naturally invites suspicion because it
has grown beyond our ability to control it, and many people
assume globalization is synonymous with cultural imperialism,
meaning the spread of capitalism and Western culture.

We can probably trace the origin of globalization to Nicolaus
Copernicus (1473–1543), a European astronomer who argued the
sun, not Earth, was at the center of our solar system and thus
offered an alternative model of the universe. His book *On the
Revolutions of the Celestial Spheres* did not cause much controversy
at the time, perhaps because Copernicus dedicated it to the Pope.
A few years later, however, the Catholic Church denounced the
book's scientific and theological errors, placed it on the Vatican's
Index of Forbidden Books, and banned it from circulation.

What exactly is globalization? Sociologist Malcolm Waters
calls it "*a social process in which the constraints of geography on social
and cultural arrangements recede and in which people become increasingly
aware that they are receding.*" Globalization transforms time and
space in our lives, which means that all kinds of distant events—

social, political, economic—have a greater effect on our lives than ever before.[5]

Following the inexorable logic of globalization, Waters described what a fully globalized world would look like. Waters wrote in 1995, so as you read, notice he is not actually describing the future but the present, or even the very recent past.

> In a globalized world there will be a single society and culture occupying the planet. This society and culture will probably not be harmoniously integrated although it might conceivably be. Rather it will probably tend toward high levels of differentiation, multicentricity, and chaos. There will be no central organizing government and no tight set of cultural preferences or prescriptions. Insofar as culture is unified it will be extremely abstract, expressing tolerance for diversity and individual choice. Importantly territoriality will disappear as an organizing principle for social and cultural life, it will be a society without borders and spatial boundaries. In a globalized world . . . we can expect relationships between people in disparate locations to be formed as easily as relationships between people in proximate ones.[6]

Technology is the only element missing. Once you plug that in, you can see we already have a single society and culture, albeit diverse and fragmented. We already have numerous and distinctive cultures, subcultures, and countercultures, with an almost infinite range of preferences, values, and norms. Technology has already redefined territoriality and continues to reconfigure spatial boundaries. In our dot-com world, we routinely develop relationships in distant locations as easily as in our hometown. Finally, the global system consistently produces a high level of chaos or entropy, meaning the amount of energy the system dissipates during political or "value-subtracted" activity.

Bragging rights for the shortest definition belong to sociologist Anthony Giddens, who defines globalization as "action at a distance."[7] Globalization is not an economic phenomenon entirely, but also a spatial and temporal phenomenon, literally transforming space and time. Driven by advances in transportation and communication technology, events happening on the other side of the world increasingly influence our personal activities. Conversely, our personal activities and lifestyles—including perverse forms of fundamentalism and nationalism—have destabilizing consequences. According to Clinton, here are a few of the *destabilizing* forces of globalization:

> Globalization can bring repression and human rights violations and suffering into the open, but it cannot prevent them. It can promote integration among nations, but also lead to disintegration within them. It can bring prosperity on every continent, but still leave many, many people behind. It can give people the modern tools of the twenty-first century, but it cannot purge their hearts of the primitive hatreds that may lead to the misuse of those tools.[8]

The growth and development of the global economy has far surpassed the development of anything resembling a global society. As the production of consumer goods and services has increased exponentially, the post–Cold War, single-superpower world has crossed the threshold into its own lopsided age of affluence (to borrow Galbraith's phrase). One symptom indicating the global system is far out of equilibrium is the increasing number of failed states that have little effective control over their sovereign territory.[9]

The Laws of Complexity

When we say the overview effect produces a global perspective or a systems perspective, what exactly do we mean?[10] Complex systems are nested; that is, they consist of systems within systems that function within an environment (which together form a matrix). This structure may include belief systems, such as the invisible laws of political economy. This structure may also include physical systems, such as the global system, which consists of countries; corporations; markets; goods; services; commodities; currencies; and, of course, billions of people. We covered this briefly when we defined politics and economics, but a more thorough explanation here will facilitate understanding of the chapters to come.

Complex systems are almost impossible to define. According to educator and diplomat Harlan Cleveland, systems consist of "interlaced webs of tension in which control is loose, power is diffused, and centers of decision plural." According to statistician and management consultant W. Edwards Deming, a system is a network of interdependent components working together to accomplish the aim of the system. Sociologist Kenneth Bailey defines a complex system as "a bounded set of interrelated components that has an entropy value below the maximum"; in other words, anything this side of anarchy.

Political scientist Robert Jervis says, "We are dealing with a system when (a) a set of units or elements is interconnected so that changes in some elements or their relations produce changes in other parts of the system, and (b) the entire system exhibits properties and behaviors that are different from those of the parts."[11] According to Jervis:

> In summary, much of our world is unintelligible without attending to three kinds of interactions which form and

generate a system. Two or more elements produce results that cannot be understood by examining each alone; the fate of an actor's policy or strategy depends on those that are adopted by others; behavior alters the environment in ways that affect the trajectory of actors, outcomes, and environments.[12]

These definitions, Bailey's in particular, may be too abstract for some readers to appreciate. One good thing about Bailey's is the way he uses "entropy value" to define the boundaries of the system. The entropy value is usually the degree of disorder or anarchy in the system. (It is possible what we call anarchy is just extremely complicated feedback beyond the arbitrary boundaries we assigned to the system—and thus beyond our comprehension.) Because a system's behavior is different from, though not necessarily greater than, the sum of its parts, we may thus define a system as one whose behavior is not fully explainable by understanding its component parts.[13]

Perhaps it would be easier to clarify what a complex system is by explaining what it is not. A complex system is not a machine, such as a mechanical wristwatch—not the kind with video games, digital camera, cell phone, and Internet access, which have few or no moving parts and are closer to computers than machines. Here "machine" means the kind of watch Rolex or Omega makes, with an analog display (hands) and mechanical movements. If you disassemble one of those, it is relatively easy to understand how it works. If the watch is broken, you can identify the damaged part, replace it, and put it all back together again, and the watch will work as good as new. Other parts may break or wear out, but with occasional repairs and regular maintenance, the watch will run forever.

If you want to understand that kind of wristwatch, you should think mechanically. The wristwatch is a machine. The wristwatch is not a complex system. It will never grow a new replacement part. It will never reject a transplanted replacement part. It will never learn from its experience. It will never anticipate the future. It will never adapt to its environment. It will never think about itself. It will never mature someday and become a grandfather clock.

A machine is the sum of its parts. The parts determine the machine's behavior. A complex system, however, is different from the sum of its parts because the system's elements engage in behavior that cannot take place outside of the system. For example, if we combine two hydrogen molecules and one oxygen molecule, we get H_2O, also known as water, which has a behavioral repertoire significantly different from either hydrogen or oxygen. Water freezes, it vaporizes, it flows. In some situations, water is a system in and of itself, whereas in other situations water is a subsystem, a building block for a larger system. For example, if you combine water, flour, salt, and sugar, ferment and bake it, you get something called sourdough bread, one of the great inventions in human history. This characteristic in which a system serves as a building block within a larger system that exists within a larger environment is common to all complex systems.

Machines have no experience to learn from but simply run through their cycles over and over again. They never reproduce themselves, never recycle themselves, and never learn. Complex systems, on the other hand, continuously reproduce and modernize themselves. Systems adapt to changes in the environment in the same way living organisms evolve. Because systems can learn from their experience, they have the capacity to change their behavior patterns and can develop different, more effective behaviors in response to external environmental forces.

Although complex systems are mostly independent, they are in constant communication with the environment. The communication flows both ways: A system sends and receives information critical to the system's performance, also known as feedback. Systems are usually subordinate to their environment, so when a system receives feedback, it learns from the experience and then adjusts its behavior accordingly. Sometimes, however, systems deny the information they receive from the environment; other times they refuse to learn, refuse to change their behavior, and force the environment to absorb the change.

Systems can learn and spontaneously engage in all kinds of unpredictable behavior. When systems operate too far (or for too long) outside their natural state of equilibrium, they will spontaneously give birth to "dissipative structures" that purge the system of accumulated chaos and enable the system to develop and modernize.[14] For example, if we arbitrarily push one variable in the system (in this case the social balance) outside its natural equilibrium state, we force other variables in the system outside their normal ranges of operation. The system will have to blow off steam.

When a system is pushed too far (or for too long) out of its normal range of operation, it will send feedback signaling that it is experiencing stress. When you climb a staircase, for example, it causes stress on your body. When the muscles in your legs work, they need oxygen. Your heart must pump faster to increase the flow of blood to your muscles because they need oxygen. When you reach the top of the staircase, the temporary change in operation returns to normal, your heartbeat returns to normal, and the symptoms of stress disappear.

That is a systemic response to short-term stress. A medium-term response to stress is like the process of acclimatization when you travel from sea level to a mountain village. For the first few days at high altitude, you may feel altitude sickness in the form of headaches, nausea, and shortness of breath. After a week or two, your body acclimatizes and begins to function as if high-altitude thin air is normal. The system's response begins as stress, but when the change persists long enough, the system adapts itself to function in the new environment. Complex systems are very robust, but they can absorb only so much stress beyond the short or medium term. Once the stress reaches a critical threshold, systems either disintegrate or develop new capabilities.

A Web of Mutuality

The purpose of systems thinking is not to predict the future by drawing false analogies from the past but to enhance our ability to address problems that are systemic, rather than symptomatic. Because we can think systemically, we know systems are always communicating with us. Unfortunately, the feedback we receive may be extremely complicated and confusing and appear to be random. How do we know what to look for? The symptoms are evident: poverty, epidemic disease, violent crime, alcohol and drug abuse, child abuse, spousal abuse, riots, police brutality, war. And, of course, terrorism, meaning violence against civilians or other noncombatants, the purpose of which is political: to express a grievance and change the status quo and thus draw attention to who gets what, when, and how.

Terrorism, said Clinton, is part of the "inexorable logic of globalization" that grows more dense, intense, and transformative on a daily basis.[15] Remember, politics is about power, and relationships are politicized when politics is introduced. Because the symptoms of chaos in the system are often political, it is tempting to respond with solutions that are political. Treating the symptom may actually make the fundamental problem worse (although the symptom may temporarily disappear) because it will be harder to respond with systemic solutions. Our case is systemic, so we must think systemically and act systemically, as Lincoln might have said.

By now, it should be plain to see why the overview effect would facilitate understanding the world—the one we are living in, as well as the one we are moving toward—as a large complex system. It should also be plain to see the tendency of politics to obscure reality, to the extent some people do not even realize when it is happening. The thing about systemic problems, however, is they require systemic solutions. If you do not think systemically, it is easy to lose sight of the system as a whole. Complex systems do not always function based on linear cause and effect. Events are not arbitrary; there are causes and effects. But real causes may be found at any time and at any location in the system, and real effects may occur randomly: sometimes immediately, sometimes well into the future, sometimes locally, sometimes not. Because the consequences of the system's behavior can be far removed in time and space, the feedback we receive can be ambiguous, obsolete, or simply beyond our comprehension.

We can illustrate this with two examples, one specific and one general. The general example is global warming, which exemplifies what happens when people fail to think systemically and when a system refuses to learn and adjust its behavior. The system—our federal government, in this case—denies information it receives from the environment about the long-term, global effects of industrialization. People deny that increases in greenhouse gas emissions, such as carbon dioxide, methane, and nitrous oxide, cause average air temperatures to rise. In turn, people deny the potentially catastrophic effects of global warming: changing precipitation patterns, gradual inundation of coastal areas, and increasing frequency of floods and droughts.

In the case of global warming, the extent to which the global environment can tolerate persistent insult—an indicator of the system's robustness—is questionable. At a speech to the National

Geographic Society, Clinton said the problem of climate change reflected the new realities of the era:

> Many previous threats could be met within our own borders, but global warming requires an international solution. Many previous threats came from single enemies, but global warming derives from millions of sources. Many previous threats posed clear and present danger; global warming is far more subtle, warning us not with roaring tanks or burning rivers but with invisible gases, slow changes in our surroundings, increasingly severe climatic disruptions that, thank God, have not yet hit home for most Americans.[16]

Clinton delivered dozens of speeches about global warming during his presidency. He delivered this particular one in 1997, years before the "severe climatic disruption" known as Hurricane Katrina destroyed large parts of the Gulf Coast in Louisiana, Mississippi, and Alabama. Regardless whether you believe global warming caused Katrina—regardless whether you believe global warming is even real—Clinton gave Al Gore all the credit for educating him:

> He convinced me in 1993 that climate change was real. And he wrote that book in '88 and they're still making fun of his book, and I remember as late as last year [2000] we had a House subcommittee that treated climate change like a conspiracy to destroy the economy of the United States.[17]

Meanwhile, Al Gore has traveled the world giving his now famous lecture on climate change, documented in the Academy Award–winning film *An Inconvenient Truth* and a book of the same title.[18] He has also served as senior advisor to Google, Inc. and a board member of Apple, Inc., and he won a share of the Nobel Peace Prize in 2007.

This leads us to a specific example of a system refusing to learn: the *Exxon Valdez*. The *Exxon Valdez* was an oil tanker that routinely transported crude oil from the Alaska pipeline to Southern California. In 1989, the tanker hit a reef and spilled millions of gallons of crude oil into Prince William Sound, killing thousands of animals, birds, otters, seals, and fish and causing one of the worst human-made environmental disasters in history. The massive *Exxon Valdez*—ten football fields long—was part of Exxon's supply chain, a system of extraction, transportation, and distribution. Failure of the system caused a monumental environmental disaster and damaged the ecosystem of Prince William Sound.

If the system had succeeded, on the other hand, the *Valdez* would have completed its voyage to Southern California, where its cargo of crude oil would have been processed and refined into petroleum products, such as gasoline, and then sold to consumers to fuel their cars and trucks. If the system had succeeded, it would have contributed to the chronic air pollution in Los Angeles and increased the greenhouse gasses that contribute to global warming. This particular example illustrates an important point about human systems: Only human systems can both succeed and fail. A natural system produces exactly what it is supposed to produce. There is no question of failure. A human system, however, can fail in one of two ways: either by not doing what it promises or by doing exactly what it promises with unintended consequences.

Our ability to see the system—our capacity to accept reality—influences our policy choices. A mechanistic philosophy of governance, which presupposes little or no uncertainty, has a bias for political intervention. Remember, our goal is to produce the maximum positive outcome while optimizing the allocation of scarce resources and minimizing waste. George W. Bush has said winning the war on terror and advancing democracy and self-government is "the calling of a new generation of Americans."[19] If so, shouldn't we set realistic goals and not waste our resources? When faced with the possibility of a prolonged conflict, shouldn't we conserve our energy? When a high level of uncertainty and unpredictability exists—as it does in the post–Cold War global system—attempting to impose order on the system often will produce more disorder, more uncertainty, and more unpredictability. Officials cannot *control* the system to the degree the mechanistic perspective implies, but they can *influence* where the system is going, and how it evolves.[20] Because not all issues are super*political*, intervention by the system's sole super*power* may be unproductive.

What should be our mission in the new era? What should be our mission when there is no cold war, no world war, and no evil empire left to fight? How do we measure success when there is no need to liberate Europe, make the world safe for democracy, free the slaves, or declare our independence and dissolve our allegiance to the British Crown? If terrorism is indeed part of the inexorable logic of globalization—as is our dependence on foreign oil—then it may be useful to combat terrorism by thinking in terms of political economy, listening carefully for feedback and filtering out the noise.

In February 1998, Osama bin Laden issued a fatwa (or religious edict) declaring holy war against Jews and Americans. In August of that year, members of al Qaeda bombed American embassies in Dar es Salaam and Nairobi. Two weeks after the embassy bombings, Clinton ordered air strikes against terrorist camps in Afghanistan and Sudan. Following the air strikes—more than three years before the 9/11 attacks—Clinton predicted more attacks because of America's leadership position and its values and openness. He called bin Laden the world's "preeminent organizer and financier of international terrorism" and said the radical groups affiliated with and funded by him shared a hatred of democracy, a horrible distortion of Islam, and "a fanatical glorification of violence."[21]

At the annual opening session of the United Nations General Assembly in 1998, Clinton flatly rejected the idea that any clash between Western civilization and Islamic civilization was inevitable. He rebuked the false prophets who would use religion—any religion—to justify their political objectives, and he urged everyone to think of terrorism not as a clash of cultures "or a divine calling," but as a deeply rooted, *systemic problem* beyond the power of the world's only superpower. Then he gave this brief analysis of why terrorists attack the United States:

> Because we are blessed to be a wealthy nation with a powerful military and a worldwide presence active in promoting peace and security, we are often a target. We love our country for its dedication to political and religious freedom, to economic opportunity, to respect for the rights of the individual. But we know many people see us as a symbol of a system and values they reject, and often they find it expedient to blame us for problems with deep roots elsewhere.[22]

This is especially interesting compared to the rhetoric of Clinton's successor. During an exchange with reporters in September 2001, a few days after the 9/11 attacks, George W. Bush said, "This is a new kind of—a new kind of evil. And we understand. And the American people are beginning to understand. This crusade, this war on terrorism is going to take a while, and the American people must be patient. I'm going to be patient." At a press conference the following month, Bush said, "We cannot let the terrorists achieve the objective of frightening our Nation to the point where we don't—where we don't conduct business, where people don't shop. That's their intention."[23] On the surface, Bush's reference to shopping seems to trivialize the situation, but he's expressing a profound insight. Terrorists want chaos. They want us to overreact, and they want the system to waste energy on political (value-subtracted) activity rather than economic (value-added) activity.

The forces of globalization—a fact of life, not a policy choice, according to Clinton—exude and exemplify change, are liberating and equalizing, but also frightening to people who are vulnerable. Said Clinton:

> The forces behind the global economy are also those that deepen democratic liberties: the free flow of ideas and information, open borders and easy travel, the rule of law, fair and even-handed enforcement, protection for consumers, a skilled and educated work force. Each of these things matters not only to the wealth of nations but to the health of freedom. If citizens tire of waiting for democracy and free markets to deliver a better life for them, there is a real risk that democracy and free markets, instead of continuing to thrive together, will begin to shrivel together. This would pose great risks not only for our economic interests but for our security.[24]

Clinton considered it an impossibility to create a global economy without *some sort* of global society. When Clinton used the phrase "global society," he did not mean it in a utopian sense but in terms of connectedness beyond business and economics. At a speech commemorating Martin Luther King, Jr., Clinton commented on a phrase he attributed to King: "the web of mutuality." It means recognizing our collective responsibilities within our national boundaries and with the rest of the world. Whatever you call it—mutuality, connectedness, or interdependence—as the process of globalization continues, it implies there will be fewer and fewer truly national economies, and those that resist will exist at the margins. It implies "we have a vested interest in the United States in advancing the welfare of ordinary citizens around the world as we pursue our economic and security interests." That is a rather astonishing thing for any American president to say, but helps explain why we have to get the economics right or risk making all our political problems worse—on a global scale.[25] In Clinton's words:

> Open markets and open trade are critically important to lifting living standards and building shared prosperity. But they alone cannot carry the burden of lifting the poorest nations out of poverty. While the forces of globalization may be inexorable, its benefits are not. Especially for countries that lack the most important building blocks of progress—a healthy population with broad-based literacy. Here in our nation this will be remembered as a time of great plenty, but we cannot forget that for too many of the world—too many in the world—it is still a time of astonishing poverty. Nearly half the human race, 2.8 billion people, lives on less than two dollars a day. In many countries, a child is three times more likely to die before the age of five than to go to secondary school. One in ten children dies before his or her first birthday. One in three is malnourished. The average adult has only three years of schooling. This is not right, not necessary, and no longer acceptable.[26]

The inexorable logic of globalization supersedes the invisible hand guiding the market. Although there is little the United States can do to protect people from their own mismanagement, we still need to make the global economy more humane. We need to find a way to moderate the global economy's cycles of boom and bust, extend the benefits of globalization to more people, and prevent further deterioration of the social balance. "Unless the citizens of each nation feel they have a stake in their economy they will resist reforms necessary for recovery," he said. If they don't have the tools to master change, they will be tempted to turn inward and close themselves off from the world.[27]

What happens when the social balance in the global system is pushed too far out of its natural state of equilibrium? If the resource distribution gap stays wide enough for long enough, people will seek ways to glorify their poverty. If the power distribution gap stays wide enough for long enough, people will seek ways to glorify their weakness. What is the most ostentatious display of powerlessness, the ultimate glorification of violence? It is the suicide attack that kills as many innocent victims as possible.

IN 1789, WHEN George Washington took the presidential oath of office, news traveled by horseback over land and by boat across the ocean. In 1993, when Clinton took the oath, millions watched the ceremony live from all over the world. "Profound and powerful forces are shaking and remaking our world," said Clinton, "And the urgent question of our time is whether we can make change our friend and not our enemy."[28] What a difference from the Reagan era, when the most urgent questions were the Cold War, Soviet aggression, and the threat of nuclear warfare. Today, the most urgent questions are globalization and the fallout from change.

My own thinking on the subject of change comes from studying Confucius (circa 551–479 BC), a philosopher, student, and teacher—not born in Austria, surprisingly, but in China, in what is now Shandong Province. Confucius, perhaps the first practical idealist, envisioned a social order grounded in modesty, self-mastery, and devotion to duty. His political philosophy emphasized limited government and impartial justice, but mostly he urged people to think for themselves, educate themselves, and come to conclusions on their own. His enthusiasm for the *Book of Change*, that three-thousand-year-old classic of strategy and statecraft, is legendary. Near the end of his long life, Confucius said, "Give me a few more years, so that I will have studied the *Book of Change* for fifty years, and I may thereby eliminate major errors."[29] This is where Chapter 5 begins.

CHAPTER 5

Reflections on Change

*A reasonably famous Italian, Niccolò Machiavelli—
whom Leon [Panetta] can read without benefit of translation—said 500 years ago, "There is nothing so
difficult in all of human affairs than to change the established order of things, for all people who will be discom-
forted by the change will immediately oppose you, and
those who will be benefited will be lukewarm, because
they are uncertain of the result.[1]*

—BILL CLINTON, 1994

CLINTON WAS QUOTING FROM Machiavelli's *The Prince*, which was
published in 1513 and was very popular for several years thereaf-
ter. Many years after Machiavelli died, however, the Catholic
Church denounced Machiavelli's works at the Inquisition; one
cardinal claimed the true author must have been Satan himself.
Let us remember: There is nothing more difficult than to change
the established order of things, because anybody comfortable

under the old conditions will be antagonistic, and everyone else will be skeptical.

Change was a recurring theme throughout Clinton's presidency. He spoke often about the many changes taking place beyond our control but also about those within our control, such as the direction of the country, the role of government, welfare, healthcare, education, and, of course, the budget. When he took office in 1993—just after the end of the Cold War—it was a tumultuous time, which in the past would likely have been accompanied by war. Without a cold war, a world war, or an evil empire to fight, Clinton worried the forces of globalization might overwhelm the country and cause our racial, regional, and class differences to fester.

Before we consider Clinton's thinking on the subject of change, however, we must complete our discussion of political economy and complexity. Once we have completed our theoretical framework, we will then turn our attention to public policy and other such practical matters for the remainder of the book.

Typology of Change

The house always wins. This is based on the law of large numbers, a discovery of Swiss mathematician Jacob Bernoulli (1654–1705), who observed long-term predictability in large numbers of random events. Specifically, when a large number of similar people or objects are subjected to events under similar conditions with the same risk, outcomes will approach and tend to cluster around predictable ratios. This is how those swanky Las Vegas casinos got that way. Casino operators control the game and as many variables in the game as they can and continuously look for new ways to increase their advantage. Thus, the house has a better chance of winning over the long term than any individual in the house has.

Complex systems, however, are not subjected to similar conditions and similar risks. Complex systems are by definition wild, meaning they spontaneously self-organize, self-generate, and self-regulate. Movement is constant; change is inevitable, and long-term outcomes are no more predictable than the weather. Based on these observations and others from Chapter 4, we can identify a few simple rules.

- Historical analogies are misleading because the future does not simulate the past.
- Unpredictability and local instability are more common than equilibrium.
- Feedback may be ambiguous or obsolete and may defy all explanation.
- Events may produce consequences that are indirect, delayed, and/or unintended.
- The system may accumulate a chain of consequences that multiplies over time.

When we say time's arrow points in one direction, we mean change is directional and irreversible, which is why the future does not simulate the past. Change is also cyclical, meaning the flow of events is not directional but rhythmic, recurring in the same sequence regardless of the length of the cycle or the size of the system. Directional change and cyclical change are both part of the inexorable logic of globalization. Furthermore, our global system of political economy is a human artifact, which means it is an accurate projection of human nature.

Likewise, the typology of change is a reflection of human nature in all its complexity. The typology discussed next comes from my study of *Book of Change* over a span of fifteen years, particularly translations by Thomas Cleary (2000), Alfred Huang (1998), and Richard Wilhelm (1924). Huang and Cleary translated their versions from Chinese directly to English. Wilhelm translated his version from Chinese to German, and then Cary Baynes translated it to English. The Wilhelm/Baynes translation is more prosaic—no doubt because of the German-influenced syntax—and thus, despite being a translation of a translation, more useful for the specific purpose of studying political economy and complexity.

The structure of this typology of change consists of four types (or states) of change, each of which consists of two complementary opposites (though every type of change has some characteristics of every other type). According to *Webster's*, a complement completes something or makes it whole. In this context, one type of change is countervailing, equivalent to its opposite, and necessary to maintain the system's natural equilibrium. For example, reactionary change is not the opposite of catalytic change (see below) but the perfect complement. Reactionary change balances the system, minimizes turbulence, and resists excessive change. Catalytic change is creative and progressive, while reactionary change is responsive and conservative. Complementarity is one of the universal laws of complex systems and a fundamental principle of political economy.

Catalytic to Reactionary

Catalytic change is analogous to Schumpeter's concept of creative destruction from Chapter 2. Catalytic change lends form to what is potential and gives actuality to intangible ideas. This type of change enables systems to modernize and increase in complexity by developing innovative structures and processes (called *dissipative structures* in systems jargon) that purge the accumulated chaos from the system. Catalytic change is dependent on entrepreneurship—creative and value-added destruction—to recognize inefficiencies, optimize allocation of scarce resources, minimize waste, and maximize performance.

Managing any type of change requires the capacity to recognize change in all its diversity: the differences, similarities, and subtle variations each type manifests. Reality sometimes presents the appearance of catalytic change and thus may be deceiving. Although the clouds indicate rain, rain does not come. Managing catalytic change is exactly like that. When waiting for the right moment to intervene, sometimes waiting is the only option. It is counterproductive to interfere before the time is ripe. If even one element is out of place, then using creative destruction will only produce an unsuccessful outcome. If even one element is out of place, then the circumstances call for a type of intervention less reliant on creativity. In this kind of situation, it is better to take precautionary measures and not attempt sweeping changes. Attempting to produce sweeping change in this situation would not produce lasting effects, so it is better to monitor the situation and, where possible, keep it from drifting out of control.

Restraining power while never losing sight of the ultimate goal is sometimes the most advantageous (though not the most direct) path to success. When we survey the field around us, we must simultaneously take inventory of our own resources. For those in positions of influence, force of habit makes it very difficult to hold back, to refrain from showy displays of power. This is one of the consequences of simultaneously misreading the situation and failing to exercise restraint. It may cause us to act in an untimely fashion, too soon or too late, when the moment for change has not arrived or has already passed. We may be so intent on movement that we rely on force to the exclusion of principle. We become tangled in the incomprehensible mess, ultimately swept away by the situation, dissipating power when we should be replenishing it.

As stated, reactionary change is not the opposite of catalytic change but the perfect complement. Reactionary change is the system's natural regulatory mechanism. It is what enables a complex system to form new structures and engage in new behaviors without undoing the system's cohesion. Reactionary change connotes a lower comfort level relative to other types of change. Reactionary change is a principle of social organization, which holds systems together over time. Just when it seems as though chaos and confusion are everywhere, reactionary change helps the system resist provocations and distractions and helps the system rediscover its core constituencies and core competencies, such as those few and well-defined powers the founders wanted the federal government to have.

Because of the system's natural tendencies, however, stagnation is a real possibility. Managing reactionary change requires a light touch to avoid aggravating the situation, but not so light that things come to a complete standstill. This requires empathizing with people without permitting them to indulge in fundamentalism: rejecting facts, renouncing science, or relying on superstition. Mismanaged reactionary change may lead to a descent into demagoguery and incite a perverse and aggressive national vanity. Managing any type of change requires care. Under these circumstances, acknowledging limitations shows wisdom, while making up false pretenses is foolish. Sometimes, there is nothing to do but sit tight, be quiet, and wait for the system to cycle through to the next phase. This requires monitoring popular opinion carefully, adjusting one's attitude accordingly, and refraining from self-deception.

Revolutionary to Developmental

Revolutionary change is difficult and can be dangerous, especially for those motivated by private gain rather than the greatest good for the greatest number. Those who turn their backs on human suffering and reject Bentham's principle of utilitarianism will be incapable of producing meaningful results. Edmund Burke had some advice on managing revolutionary change. (If you recall from Chapter 3, Burke was not resistant to all change but to excessive change, which he defined as rebellion against *legitimate* political authority.) No political or economic institution forfeits its legitimacy as long as it serves society to any tolerable degree. Thus, no political or economic institution deserves destruction unless it is so incapable that it is unfit for reform (see Limited to Evolutionary later in this chapter). Revolutionary change may gather so much momentum that it becomes unmanageable. Those caught in this trap may enjoy some success, but it will be ornamental, shining brightly for a moment before burning itself out.

Revolutionary change is like those wildfires that burn through Southern California every year. Fueled by dry chaparral and swept by the Santa Ana winds, they burn brightly but not very long, because they depend on exactly the right conditions. They consume so much fuel, they have to keep moving or else burn out. Sometimes the cause is natural, sometimes not, but for those who live in transitional areas wildfires can be incredibly destructive in terms of property damage and lost human life. Just like revolutionary change, however, wildfires promote the introduction of new life forms and are thus part of the natural ecosystem. The new life forms may resist fire or may encourage more fire, which makes managing this type of change a heavy responsibility.

Revolutionary change is unpredictable except in one respect: It consumes anything useful in its path and makes no distinction between good and evil. The pressure to go along with this type of change can be overwhelming. We must not permit ourselves to be swept away by those who have allowed themselves to be swept away. Revolutionary change is serious business that should only be attempted when it is absolutely necessary and when the time is right, and only as a last resort. Not every generation is called to the task, but if we are among the chosen few, we should steer the revolution toward the greatest good. Revolutionary change is a time of climax, but also of perfect, albeit unstable, equilibrium. The moment will not last very long, so we should make the most of it, be watchful for symptoms of entropy and decay, and take precautions for the inevitable turn of events.

Developmental change is the perfect complement to revolutionary change and refers to the process of self-development as well as the gradual unfolding of events. The best way to describe this type of change is to picture yourself standing beside a mountain stream in a steep ravine. There appears to be no way forward—no way to overcome the insurmountable obstacle. What should you do? You should keep still and observe the water. You should watch the water slowly rise at the base of the mountain. It does not immediately overcome the obstacle in front of it but slowly fills the basin, flowing into every crack and crevice. The water rises slowly until the basin becomes a pool and the pool becomes a lake. When the lake is full, the water keeps flowing until it finds the outlet, which no longer presents an obstacle, but a flow line allowing the water to proceed toward its destination.

This metaphor depicts the best way to manage developmental change: Don't rush forward, but build capacity and accumulate knowledge, skill, and wisdom before proceeding. This helps to recognize the obstacle not as a nuisance, but as an inherent part of our chosen path. As it is with other types of change, managing developmental change requires adopting a certain attitude. First, know your limitations; second, learn how to change yourself. This may be frustrating for those eager to show progress—or at least show vigorous activity—but sometimes the problem is internal; sometimes the problem is an inevitable result of the strategy we have chosen to implement. Learning requires receptivity on behalf of the learner, a willingness to accept instruction, a willingness to master the lessons one by one until the obstacle is no longer an obstacle.

The conflict in developmental change is inherent but latent. Conflict may be unavoidable depending on the personalities involved—the change agents who themselves are unwilling to learn. Those unschooled in the typology of change may try to overcome the obstacle through direct attack rather than increased capacity and thus create resistance. Convinced of their righteousness, they may not engage in open conflict, but instead resort to high-handed or underhanded maneuvers. Even if those unschooled in the typology of change successfully impose their will, it will lead to unintended consequences. Even if they are right, even if they advocate change that is necessary, such maneuvers may cause acrimony and conflict.

Managing developmental change requires leadership, but not necessarily from the chief executive. It may come from a less senior officer in the hierarchy. To see this type of change through to a successful outcome, there must be no perception it is coming from the top down, but instead from the middle of the organization. Change agents who are second-tier officers (or lower) in the organizational hierarchy have less formal authority, which forces them to rely on their powers of communication and persuasion. This enables them to earn the trust and confidence of people at all levels and creates a comfort level across the organization. The objective is for people to be comfortable with change, so they neither back away from it nor rush through it. This is self-mastery on an organizational scale.

Managing developmental change requires an organization to undergo one rigorous test after another. This helps optimize the organization's performance and protects it from external threats, but it cannot go on forever. Once we have overcome the adversity or removed whatever external threat we faced, it is imperative to let up on the accelerator. One side effect of developmental change is exhaustion, which requires leaders to make sure the organization does not go further than necessary. It helps to remember the goal of political economy: to produce the maximum positive outcome while conserving energy and minimizing waste.

Adversity builds capacity and serves as the foundation for future successes, which is one reason we want to teach organizations not to back away from change. The kind of adversity associated with developmental change can easily break an organization. However, an organization that learns how far it can bend without breaking learns something very important about itself. It learns resilience, which fuels a culture of self-confidence. As usual, it is important not to overdo it, not to let the confidence deteriorate into overconfidence and complacency.

Limited to Evolutionary

Limited change is a call for reform rather than revolution. It is a teachable moment on a social scale, a time when people are most likely to learn something new. To make the most of this moment of educational opportunity, people need a framework—such as a coherent governing philosophy—to be already in place. Whether the framework is based on the most primitive impulses of human nature, the most complex expressions of human development, or the principles of some defunct economist, people need a theoretical framework. Why is this? As W. Edwards Deming explains, "Without theory, experience has no meaning. Without theory, one has no questions to ask." Without theory, there is nothing to compare, nothing to revise, and nothing to learn.[2]

This type of change can be difficult, because it deals with the symptoms and consequences of arbitrary differences in political and economic status. I should add, just because the differences are arbitrary does not mean they are meaningless. The post–Cold War political and economic system is not designed to bring about universal equality. A certain degree of resentment and resistance is predictable. If we read the situation accurately, however, it is possible to achieve a successful outcome. When we encounter resistance, it is better not to buffalo our way forward. Instead, we should look for the polarities that would occur naturally and symmetrically within the system. Reconciling these opposing forces—as if they were always meant to be complementary—is the key to implementing successful reform.

When it comes to managing this type of change, simplicity is essential. Where there are arbitrary differences, there will be aggressive competition for scarce resources. Rather than covering it up or trying to deny it, rather than presenting false appearances, we should acknowledge the injustice and not try to minimize the problem in any way. With this in mind, we should try to understand the origins of the problem and make them public. We should forego grandiose schemes and instead focus on specific problems where it is possible to reach a consensus—and draw strength from that. The factor constraining this type of change is the inadequate framework that impedes learning and limits the potential for cognitive development. Without an adequate framework, the majority of people will fail to understand the feedback the system is communicating.

Clinton's frequent exhortations on the subject of personal responsibility and the need for fiscal discipline were his way to call for limited change (or reform). If you recall from Chapter 3, part of the Hoover Institution's definition of conservatism included limited government, one that recognizes its limitations and concentrates on its core functions. If you recall from Chapter 2, Rousseau said people would be happier and more productive if they relinquished some of their freedoms and submitted to the sovereign will of the people, while Smith said the government had a fundamental duty to maintain a system of law and order, protect individuals, and defend their property rights. The purpose of the social contract is to establish a system of political economy that protects and defends individuals and their property without imposing excessive limitations on individual freedom. Thus, freely imposing limitations on ourselves is a prerequisite if we expect to enjoy the benefits of the social contract.

Evolutionary change is the perfect complement to limited change. Evolutionary change implies directionality, indicated by increasing diversity, complexity, and organization. Each successive stage of evolution produces greater depth (more systems within systems), greater interdependence between subsystems, and a longer and larger chain of consequences. Evolutionary change is very gradual—almost imperceptible—and thus very powerful. Evolutionary change takes place in *ecological time*, generally on the order of tens to hundreds of years. Because evolutionary change is largely impervious to human intervention, the best response is not to "manage" it in the conventional sense, let alone try to control it, but to emulate it.

The most outstanding attributes to emulate are patience and persistence. Evolutionary change manifests itself with an air of inevitability. The most effective response to this type of change is respectful, receptive, and observant. The term *evolutionary change* implies no positive or negative connotations. The term merely describes a type of change that takes place gradually and unavoidably. Regardless whether the change that takes place is for better or worse, inevitability is the source of its power. In this situation, it is wisest to retreat. Rather than interfere in a situation we are powerless to change, we should pull back to avoid being drawn in. Evolutionary change is reminiscent of the Borg, the fictional race of cyborgs on *Star Trek*; as the Borg queen says, resistance is futile.

When the forces of change have an overwhelming advantage,

it is pointless to exhaust our resources. It is much wiser to with-draw—as long as it is the right kind of withdrawal: not the kind of withdrawal after suffering a defeat, but the kind where we can reposition our forces. Such a retreat is a show of strength that requires careful timing. Retreating when our forces are still strong but our position is indefensible is not the same thing as abandon-ing the field. If our timing is good, we should be able to retreat without signaling weakness and without provoking an aggressive response. One thing we can be sure of is that the situation will change again, so timing and organization are important. A well-timed, well-organized retreat will conserve resources and buy time to think.

In times of evolutionary change, remember not to resist. Leave that to our adversaries, and watch them carefully for signs of exhaustion or complacency. If they have misinterpreted the situa-tion, they may leave themselves in a compromising situation. Watch what happens and prepare to take the initiative when con-ditions change again, as they inevitably will. Evolutionary change requires reflection and sometimes action—such as retreating—that may appear to move us further from our goal. It is an oppor-tunity to consider whether the difficulty is internal rather than external. While those unschooled in the typology of change will typically blame peripheral factors—unfavorable market condi-tions or the like—it would be wiser to look into the mirror, ques-tion our own motives, and reconsider the flaws in our own strategy.

Although executives are often restless and not naturally intro-spective, withdrawing from the situation is a prerequisite for thinking systemically. Coping with evolutionary change requires critical distance to observe the dynamics of the system at work. Withdrawing helps focus our attention on the big picture, so we will not be distracted by extraneous details or insignificant per-sonalities. Evolutionary change, by definition, produces long-term consequences, which requires long-term planning. Rather than exhaust ourselves trying to exert influence on the immediate situation, it would be wiser to develop contingencies based on alternative scenarios of the future.

Although "you must become the change" is a cliché, there is a reason it became a cliché in the first place. In this context, it means emulating the characteristics of evolutionary change. Picture a tree growing on a mountain. Two lessons come to mind. Lesson one: The tree enjoys a commanding view of the landscape in every direction and thus is visible from every direction. Lesson two: Everything in the landscape took years to develop. Because evolutionary change takes place in *ecological time*, anyone who hopes to manage it successfully must be equal to it. Unfortunately, this is rare in the age of television. Our market system is not particularly generous to individuals with this gift, even if they express an interest. More often (but not always), the wrong people rise to prominence. That too is part of the challenge and requires emulating the characteristics of evolutionary change.

Robust to Chaotic

In systems jargon, *robustness* indicates the dependability of a system to continue functioning under stressful or unreliable conditions. We consider a system robust if it remains relatively stable when the environment fluctuates. It may seem as though *robust* is a contradiction in terms for this type of change because the situation appears unsustainable. Like all types of change, however, this too is multifaceted and dynamic. When dealing with situations such as this, remember that even though all types of change will have superficial characteristics that make the situation appear unique, the key to change management requires first using the typology to recognize the deep structure of the change, then formulating (and then implementing) a strategy corresponding to the type of change.

Robust change does not weaken but becomes stronger with longevity. In the jargon of complex systems, robust change is *autopoietic*, meaning it regenerates itself naturally. Robust change is cyclical, but that may not be evident to the untrained eye, depending on the length of the cycle. The analogy I mentioned in Chapter 4 is the solar system. The Earth spins on its axis, giving us night and day, and orbits around the sun, giving us winter, spring, summer, and fall. Each phase has a beginning and an end, and although the duration of each phase may vary year to year, the sequence never does. It helps to remember those Biblical verses American folk singer Pete Seeger set to music: To every thing, there is a season, and a time to every purpose under the heaven (Ecclesiastes 3:1–8).

Robust change is mobile, which may seem like another contradiction in terms, but the contradiction teaches us how to manage it. The characteristics that define robust change are its structure (systems within systems), long-term equilibrium (with local instability and unpredictability), and an accumulation of effects (a chain of consequences that multiplies over time). While the internal effects of robust change may be invisible, the external effects surely are not. Success in this instance requires adaptability and persistence: never rushing, never idling, and thus making time our ally. Historic achievements are possible if we align ourselves with the system's natural tendencies and use the long cycle to our advantage. However, we must exercise caution in the process of strategic planning, fine-tuning our policies and strategies to the long cycle in order to lend power to our goals. The results may be gradual and inconspicuous at any given point in time, but the cumulative effect will be nothing short of miraculous.

Chaotic change is the perfect complement to robust change. Chaotic change has a high entropy value because it consists almost entirely of potential. This type of change is in its emergent phase, full of pent-up tension. It is very difficult to manage because of the abundance of energy struggling to take form. Everything is in a state of motion, unruly, volatile, and weird. The situation is not completely confused, however, because there is a natural order in the situation, which is intrinsic and latent. Once again, managing this type of change requires holding back until the time is right. This does not imply looking on passively. The situation calls for action, but not a shock wave—more like an isometric exercise, with tightly controlled exertion over an extended length of time.

Managing any type of change is rarely a solitary endeavor. It often requires members of a community to work as a team and adapt to the demands of the situation. Overcoming obstacles together requires bringing members of the community together. Unity does not emerge simply by purging dissent, eliminating factions, or overcoming resistance by force. We must learn to recognize the difference between disagreement and disloyalty. To perform effectively in this context, it is important for individual team members and the team as a whole to follow a middle path between the extremes of aggression and submission. Chaotic change is full of potential that can switch from victory to defeat and back again, so every member of the team must be aware of (if not make sense of) the extremely complicated feedback.

That is another curious thing about chaotic change. Though it appears completely disorganized on one level, it is following a pattern on another level, cycling through its phases one after another. It emerges full of potential, full of energy struggling to take form, and then comes the turning point. What was pure entropy completes its cycle naturally with minimal intervention. In some ways, managing chaotic change requires the opposite of chaos. It requires people to work in harmony, allowing the system to accumulate energy, then dissipate it, accumulate it, and dissipate it again in regular (if not entirely predictable) intervals. Doing nothing while the world is falling apart can be exhausting and sometimes humiliating, because people expect their leaders to show activity.

Nothing challenges one's management skills like chaotic change, especially when chaotic change appears in its most baffling camouflage. If your internal bullshit detector is not in perfect working order, your instincts may lead you in the wrong direction. Chaotic change is like springtime. There is so much uncertainty; when everything seems to be sprouting and growing, it is nearly impossible to know for sure which new developments to cultivate, which ones to ignore, and which ones to eradicate. Managing chaotic change requires an able and adaptable team, so it is important to identify the right people. We can learn a great deal about potential teammates by observing which sides of their personality they choose to cultivate and which sides they disregard or deny. In times of chaotic change, people tend to revert to type and will ostentatiously display sides of themselves they regard as especially important. Intellectuals, for example, will not only overestimate the value of intelligence but will also overestimate their own intelligence.

After a while, the systems thinker begins to see patterns all around—systems nested within systems within a matrix. One begins to recognize the various types of change and the permutations of each type and then begins to cultivate the ability to recognize the boundaries of a system. The boundaries of a system have no time limits, meaning the immediate effects of managerial intervention today may be negligible or erroneous, while the long-term effects may be unknown for months or even years. When we say boundaries of the system, we don't mean the physical structure but instead dynamic complexity, which may include events that have yet to take place and consequences that have yet to take effect. When in doubt, we should remember the words of management consultant W. Edwards Deming: "A system includes the future."[3]

Future Preference

Clinton formed his ideas on change as a freshman at Georgetown University. He often related the story about a course he took, History of Civilization. He remembered the professor (Carroll Quigley) saying that one of the distinguishing characteristics of Western civilization is the propensity for "future preference," the idea that the future will be better than the past and that every individual in society has a duty to make it so.[4] This transforms the social contract from an agreement between members of society into an agreement between generations.

In the fall of 1995, Clinton borrowed from Proverbs 29:18 to summarize his thoughts on the need to manage change:

> You know, the Scripture says, "Where there is no vision the people perish." Whether you believe that or not, it is perfectly clear that no change occurs that is positive unless someone has imagined it. And at a time when things are changing anyway, when the way we work and live and relate to each other and the rest of the world is very much in flux, it is absolutely imperative that we have citizens and leaders who can imagine the future in a different way, so that we can shape it in the way that we want our children to find it.[5]

The purpose of politics, he said, is to imagine the future and then articulate a unifying vision that helps people achieve their common destiny.[6] Imagining the future is particularly difficult when the stars that used to guide our policies have disappeared.

At a 1994 meeting of the Asia-Pacific Economic Cooperation (APEC) forum, Clinton described what happens when you arrive at the intersection of continuity and change only to discover your map is obsolete:

> These moments are always hard, because change is always hard, because they are steeped in controversy, because they are often full of risk. We know and regret the moments when our Nation has chosen unwisely in the past, such as when we turned the world toward protectionism and isolationism after World War I or when we failed for so long to face up to the awful consequences of slavery. We celebrate the chapters of American history in which we chose boldly: the Declaration of Independence, the Louisiana Purchase, the containment of communism, the embrace of the civil rights movement.
>
> Now we have arrived again at such a moment. Change is upon us. We can do nothing about that. The pole stars that guided our affairs in the past years have disappeared. The Soviet Union is gone. Communist expansionism has ended. At the same time, a new global economy of constant innovation and instant communication is cutting through our world like a new river, providing both power and disruption to the people and nations who live along its course.[7]

In a commencement address at UCLA some months later, Clinton described the "bewildering, intense, sometimes overpowering change" confronting the young graduates. With the fiftieth anniversary of the allied invasion of Normandy less than two weeks away, Clinton wanted the young graduates to remember the *greatest generation* rather than the *lost generation*. The allied invasion of Normandy exemplified sacrifice and personal courage, mostly by citizen soldiers, some still in their teens and many others not much older than college students. These people grew up in the false prosperity of the twenties and the bitter realities of the Great Depression, said Clinton, "But they rallied that day to a cause larger than themselves. And when they had done the job they were sent to do—to save their country, to save freedom, to save a civilization—they came home and got on with the business of making lives for themselves, their children and their children's children."

Following the devastation of WWI, "America withdrew from the world, seeking security and isolationism and protectionism," said Clinton. "An ugly withdrawal occurred here at home as well—a retreat into the trenches of racial prejudice and religious prejudice; of class bigotry and easy convenience; and a simple refusal to prepare our people to live in the world as it was." Following our victories in Europe and the Pacific, however, the greatest generation came back to work wonders at home. These individuals reached out to the world, helped allies and former enemies alike rebuild from the ruins. They created the GI Bill, which helped war veterans get a college education, helped them buy homes and created the strongest economy and the greatest middle class the world has ever known. They transformed the American economy into a global powerhouse, which proved to be the decisive factor in the Cold War.[8]

Although the Great Depression and WWII taught us valuable lessons, we did not learn them completely, because Russia and China, two of our former allies from WWII, became our enemies. Four decades later, the Berlin Wall fell and the Cold War ended, bringing more change, new opportunities, new fears, and new challenges. First came 9/11, then the invasions and occupations of Afghanistan and Iraq. Then came too many natural disasters to count, followed by turmoil in the financial market, the housing market, and the energy market.

What shall be our response? Do we reach out and build bridges or do we retreat and build walls? Somewhere, there is always a fledgling democracy, with people trying to stand up and be brave, and it is our responsibility to stand with them. Furthermore, just as we have leadership responsibilities in the world, we have leadership responsibilities in our neighborhoods. The future depends on our response—though we know it is an imperfect world. According to Clinton:

> History will look back on us and judge how well we responded to this time of intense economic transformation. It is the most intensive period of economic change since the industrial revolution. The revolutions in communications and technology, the development of nonstop global markets, the vast currency flows that are now the tides of international business, all these have brought enormous advantages for those who can embrace and succeed in the new global economy. But these forces have also made all our societies more vulnerable to disturbances that once may have seemed distant but which now directly affect the jobs and livelihoods in every nation in the world, from the richest to the poorest.[9]

The forces of globalization are making it more difficult to maintain the social contract—from combating terrorism to eliminating violence in our schools and providing security for our children. The world is changing fast—and will change again—and eventually terrorism will be just one of many challenges we face, not the all-consuming problem it has become since 9/11. What will not change are the fundamental laws that govern political economy and complexity. Politics is about power. Economics is about resources. Complexity is ubiquitous.

When globalization is so powerful and change is so prevalent, it is easy to see why some people wish they could make the world go away. Clinton said:

> Well, there are two problems with that. One is nothing ever stays the same anyway, ever, not in an individual life, not in the family's life, not in a business, not in a state's life, not in a nation's life. The second is all you have to do is pick up the paper every day to know that things are changing quite a lot around the world and there are a lot of outcomes that aren't clear.[10]

Our ultimate goal is not to control reality, but to master the moment of change and put our propensity for future preference to good use. There is a moment between stimulus and response where people—free people—have that power. What shall we do with our moment? Let's find out in Part 2.

Public Policy

CHAPTER 6

The Role of Government (A)

Robert Morris of Pennsylvania was really one of the major financial backers of the Revolutionary War—of our side . . . and he was also the first budget balancer. He resigned from the Continental Congress in 1778 because he thought they were printing too much money. My kind of Democrat.[1]

—BILL CLINTON, 1996

WE OFTEN HEAR ABOUT THE principles of the founding fathers. Rather than place our trust in think tanks or talk shows—never mind our memories from high school civics—we should reread what the founding fathers actually wrote about the principles of government. Beginning in 1787, Alexander Hamilton, James Madison, and John Jay wrote a series of essays to support ratification of the new U.S. Constitution collectively known as *The Federalist Papers*. Before then, each state retained its sovereignty according to the Articles of Confederation, a collective security agreement created in 1777 by the Continental Congress. The central government had no power of taxation but instead relied on the thirteen state legislatures for revenues, which left the central government weak and chronically in debt.

There are eighty-five *Federalist Papers* covering a wide range of issues regarding each branch of government. *Federalist Paper No. 84* (by Hamilton) is particularly interesting because it argues against the necessity for a Bill of Rights, which was not part of the original Constitution. The Bill of Rights (the first ten amendments to the Constitution) explicitly guarantees freedom of speech, press, and religion; protects our right to own weapons; protects against unlawful search and seizure; guarantees the right to a speedy trial and a trial by jury; and protects against excessive bail, as well as cruel or unusual punishment. No. 84 proves the founding fathers did not agree on everything and should make us suspicious any time someone invokes the founding fathers to make their case. Hamilton argued that the rights specified in the first ten amendments were not only unnecessary but also dangerous—and he was particularly skeptical about guaranteeing freedom of the press. Reagan and Clinton would both agree it is a good thing Hamilton lost this argument. Reagan was emphatic that people had certain natural, unalienable rights that no government could take away.

In addition to protecting the rights of individuals and states, one of the federal government's primary functions is to protect property rights. No. 10 and No. 54, both written by Madison, concern property rights. In No. 10, he wrote, "The diversity in the faculties of men, from which the rights of property originate, is not less an insuperable obstacle to a uniformity of interests. The protection of these faculties is the first object of government." In No. 54, Madison stated, "Government is instituted no less for protection of the property, than of the persons, of individuals."

The federal government's other primary function is national

security. In No. 23, Hamilton asserted, "The authorities essential to the common defense are these: to raise armies; to build and equip fleets; to prescribe rules for the government of both; to direct their operations; to provide for their support," and because it is impossible to always foresee the circumstances that endanger the safety of the nation, "these powers ought to exist without limitation." Of all the arguments in favor of an energetic government, this is the strongest.

In No. 2, John Jay pointed out, "Nothing is more certain than the indispensable necessity of government, and it is equally undeniable, that whenever and however it is instituted, the people must cede to it some of their natural rights in order to vest it with requisite powers." This is Rousseau's social contract, which claims that people are better off when they relinquish some of their natural rights to legitimate government authority. Why institute government at all? Without government, according to Hamilton in No. 15, "The passions of men will not conform to the dictates of reason and justice." According to Madison (No. 51), "If men were angels, no government would be necessary. If angels were to govern men, neither external nor internal controls on government would be necessary. In framing a government which is to be administered by men over men, the great difficulty lies in this: you must first enable the government to control the governed; and in the next place oblige it to control itself."

Although the founders believed government was an indispensable necessity, they worried the federal government might exceed its authority and make tyrannical use of its powers (No. 33, by Hamilton). This is why they decentralized government authority and limited its jurisdiction "to certain enumerated objects" (No. 14, by Madison). Not only did the new constitution contain a system of checks and balances within the federal government, there was also a system of checks and balances between the federal government and the thirteen states. According to No. 45

(Madison), "The powers delegated by the proposed Constitution to the federal government are few and defined. Those which are to remain in the State governments are numerous and indefinite." The founders worried about the federal government becoming too powerful but also worried about it becoming too weak. In No. 17, Hamilton asserts, "It will always be far more easy for the State governments to encroach upon the national authorities than for the national government to encroach upon the State authorities."

The founders envisioned a central government that was not too strong, but also not too weak. According to No. 1 (Hamilton), "The vigor of government is essential to the security of liberty." According to No. 70 (Hamilton), "Energy in the Executive is a leading character in the definition of good government." Under the old Articles of Confederation, the central government could not levy taxes, which left it weak and broke. Although the founders wanted the federal government's powers to be "few and defined," one of those was the power of taxation. According to No. 31 (Hamilton), "The federal government must of necessity be invested with an unqualified power of taxation." They considered money to be "the vital principle of the body politic," which sustained its life and enabled it to perform its essential functions. Thus, they regarded a "complete power" to procure a regular and adequate supply of money to be an indispensable ingredient in the Constitution (No. 13, by Hamilton.) Without adequate funding, the federal government would "sink into a fatal atrophy, and, in a short course of time, perish." In No. 30, Hamilton writes:

> How is it possible that a government half supplied and always necessitous, can fulfill the purposes of its institution, can provide for the security, advance the prosperity, or support the reputation of the commonwealth? How can it ever possess either energy or stability, dignity or credit, confidence at home or respectability abroad? How

can its administration be any thing else than a succession of expedients temporizing, impotent, disgraceful? How will it be able to avoid a frequent sacrifice of its engagements to immediate necessity? How can it undertake or execute any liberal or enlarged plans of public good?

What did the founders say in response? There is nothing in political economy and nothing in the field of public administration more important than the business of taxation. It requires understanding the resources of the country, as well as the genius, habits, and modes of thinking of the people. Political leaders who understand taxation are most likely to be fair and least likely to be impulsive. Finally, the lower the tax burden, the better. In the words of Alexander Hamilton, author of No. 35,

> There is no part of the administration of government that requires extensive information and a thorough knowledge of the principles of political economy, so much as the business of taxation. The man who understands those principles best will be least likely to resort to oppressive expedients, or sacrifice any particular class of citizens to the procurement of revenue. It might be demonstrated that the most productive system of finance will always be the least burdensome.

As we know, the business of taxation was fundamental to Reagan's governing philosophy. Conservative columnist George Will considered Reagan's views on tax reform one of the wonders of American politics. "No previous President has stressed as much as Ronald Reagan has the possibility and importance of changing society by changing the tax code." Like Reagan, Will does not arbitrarily separate politics from economics. Will's insight is important, but we have to take into consideration that he also considers the political part of "political economy" superfluous, because economic relationships—such as contracts, corporations, or trade unions—are inherently political.[2] Will's point is that economic influences—in this case reforming the tax code—are often more reliable than political influences. If not for Clinton's party affiliation, Will might have said no previous president had stressed the importance of changing society by balancing the budget, cutting the deficit, and reforming the welfare system.

The End of Big Government

The era of big government symbolically ended on January 20, 1981, the day Ronald Reagan's presidency began. Reagan's inaugural address was built on the same themes he had been communicating since his 1964 political debut. He denounced the unnecessary and excessive growth of government and announced his intention to restore the proper balance between the federal and state governments. Of course, the source of the problem was deficit spending and the symptom was inflation, which discouraged saving and eroded the value of pensions and fixed incomes and was thus especially cruel for people dependent on Social Security. Piling deficit upon deficit, he said, would guarantee social, political, and economic upheaval.

Up to this point, there is nothing Clinton would vehemently disagree with—that is, until Reagan said, "Government is not the solution to our problem; government is the problem." Reagan's famous phrase is the hinge that connects Reagan and Clinton, so let's reread the complete quotation:

> In this present crisis, government is not the solution to our problem; government is the problem. From time to time we've been tempted to believe that society has become too complex to be managed by self-rule, that government by an elite group is superior to government for, by, and of the people. Well, if no one among us is capable

of governing himself, then who among us has the capacity to govern someone else? All of us together, in and out of government, must bear the burden. The solutions we seek must be equitable, with no one group singled out to pay a higher price.[3]

Reagan was a master of the English language, and his use of the prepositional phrase "in this present crisis" is intentional and specific. He knew some people (carelessly or deliberately) would misinterpret his words. It was not Reagan's intention to do away with all government, but to remove the roadblocks that hindered economic growth and threatened political freedom. It was not his intention to solve the entire problem at once, but to reverse the trend and try to bring interactions among federal, state, and local governments closer to the founding principles of federalism.

CLINTON'S 1994 ANNUAL message was a condensed version of every speech he gave in 1993. As usual, Clinton disparaged his predecessors' policies, which built a false prosperity on a mountain of debt. According to Clinton's version of events, the voters woke up in 1992 and demanded change. As a result, he said, "We replaced drift and deadlock with renewal and reform."[4] Of course, the 1994 midterm elections were still nine months away.

Several weeks before the 1994 midterm elections, Republican leaders released the Contract with America and turned the election into a national referendum. Most Republican House members and all challengers running for office signed the contract seeking a "mandate for reform" from the voters. Dissatisfaction with the Democratic leadership in the House of Representatives led to the defeat of dozens of Democratic incumbents and several powerful party leaders, including house speaker Tom Foley. Republicans won a majority of seats for the first time in forty years.

Newt Gingrich of Georgia became the new speaker and promised quick action on a range of issues that would restore trust in the government and accountability in Congress.

Here is Clinton's shell-shocked analysis of the election:

> The voters clearly all along had wanted smaller, more effective, less intrusive government that reflects both our values and our interests—governmental action that brings stability into their lives and doesn't create too many problems because most folks think they've got enough problems already. But they plainly also want us to be strong and secure and to lead them into the next century in a country that is strong and secure, with the American Dream alive.[5]

Clinton's early analysis told him voters wanted change but were impatient. The same forces that prematurely ended George H.W. Bush's presidency and swept Clinton into power ended four decades of Democratic rule and swept Newt Gingrich and the Republican Party into power. Clinton commented their message was "government is the enemy," quite a departure from Reagan's message that "government is the problem."

The Contract with America was a patchwork of proposals mostly drawn from Reagan's old State of the Union messages, a testament to Reagan's enduring political influence since his presidency.[6] According to the contract, the election was an opportunity to end "four decades of one-party control" and end "government that is too big, too intrusive, and too easy with the public's money."[7] Broad issues included fiscal responsibility and taxes; crime reduction; welfare reform; tort reform (discouraging frivolous lawsuits and limiting punitive monetary damages); term limits; and a pledge to eliminate government waste, fraud, and mismanagement. The contract also included ten specific bills, with such down-to-earth titles as the Family Reinforcement Act and the American Dream Restoration Act, that Gingrich promised to bring to a vote within the first one hundred days of the new session.

Again, there does not seem to be much in the substance of the contract that Clinton could have disagreed with—but he found a way. As a reminder, social science requires at least two people, and political science at least two oppositional people. In politics, having an adversary is not an inconvenience, but a requirement. To much laughter, this is what Clinton said about the easy promises of the Contract with America:

> Now, what will they do if we give them power? Have you seen their "Contract for America"? They promise everybody a tax cut, mostly the wealthiest Americans. They promise huge increases in defense spending. They promise everybody everything—a trillion dollars. And you say, well, how are you going to pay for this? And they say, we'll tell you later. Well, you know it's election year, folks. I'd like to make you a trillion dollars worth of promises, too. I could show you a good time with a trillion dollars. We could have a lot of fun.[8]

Clinton wanted his party to stay faithful to its values but very much wanted it to modernize its approach, "to focus less on preserving the party's industrial-age achievements and more on meeting the challenges of the information age, and to clarify our commitment to middle-class values and concerns."[9] He relished the opportunity to compare his approach to our economic and social problems against the Contract with America. He recognized one of the problems with creating government programs is that after they've served their purpose, the organization inevitably engages in self-preservation. This is one of those fundamental

laws of bureaucracies and happens to many kinds of organizations, including private sector companies, not just government
bureaucracies. It happens to agencies created by both political
parties, and it happens to military and intelligence organizations,
just like any other kind of government organization.

The Contract with America had a certain superficial attraction
because it indulged the present instead of preparing for the future. It was, Clinton said, "nothing more than the second verse
of trickle-down economics." Years later, Clinton reflected on the
Contract with America in his autobiography.

> I agreed with many of the particulars of the contract. I
> was already pushing welfare reform and tougher child-
> support enforcement, and had long supported the line-
> item veto and ending unfunded mandates. I liked the
> family tax credits. Though several of the specifics were
> appealing, the contract was, at its core, a simplistic and
> hypocritical document.[10]

Looking back on his first presidential campaign, Clinton once
said his goal was to take the country's (and his party's) main-
stream values and "marry them to modern ideas and policies." If
you don't win you can't govern, which is why Clinton prized
being "relevant and effective" above all else. It is one reason why
Clinton sounded like a conservative at times, with all his talk
about personal responsibility. It is another reason why there was
no way Clinton would permit Newt Gingrich to get around his
right flank. After the stunning upset, Clinton did his best to reas-
sure members of the Democratic Leadership Council (DLC), reminding them "the Democratic Party's fundamental mission is to
expand opportunity, not government." Then in November 1995,
he test-marketed the phrase that would later become the signature phrase of his governing philosophy: "We have given you a

modern government. *The era of big government is over* . . . but the era of good government and strong government cannot be over, because the public interest still must be advanced by the American people working together through their elected representatives."

In January 1996, two weeks before his annual message, Clinton paid a visit to the National Democratic Club and took a predictably partisan tone. He urged his fellow Democrats not to let Republicans take credit for ending big government. "That is done," he said. "And the Democrats did that for you, and nobody even noticed because we did it in the right way with no suffering of government services and without putting good public employees out on the street and treating them like they were disposable products."[11] If this excerpt seems familiar, it should, because it mirrors Reagan's sentiments regarding arbitrarily cutting state government payrolls in California after passage of Proposition 13.

Perhaps we can forgive Clinton for being less than presidential. Perhaps his gratuitous partisan shot was a belated response to something Reagan said a few years earlier, when Reagan accused Democrats of being "addicted to big government, high taxes, and inflation" and said, "Big government has become the Democrats' pet." Perhaps we can forgive Reagan as well, because he had a great sense of humor. At a speech to the National Association of Broadcasters in 1988, toward the end of his presidency and with his political battles soon behind him, he said he never liked big government. "Yet sometime before I leave office, I do intend to enact a very important new regulation: one limiting the number of commercials during my old movies."[12]

Here is the big government money shot from Clinton's 1996 annual message:

> We know big government does not have all the answers.
> We know there's not a program for every problem. We

know, and we have worked to give the American people a smaller, less bureaucratic government in Washington. And we have to give the American people one that lives within its means. The era of big government is over. But we cannot go back to the time when our citizens were left to fend for themselves.[13]

Clinton liked the line about big government so much he said it twice in that annual message, and both times he said there was no turning back. Big, centralized bureaucracies—in countries with centrally planned and market economies alike—were more and more going to be part of the past. Of course, Clinton's assertion about the era of big government grabbed a lot of attention. It did so at the expense of the following line about not abandoning people to fend for themselves. The end of big government did not mean the end of effective government or responsible government. Smaller government did not mean weaker government, but one more focused and more oriented toward future challenges. According to Clinton, "It can be smaller, it can be less bureaucratic. We can be giving more power to state and local governments, more power to people in the private sector, more power to groups that can solve social problems at the grass-roots level. But we don't need to walk away from America's challenges."[14]

The era of big government was over not because the president declared it so, but because the world had indeed exited one era and entered another. The difference is the calendar. However, it would be misleading to suggest size was the only issue. A smaller government did not simply walk away from its responsibilities. Deliberately weakening the Federal Emergency Management Agency (FEMA), for example, would leave it unable to respond in times of crisis and was thus unnecessary and irresponsible. Unfortunately, not everyone got the message.

In 2003, conservative pundit Fred Barnes coined the phrase "big government conservative" to describe George W. Bush's incoherent policies that combined tax cuts, huge loans, and huge deficits.[15] According to Barnes, big government conservatism uses liberal methods—meaning government activism—to accomplish conservative goals. When Hurricane Katrina made landfall in August 2005, it flooded and destroyed large parts of New Orleans; brought terrible destruction along the Gulf Coast in Louisiana, Mississippi, and Alabama; caused billions of dollars of property damage; and killed hundreds of people. When Bush visited the area the following month, he unwittingly provided a concise definition of big government conservatism: "The Federal Government's job is big, and it's massive, and we're going to do it. Where it's not working right, we're going to make it right. Where it is working right, we're going to duplicate it elsewhere."[16] Safe to say, both Reagan and Thatcher would have considered "big government conservatism" to be ridiculous.

In a 1983 essay entitled "The Emergence of Two Republican Parties," Irving Kristol wrote, "Not since Theodore Roosevelt has the Republican party shown the faintest comprehension of the nature of presidential leadership in a modern democracy. It has failed to understand that the idea of limited government is not contradictory to the idea of energetic government or (what comes to the same thing) responsive government."[17] According to Clinton, the great debate in American politics since the early eighties was trying to resolve our differences regarding the national government's responsibility. "I have to tell you that I think that is the wrong debate," he said. "The era of big government is over." In effect, Clinton wanted a new debate—not about big government versus small government, but about a new philosophy of government appropriate to the new century. According to the new philosophy, there would be a revised relationship between citizen and government, which reconfigured the relationship from welfare provider to equal partner. Following up on his annual message, Clinton said this:

> A great part of this debate in Washington is about what the national government's responsibility is. And the way you've heard this debate over the last fifteen years has often been: big government is getting in the way of the American economy; big government is undermining the independence of the American community; big government is weakening, not strengthening, the American family. I have to tell you that I think that is the wrong debate. The era of big government is over. Our administration has eliminated 16,000 pages of federal regulations, hundreds of programs, thousands of unnecessary offices. The government is over 200,000 people smaller today than it was the day I took the oath of office as President. But the issue is not big government versus small government. The issue is, what is your responsibility through the national government to work to help people make the most of their own lives, to work to help communities solve their own problems and meet their own challenges. That is the issue.[18]

In his second term, Clinton touched on the limited government theme to explain Republican and Democratic differences on gun control, specifically the Brady Handgun Violence Prevention Act, otherwise known as the Brady Bill, named for Reagan's former press secretary Jim Brady, who was wounded and permanently disabled in the 1981 assassination attempt on Reagan. The Brady Bill required people to undergo a background check and waiting period before buying a handgun from a federally licensed firearms dealer. "But governments ought to be limited, they ought to be limited in scope, limited in power, limited in reach, but they should do those things that we cannot do alone. And sometimes, in order to advance our collective life, liberty, and happiness, individually we have to make a few sacrifices. That's really what the Brady Bill is all about."[19]

According to the Republican philosophy Reagan popularized, government is the source of our problems, and we would all be better off if there were less of it. Republicans claimed big government was riding on our backs, smothering opportunity, stifling productivity, piling deficit upon deficit, and mortgaging our future. According to political scientist Benjamin Barber, Reagan "evoked an America without government, an America of individuals all pulling their load," while Democrats had no viable political philosophy. According to Clinton, "It was very powerful rhetorically, but the American people never knew what it meant until the other party won the Congress in 1995 and had the Government shut down twice over the battle of the budget."

During an early reelection campaign visit to New Hampshire, Clinton wanted to remind voters he "was not a Democrat who believed in preserving the status quo and every bureaucratic program that ever existed." Even after three years in office, there were still too many unneeded regulations, too many unnecessary programs, and too many bureaucracies. At a Democratic Party fundraiser a few months later, Clinton said, "I'm glad that we *proved* that the Democratic Party is not the party of big government."[20] Then a few weeks before the election, Clinton put it this way:

> And our friends in the other party, they always say government is the problem, government is the enemy, government is bad. But you know what? We've done more to reduce the size of government than they ever did. It's the smallest it's been since John Kennedy was President. We got rid of more regulations, ended more unnecessary programs, gave back more authority to states and local

governments to run their own affairs than our Republican predecessors did. But what we did not do is to give you a government so weak it could not build a strong economy, invest in education, protect the environment, and take care of the people who have earned the right to a little help from the rest of us.[21]

In the 1996 presidential election, Republicans nominated Bob Dole, the decorated WWII combat veteran, former member of Congress, and former senator (and majority leader) from Kansas, who was also Gerald Ford's running mate in 1976. The dynamics of the 1996 election were similar to those of 1992, when Ross Perot also ran as an independent. Perot's candidacy split support among Republicans, though not to the extent it did in 1992. Although Clinton won less than 50 percent of the popular vote again, he won the Electoral College vote overwhelmingly.

At his second inaugural address, Clinton said the great debate over the role of government was over. "Today we can declare: Government is not the problem, and government is not the solution." What we needed, he said, was a "new government for a new century," which would guarantee not success but opportunity for everyone. This required "responsible citizenship" from everyone. "If we're going to rebuild the American community, we have to have more rights and responsibility. And you can't have one without the other."[22]

A few days after his second inaugural, Clinton spoke to the Democratic National Committee and gave his analysis of the Republican political strategy. He accused Republicans of trying to "divide our people" from each other using race, religion, and taxes. In fact, what Republicans were doing was no different from what Democrats were doing, which was trying to build a political coalition from disparate, sometimes overlapping groups with distinct interests. Since 1981, Republicans used two arguments—

among others—with considerable success. One argument was supply-side economics: Tax cuts would stimulate growth and off-set lost revenues. The other was limited government: Government was too big, too bureaucratic, and too expensive. Until Bill Clinton came along, no Democrat at the national level was able to make a more compelling counterargument.

The New Covenant

A year before the 1992 presidential campaign, Clinton delivered a three-part lecture series at Georgetown University outlining his political philosophy. The three speeches are somewhat analogous to Reagan's endorsement speech of Goldwater, though Clinton had already served as governor for more than a decade by then. The first speech introduced the New Covenant in general; the second dealt with economic change and the third with foreign policy. According to Clinton, our principles and ideals were tri-umphant abroad, but twelve years of Republican rule left "a hole in our politics" at home. The eighties and early nineties were an age "of greed and selfishness, of irresponsibility and excess, and of neglect." Presidents Reagan and Bush permitted our national debt to spiral out of control despite their promises of fiscal re-sponsibility, and thus they betrayed their own principles for the sake of political power. Whereas Republicans brought the government "to the brink of bankruptcy," Clinton promised, amazingly, that Democrats would follow the lead of our best companies, eliminate unnecessary layers of bureaucracy, impose fiscal discipline, and make government more cost-effective.

Clinton proposed rewriting the social contract and revolution-izing the way the federal government did business. He saw the fall of the Berlin Wall not simply as a rejection of authoritarian communist rule but as a repudiation of all top-down bureaucracy. Our founding fathers wrote our first social contract, Lincoln gave it a second birth, and then Franklin Roosevelt promised a New Deal. Now, we needed a New Covenant to repair the bond between the people and their government, restore our basic values, and remind people that "the future can be better than the present and that each of us has a personal moral responsibility to make it so."[23] "Make no mistake," he said, "this New Covenant means change, change in my party, change in our leadership, change in our country, change in the lives of every American."

Here is a good one-paragraph summary:

> To turn America around, we've got to have a new approach, founded on our most sacred principles as a nation, with a vision for the future. We need a New Covenant, a solemn agreement between the people and their government to provide opportunity for everybody, inspire responsibility throughout our society and restore a sense of community to our great nation. A New Covenant to take government back from the powerful interests and the bureaucracy and give it back to the ordinary people of our country.[24]

In this global economy, where we are competing economically with our former Cold War adversaries, sustainable economic growth does not come from government spending. The new era demands an alternative approach to liberal (meaning tax-and-spend) and conservative (meaning supply-side) economics. Clinton promised "a new radical approach to economics" that was neither liberal nor conservative. "The old economic answers are obsolete. We've seen the limits of Keynesian economics. We've seen the worst of supply-side economics. We need a new approach." His new approach—dubbed invest-and-grow economics—was not all that radical. In terms of domestic policy, it meant getting spending under control, reducing the deficit, and investing more in education. In terms of foreign policy, it meant engagement in and leadership of the global economy.

Clinton based his engagement strategy on several assumptions: The collapse of communism would bring instability and new threats, economic power would be as important as military power, the power of ideas would rule the information age, and our foreign policy would be inseparable from our domestic policies and consistent with our moral principles. In general, Clinton agreed with incumbent George H.W. Bush on a number of foreign policy issues, such as redefining NATO's role in the post–Cold War era, supporting NAFTA, and pursuing Middle East peace talks. Clinton's praise for Bush's management of the first Gulf War was unequivocal: "I think he did a masterful job in pulling together the victorious multilateral coalition." It is a cliché to say Clinton was more comfortable with domestic policy than foreign policy, but that is through no fault of his own. The intersection of politics and economics is the epicenter of Clintonomics; thus, it should come as no surprise that Clinton would claim, "Our economic strength must become *a central defining element* of our national security policy."[25]

Clinton's New Covenant is reminiscent of the values and mission statements of many African American churches, which emphasize self-sufficiency and personal responsibility and encourage members to contribute to the community. His emphasis on opportunity and responsibility draws on Biblical themes of individual initiative and obligations to the public interest. If it seems vaguely Republican, that is because Clinton quoted John Winthrop (Governor of the Massachusetts Bay Colony in 1630), who told his shipmates we must "rejoice together, mourn together, labor and suffer together, always having before our eyes our community in the work, our community as members of one body." Winthrop was one of the Pilgrims who fled religious persecution in Europe and founded a new colony in North America, the same John Winthrop from whom Ronald Reagan appropriated the "shining city upon a hill" metaphor for both his 1988 annual message and his 1989 farewell address.

Clinton's New Covenant was indeed based on an old idea—the idea that with opportunity comes responsibility. Clinton wanted to create a leaner, not meaner government. He said it was "basically an old-fashioned social compact about citizenship—citizenship for the twenty-first century—that requires us to get rid of yesterday's government and replace it with a new government." In practice, this meant downsizing the federal government, cutting unnecessary and wasteful spending, and bringing down the deficit. It also meant education would be "our most important tool" in the new compact (or "basic bargain," as he sometimes called it). Of course, one of the effects of shrinking the federal government bureaucracy is giving more authority to state and local governments and to the private sector, something Reagan would have appreciated. Clinton once even referred to himself as "the man who downsized the government more than President Reagan did."[26]

Clinton worried the federal government was antiquated and responsive only to people who played power games in Washington. What Clinton wanted to do was eliminate as much of the federal bureaucracy as possible as a way to minimize the corrosive influence of organized special interests. Clinton also wanted to accomplish what Reagan accomplished, which was to create a new political and economic coalition that would last beyond his presidency. One of Clinton's methods was to push decision making as far down the hierarchy and as far away from Washington as possible. As he said to a national meeting of governors, what he wanted was to regulate less, empower more, and give more responsibility to state and local governments. "We need to help move programs down to the point where states and communities and private citizens in the private sector can do a better job. If they can do it, we ought to let them do it."

The New Covenant was a convenient political slogan, but it was also part of the debate about the role of government: how we should educate our children, administer our justice system, and reform the welfare system. Clinton placed himself right in the middle of the debate. On one extreme was the old, discredited Washington view that a big, bureaucratic government could solve all our problems. On the other extreme was the contract that said government was the source of all our problems, and if we starved it to death, all our problems would miraculously solve themselves. The proper role for the national government was not savior or "government knows best" and "one-size-fits-all." "Our problems go way beyond the reach of government," Clinton said. "They're rooted in the loss of values, in the disappearance of work and the breakdown of our families and our communities."[27] What Clinton proposed was a partnership in which the federal government would be a partner to people in their private lives as citizens and a partner with state and local governments. In his words:

> I believe in a government that promotes opportunity and demands responsibility, that deals with middle class economics and mainstream values; a government that is different radically from the one we have known here over the last thirty to forty years, but that still understands it has a role to play in order for us to build strong communities that are the bedrock of this nation. That's what the New Covenant I talk about all the time is really all about—more opportunity and more responsibility.[28]

He rejected the laughable idea that all our social problems, such as teen pregnancy or welfare dependency, were the result of *too much* government trying to help people. Black religious leaders were and still are fully cognizant of the problems of teen pregnancy and out-of-wedlock births and the need to help people break the cycle of dependency and escape the welfare system. Clinton said:

> What ought to be the greatest joy of life, giving birth to a child, has now become a great social drama for us. This is not a partisan political issue. It is not a racial issue; it is not an income issue; it is not a regional issue. This issue is eating the heart out of this country. You don't have to be in any particular political camp to know we're in big trouble as a society if we're headed toward a day when half of all the kids in this country are born outside marriage.[29]

These and other questions are fundamental to who we are as a people, what kind of government we want, and what kind of country our children should have. Clinton believed that to respond to these questions, we needed to "get rid of yesterday's government" in order to meet the problems of today and the challenges of tomorrow. In other words, we needed a New Covenant that offered more opportunity; demanded more responsibility; and created a more effective, less bureaucratic system of governance. "This New Covenant can only be ratified in the election of 1992," Clinton said, "and that's why I'm running for president."[30]

Just when you thought there was nothing left to learn about Clinton's presidential ambitions, there he goes again. Why is getting rid of yesterday's government so important? We'll continue this discussion in Chapter 7.

CHAPTER 7

The Role of Government (B)

*Is the government inherently bad and part of the problem
and totally irrelevant to this modern, high-tech entrepreneurial world; or is the government inherently neither
good or bad, simply the servant of the people that has a
role to play, but not the only role in the partnerships that
we have to create?*[1]

—BILL CLINTON, 1996

IN *THE BROTHERS KARAMAZOV* (1879–80), by Russian novelist
Fyodor Dostoyevsky, there is a poignant chapter called "The
Grand Inquisitor," the scope of which parallels our field of inquiry, at least when it comes to the most primitive impulses of
human nature. The chapter describes a fictional story in which
Christ returned to Earth at the time of the Spanish Inquisition—
not the second coming but a brief visit fifteen hundred years after
the crucifixion. People recognized Jesus, threw garlands to him,
and flocked to him. However, the grand inquisitor was worried
about the risk of civil unrest. He had him arrested, imprisoned,

and sentenced to death—to be burned at the stake. The grand inquisitor visited Jesus in his prison cell, mocked him, and tried to question him, but Jesus sat in amused silence. "Don't answer; be silent," said the inquisitor. "What could you say anyway? People would consider anything you said now to be evidence of a miracle. Anything you said now would only confuse people and shake their faith, and corrupt everything you said before."

The inquisitor accused Jesus of misjudging human nature and underestimating the level of security most people need—even though his teachings tried to show the path to freedom. Nothing confuses people more than having too much freedom, the inquisitor said, nothing frightens them more than having no authority figure to surrender their freedom to in exchange for security. Given the choice between freedom and security, he said, most people will choose security every time.

The old cardinal's tirade goes on like this for several more pages. When he is finished, he waits expectantly for the prisoner to answer, to say something, anything, no matter how bitter and terrible. Jesus says nothing; then he suddenly approaches the inquisitor and gently kisses him on the lips. First, the old man shudders; he hesitates, and then he opens the door of the cell and says, "Go, and come no more . . . Come not at all; never, never!" and releases the prisoner through a dark alley.[2]

The theological implications of "The Grand Inquisitor" are mind-blowing and beyond the scope of our study. What concerns us is Dostoyevsky's radical interpretation of human nature, specifically the security-freedom spectrum that marks the horizontal limits of political economy. It forces us to the root of the matter, back to John Locke's principle of limited government. It also forces us back to utilitarianism, Jeremy Bentham's principle of the greatest good for the greatest number. We know where Ronald Reagan stood on the matter: Pursuing the greatest good for the greatest number smacks of socialism, which Reagan considered contrary to human nature—and even a form of insanity.

Remember, Dostoyevsky was writing in the late nineteenth century, almost forty years before the Russian revolution began and more than a century before the Cold War ended. The dissolution of the welfare state and disintegration of the communist bloc in the late twentieth century swept away the old certainties. Although this precipitated an ideological crisis, it also stimulated new thinking about our high-tech, decentralized global economy and sparked an ideological renewal—first to make sense of the new system and then to make the most of it. In the early twenty-first century, there is no need to follow freedom and security to their logical extremes, no need to choose between total control and total anarchy.

Clinton's challenge was to articulate a coherent governing philosophy equal to the inexorable logic and complexity of globalization. He believed we needed to transcend the simplistic debate between liberalism, which seeks to expand government, and conservatism, which seeks to eradicate it. This means not only reforming and modernizing government but also giving people a greater sense of direction and purpose. Because there is no constitutional principle requiring separation of market and state, Clinton wanted to promote competition and encourage an entrepreneurial culture through investment in education and the public infrastructure. He also wanted to make use of market-based solutions. This does not mean limiting our thinking to privatization: the transfer of ownership and control of government operations to the private sector. It means using tools and techniques from the private sector to make government more efficient and more cost-effective.[3]

The Third Way

In April 1999, the Democratic Leadership Council (DLC) hosted a roundtable discussion on the third way, with Bill and Hillary

Clinton, Tony Blair, Gerhard Schroeder, and other European political leaders.[4] There is no single European version of the third
way but instead several national variations of social democracy—
all of which are works in progress. Because the third way is a
global phenomenon, it is hard to pin down a good working definition, but there is an *American* definition, thanks to the DLC and
its affiliated think tank, the Public Policy Institute.[5] Their definition rests on three cornerstone ideals: (1) equal opportunity for
all and special privileges for none; (2) mutual responsibility,
meaning rejection of the politics of entitlement and the politics
of social abandonment; and (3) encouraging citizens and communities to play active roles in public life. In general, proponents
believe the left-right debate is obsolete, ill suited to the challenges
of the information age and unresponsive to the powerful forces
shaping American society and the global economy. Proponents
reject conservative efforts to dismantle government and instead
envision an alternative form of government that emphasizes
technological innovation, competitive enterprise, and education
as a means to spread economic opportunity and ensure economic security. On questions of values, the third way encourages
tolerance and civility and respects traditional moral and family
values but resists attempts to impose values on others.

According to one key document, the third way was (and still
is) a new model of governance that uses the flexibility and inge-
nuity of the market to serve the public interest. This is one of the
most interesting aspects of the third way, because this is where it
intersects with reengineering. According to Adam Smith, prophet
of the invisible hand, people promote the public interest by pursuing their self-interest—without intending to and without even
knowing it. Not only that; by pursuing their own interest, according to Smith, people promote the public good *more effectively* than
when they actually intend to do so. According to the DLC, how-

ever, there is no invisible hand to create equal opportunity, confront special interests, or preserve the social balance.

Here's an interesting excerpt, a brief history of the DLC, which Clinton and others founded expressly for the purpose of winning presidential elections:

> The first thing we wanted to do was to broaden the base and change the rhetoric and the substance of a lot of the policies of the Democratic party. We thought we had been typecast too much as the big government, pro-tax, government can solve all the problems party. We needed to broaden our base and prove that we could spend tax money with discipline, grow the economy, be tough on crime and bring the American people together across regional and racial and party lines, and move the country forward. Instead of always having a left-right argument, in a time of transition, you need to be moving ahead.[6]

Twice Clinton mentions the need to broaden the democratic base, an absolute necessity if you're going to win national elections. He also mentions the Democrats' image makeover, from "tax and spend" to fiscal discipline, economic growth, and getting tough on crime—without big government. Finally, he reveals his philosophy of change management: In a time of transition, when others are busy having a left-right argument, find a way to push the dialogue forward, and challenge your adversaries to do the same. This seems like a textbook definition of triangulation (the strategy political advisor Dick Morris advocated), which means preventing your political opponents from coalescing by appropriating some of their ideas. In Clinton's autobiography, however, he dismissed the significance of triangulation unequivocally.

> Actually, it was just another way of articulating what I had advocated as governor, with the DLC, and in 1992

during the campaign. I had always tried to synthesize
new ideas and traditional values, and to change government policies as conditions changed. I wasn't splitting
the difference between liberals and conservatives; instead, I was trying to build a new consensus.[7]

Building a new consensus required broadening his political
and economic base. Clinton wanted businesses to tear down the
barriers of discrimination and target new markets, particularly
underserved populations at home or abroad. Despite the attraction of overseas markets, Clinton believed there was a huge un-
tapped market right here in America. In his words, these were
"people who live in our cities, people who live in our isolated
rural areas; people with productive capacities who, if they can
become consumers, can explode the American economic growth
rate well into the next century."[8]

The new base would be built on ideas such as equal opportunity, personal responsibility, and community. This is precisely
what Clinton meant when he said citizenship entailed responsibilities as well as rights, and the national government's primary
responsibility in the era was to empower people while neither
solving nor ignoring their problems. The third pillar of the
base—community—implied seeing ourselves not as isolated individuals but as members of many interdependent communities,
locally, nationally, and globally. Asking the government to put
up a wall is futile. In fact, expecting any government or any other
big bureaucracy to solve our problems is futile.

The American version of the third way followed a few simple
principles: a pro-growth economic policy with close ties to the
private sector; world leadership with limited intervention; a balanced budget and a smaller, less bureaucratic, more entrepreneurial federal government; and reduction of economic inequality
through education, investment in technology, healthcare reform,

and welfare reform. Although there is no unified statement of principles for the third way, the American and European versions share an overarching agenda to privatize the economy; support international trade and investment; limit government intervention in the labor market; reform the welfare system; and, of course, cut the deficit and balance the budget. In general, both versions agree that government should not block change and should not subsidize uncompetitive industries, companies, or workers. It should embrace economic change but support people disadvantaged by change through education, training, and lifelong learning. The third way is a "political hybrid," says Robert Reich, whose central faith is that free market policies will promote *shared* economic growth across society that is neither arbitrary nor inequitable.[9] This is no problem, as long as the theory remains a theory. Implementation is problematic, because third way economic policies have no natural political coalition that would support a new social contract.

A case in point: Clinton raised the issue of lifelong learning as it relates to economic competitiveness during a speech at a community college in Chicago, Dan Rostenkowski's old district. Continuing along the "big government is over" theme, Clinton said, "It is not up to me to know or to make judgments about all the things that are of concern to the people of Chicago, the people of this neighborhood." This was false modesty, because Clinton definitely believed it was his responsibility to know what concerned the people of Chicago. Clinton also knew it was up to him to flatter Dan Rostenkowski, who at the time was chairman of the House Ways and Means Committee. Without Rostenkowski's support, Clinton's legislative agenda—which included gun control; more police officers on the street; voter registration; family and medical leave; welfare reform; healthcare reform; and, of course, deficit reduction—would go nowhere.

Other than that, why should the people of the 5th Congressional District of Illinois care about globalization? Globalization is accompanied by some harsh economic realities—such as outsourcing—whose effects are sometimes felt close to home. One of the reasons why it is so tempting for General Motors, for example, to outsource jobs to developing countries is the high cost of healthcare in America. Just like Japanese automobile manufacturers, General Motors must compete in an increasingly cruel global economy. Even though Clinton's pollsters told him most Americans "didn't give a rip" what was happening in other countries, Clinton thought it was important for people in Chicago or Detroit to know *how much healthcare* goes into every automobile manufactured here or in Germany or Japan.

This was a relatively easy way for Clinton to explain his thinking and his policies and make the link between globalization and the third way.

> We have worked hard in our respective nations and in our multinational memberships to try to develop a response to globalization that we all call by the shorthand term, the Third Way. Sometimes I think that term tends to be viewed as more of a political term than one that has actual policy substance, but for us it's a very serious attempt to put a human face on the global economy and to direct the process of globalization in a way that benefits all people.[10]

The third way is policy-wonk shorthand, as Clinton said, a way to direct the process of globalization and make multilateral coordination among the advanced industrialized economies a little easier.

It is also shorthand for reciprocity, the golden rule of international relations, which recognizes our mutuality and our interdependence and connection to the world. Directing the process of globalization requires leadership, and leadership requires discipline. In practical terms, this means preventing the government from accumulating too much debt in order to free up capital for private sector investment. When the government borrows so much, we surrender leadership, lose control of our economic destiny, and risk concentrating a dangerous amount of economic power in unfriendly hands. In a world of twenty-four-hour markets, it is nearly impossible to overstate the importance of fiscal discipline, because the global financial markets inevitably punish countries with irresponsible economic policies, large deficits, low investment, and profligate spending. In theory, everybody wants a tax cut, but does anyone want one knowing it would saddle later generations with an unsustainable economic burden?

The Two Friedmans

"My basic belief is that the government ought to do more to help people help themselves," Clinton said, "to reward responsibility with more opportunity, and not to give anybody opportunity without demanding responsibility." According to Clinton, government is neither the primary problem nor the primary solution. Clinton believed government could be "an instrument of democratic destiny," and he presented his version of the third way as an alternative to the conventional political dichotomy, which could help the country break free from "that old false choice, between tax and spend and trickle down; between abandonment and entitlement."

For Clinton to accomplish his political goals, he had to reform the Democratic Party and redefine what it meant to be progressive, but also generate support across party lines. Clinton decried the "miserable condition" of his party and implored fellow Democrats to "imagine the future and then try to define it." Ideas and arguments coming from both parties were stale, stuck on liberal versus conservative and left versus right, what Clinton called *old think*. (It was okay with Clinton to have differences with friends and adversaries alike as long as it was not *yesterday's difference*.) He had to change his party's image from the "cardboard cutout" that Republicans pasted on the face of every Democratic candidate at election time. He had to change the perception that Democrats were weak—weak on crime, welfare, foreign policy, and the budget.

Accusations that Clinton was a liberal are silly, because he routinely looked across the political spectrum for solutions. Nothing would have made Clinton happier than if he were unable to tell who was Republican or Democrat, but Republicans and Democrats alike had become caricatures of themselves. Rather than identifying points of contention in society—the so-called wedge issues—and forcing people to choose one side or another, Clinton sought to develop new ways of thinking and acting, to go "beyond false choices . . . imposed on us by limited thinking and beyond old conflicts."

He did not require any good idea to be consistent with liberal or conservative orthodoxy. "The issue is not what is liberal or conservative, but what will move us forward together," he said. "These are ideas at the vital American center, ideas that have broken the gridlock that gripped Washington for too long. For years politicians treated our most vexing problems here, like crime and welfare and the budget deficit, as issues to be exploited, not problems to be solved."[11]

One of the best ways to discover Clinton's values is to read about the Republican presidents he admires. "On occasion," said Clinton, "the Republican Party has been the party of true and progressive change." For example, Clinton's ranking of Abraham Lincoln as the "greatest Republican President" says something about race relations in the United States. He also admired Teddy

Roosevelt for his environmental activism (he was responsible for the creation of numerous national parks) and because Roosevelt was "a man who understood the dangers of great concentrations of power," a reference to Roosevelt's progressivism. He admired Dwight Eisenhower for his effort to build a bipartisan foreign policy, win the Cold War, and "move us away from the military industrial complex." Clinton even gave credit to Richard Nixon for signing legislation to create the Environmental Protection Agency.

Executives in all kinds of organizations cannot simply pull strategy out of a textbook. Instead, they must absorb new information and new ideas and adapt their thinking to conform to the complexities of a dynamic, modern world. In the new era, we need to find new ways to promote security—personal, family, community, and national security—in order to cope with changes taking place at home and abroad. In 1993, Clinton presented his analysis of the profound structural forces at work in the world at a Democratic National Committee meeting.[12] Despite troubled spots around the country having too much unemployment and too little economic development, America's middle class grew with relative stability in the decades following WWII and the Great Depression. Clinton commented on the rise of violence among young people and the increasing number of children born to single parents, the latter a trend Daniel Moynihan identified among African American families almost thirty years earlier.[13] (Moynihan wrote about the breakdown of the African American family in the midsixties, so blaming Reaganomics for it is obviously ridiculous.)

Two other excerpts from a speech Clinton gave to a party caucus in 1998 offer a fascinating if selective version of American history. They explain his political battles with Republicans but also describe battles within his own party. The excerpts explain the natural tension between strategic planning, which is forward looking by definition, and historical principles transfixed in time:

> What is the purpose of a political party? I spent a lot of time last year reading about the nineteenth century and about places in the 1800s, periods of time that most Americans don't know much about anymore. I've spent a lot of time studying the history of our party. I believe the purpose of our government and, therefore, the purpose of any political party, at every important period in our history if you look back through it, has been three-fold: to widen the circle of opportunity, to deepen the meaning of freedom, and to unify the nation.
>
> Now, any honest Democrat will say that the Republicans did more of that than we did, from Abraham Lincoln through Theodore Roosevelt. And, frankly, I'm sure we had a lot of nice people in our party during a lot of that period, but they were asleep at the switch. But from Woodrow Wilson to Franklin Roosevelt to Harry Truman to John Kennedy to Lyndon Johnson to Jimmy Carter to the present day, through all of our leadership in Congress in the twentieth century forward, our party—we haven't always been right, we haven't always been up to date, but we have always been for widening the circle of opportunity, deepening the meaning of liberty and freedom, and uniting and strengthening the United States of America.[14]

Summing it up—with no endorsement implied by the author—American political parties exist to protect the Constitution, promote equal opportunity, and unify the country. The Democratic Party was "asleep at the switch" for almost fifty years, from 1861 to 1909. However, starting with Woodrow Wilson in the progressive era, through the Great Depression and WWII under Franklin Roosevelt, the early years of the Cold War under Truman, the New Frontier under Kennedy, and the Great Society under Johnson, the Democratic Party, Clinton reckons, did a better job meeting the challenges of the day.

In 1985, Reagan made similar remarks at a White House reception welcoming new members of the party. He had a little fun playing with the "new converts," as he called them, recalling his own reasons for becoming a Republican in the early sixties, saying that he did not leave the Democratic Party, the party left him. He accused Democrats of having special interests, entrenched interests, and power brokers, and he outrageously claimed, "We don't have any of that." Reagan offered his own fascinating if selective version of American history. "You've joined a party that was once rather sedate," he said, or at least it was until the current party leaders began lobbing intellectual hand grenades, stopped talking about economic justice and started creating the conditions that made it possible, and stopped talking about challenging the communists and started doing something about it. "You've joined a robust and rambunctious party," he said. The Republican Party is not perfect, "but more often than not, we've been on the right side and fought the good fight, and it's wonderful to see our new recruits."[15]

The similarity of these two highly selective histories reminds me of something Abraham Lincoln wrote during the Civil War: "The will of God prevails. In great contests each party claims to act in accordance with the will of God. Both may be, and one must be, wrong. God can not be for, and against the same thing at the same time."[16] Lincoln wrote this meditation on divine will in early September 1862, shortly after the Second Battle of Bull Run—another victory for confederate general Robert E. Lee and the Army of Northern Virginia and another defeat for the Union.

Lincoln would not issue the Emancipation Proclamation until January 1863, and he could not do so without a Union victory. The moral: Both Reagan's and Clinton's selective versions of history *may* be wrong, but one of them *must* be wrong.

In Clinton's 1995 annual message, he recalled the origin of Roosevelt's New Deal, which responded to the country's economic crisis and redefined the relationship between the government and the people for the next fifty years. However, different problems require different solutions. What was a good strategy yesterday may not be such a good strategy today. Clinton wondered what Franklin Roosevelt would have contributed to the ongoing debate about the role of government. In Clinton's words:

> FDR would have loved this debate. He wouldn't be here defending everything he did fifty years ago. He wouldn't be here denying the existence of the Information Age. Should we reexamine the role of government? Of course, we should. Do we need big, centralized bureaucracies in the Computer Age? Often we don't. Should we reassert the importance of the values of self-reliance and independence? You bet we should. He never meant for anybody—anybody—to become totally dependent on the government when they could do things for themselves.[17]

FDR's old top-down bureaucracy became almost constitutional, so pervasive some people were unable to imagine any other way of government. In a global economy, however, "We know that we no longer need the same sort of bureaucratic, top-down, service-delivering, rule-making, centralized government in Washington that served us so well during the industrial age, because times have changed."[18] Big, centralized bureaucracies are not as necessary as they used to be, including the federal government's big, centralized bureaucracies.

Speaking of which, Lyndon Johnson declared war on poverty in his 1964 annual message. Poverty was a national problem requiring a national solution, and he proposed programs to offer better healthcare; improve job training; and upgrade schools, libraries, hospitals, and public transit. "Our aim is not only to relieve the symptom of poverty," Johnson said, "but to cure it and, above all, to prevent it." The war on poverty actually preceded Johnson's announcement of the Great Society, which did not occur until a few months later at the University of Michigan (the same place John Kennedy announced his intention to establish the Peace Corps during the 1960 presidential campaign). Johnson intended the Great Society to advance American civilization toward his grandiose vision of our national destiny—the ultimate triumph of the welfare state. The ambitious but specific goals of the war on poverty—to end poverty and racial injustice—are modest by comparison. One thing people seem to have forgotten, however, is that when Johnson announced the war on poverty, he also asked for a tax cut to reduce the withholding rate from 15 percent to 14 percent. "We need a tax cut now to keep this country moving," he said.[19]

Like Ronald Reagan, Milton Friedman strongly objected to Johnson's Great Society programs. Friedman was a Keynesian early in his career and considered Keynes "one of the great economists of the twentieth century."[20] Like Reagan, Friedman also supported the New Deal, but he argued the facts we have today were not available to Keynes or other economists in the middle of the Great Depression. "We now have several decades of experience with governmental intervention," he said. "It is no longer necessary to compare the market as it actually operates and government intervention as it might ideally operate. We can compare the actual with the actual."[21] According to Friedman, the difference between government intervention *in theory* and government intervention *in practice* proves the New Deal and Great Society failed to achieve their objectives. Perhaps this is what Clinton meant when he said the Democrats have not always been right or always up to date.

Clinton was not at his best complaining about the situation that he found when he took office or blaming Republicans for refusing to "close loopholes for three-martini lunches." At a California fund-raiser, Clinton said the Republicans talked tough but acted weak. "They would talk like our parent and then act like our child—telling us exactly what we wanted to hear as if it were tough medicine, and then writing us a check and never worrying about who was going to pay the bill."[22] He sounded bitter when he accused previous administrations of being irresponsible and unwilling to make difficult decisions, of running the middle class into the ground, creating a new class of poverty, and robbing our country of opportunity. Clinton sounded less angry when he talked about what he wanted to do. Some of Clinton's best moments, for example, came at fund-raising events. Even when he was expressing gratitude to donors, there was a hint of impatience—or perhaps annoyance—over the two-term limit he realized would restrict what he could accomplish. Here is Clinton at his best, fitting his political philosophy into fewer than 150 words. First, he dissects the strengths and weaknesses of his political opponents and his political allies. Then, he explains his unique position at the "vital center" of the newly redrawn political map.

> And essentially what I thought was that the Republicans understood the importance of the market, but were blind to the need to give everybody the tools and conditions to take advantage of the market; but the Democrats understood the importance of compassion and of trying to take care of everybody and the social contract, but too often were unwilling to make the tough decisions to get

the economy going, which is still the best social program for everybody who has got a good job; and that somehow we had to reconcile that and develop a dynamic approach to politics so that we could have this debate between the two parties, and one would be more liberal and the other would be more conservative, and the debate would go on, but at least it would be about the real choices facing the country and the real lives of people.[23]

The social contract is still important—we cannot neglect it. The best social program is still a strong economy, a good job, and a good education. However, we need a new approach to politics, not the same old debate that gets us nowhere. Globalization is bringing us closer together. The global economy was "growing by ideas" and the Internet was the fastest-growing social organism in history precisely because it was rooted in new ideas. However, Clinton issued this caution: "In an economy that is increasingly based on ideas and information and organization, the human element can get left behind. One of the things our party has always done is to remind people of the human element."[24] In Clinton's words:

> In a world transformed by trade and technology it is no longer possible for a young person to go to work and keep a job until retirement, or even often to stay with the same company. The economy is creating and losing millions of jobs constantly. Most people now who are laid off from their jobs never get the same old job back. Young people beginning their careers, on average, will change work seven times in a lifetime. The best jobs those young people here in the audience may ever have may be jobs yet to be created in companies yet to be founded based on technologies yet to be discovered.[25]

As Clinton himself acknowledged, Republicans understand and talk about the market better than the Democrats do, despite the third way emphasis on market-based solutions. The phrase "market-based solutions" would seem to give the Republicans an ideological home field advantage. However, if we make a side-by-side comparison of party platforms, there is a subtle difference. Under the general heading "Protecting Our Environment," the 2000 Democratic platform asserted that serving as "stewards of God's creation" is our most solemn responsibility. This requires protecting our air, water, and food supplies; cleaning up toxic waste dumps; and negotiating an international treaty to combat global warming "in a way that is market-based and realistic, and does not lead to economic cooling."[26] In this excerpt, the juxtaposition of global warming and economic cooling is catchy, but meaningless. The definition of market-based is vaguely synonymous with realism.

Perhaps by coincidence, the Republicans also advocated market mechanisms to promote environmental protection. Under the general heading "Stewardship of Our Natural Resources," the 2000 Republican platform said, "We support the federal, local, state, and tribal responsibilities for environmental protection. We believe the government's main role should be to provide market-based incentives to innovate and develop the new technologies for Americans to meet—and exceed—environmental standards."[27] The last sentence is clear and emphatic: The government's role is to provide market-based *incentives* to develop the new technologies. This anecdote does not prove anything, but it does suggest why Clinton would imply Republicans have a better understanding of the market.

If political economy is one indivisible thing, not two separate entities with interchangeable parts, then economic reform cannot take place without government reform (or reengineering or reinventing or whatever). Midway through his first term, none other than George W. Bush provided a useful, working definition of this. He sent a memo to his department heads calling for an "active but limited" government that empowers states, cities, and citizens and promotes accountability, innovation, and competition. It said that a reformed government follows three guiding principles: It is citizen centered rather than bureaucracy centered; results oriented rather than process oriented; and market based, meaning the government actively promotes innovation and competition. Bush sent another memo to his department heads restating those same three principles and giving five new government-wide reform goals: strategic management of human capital, budget and performance integration, competitive sourcing, expanded use of the Internet and computer resources to provide services, and improved financial management.[28] This approach comes straight from best practices taught in business schools, which gives new meaning to "market based." This is not the market guided by the invisible hand but by professionally trained executives. This is not the market of Milton Friedman, but Thomas Friedman.

In *The World Is Flat*, Thomas Friedman analyzes the profound structural forces at work in the world since the end of the Cold War. In some ways, *The World Is Flat* is the sequel to Francis Fukuyama's *The End of History*. Both authors chose larger-than-life metaphors, which unfortunately are easily misunderstood. Like Fukuyama, Friedman did not literally mean that the world is flat but that it is changing politically, economically, and culturally in ways we have not seen before. Most of the book describes the flatteners: the advances in technology, software, logistics, and supply chain management that are changing the way people live and work and the way organizations do business.

In one passage, Friedman says meeting the challenges of the new era will require a new kind of executive and new role for government adapted to the times. In order to take full advantage of the opportunities the new flat world will present, we need a president who understands that educational requirements in a flat world—math, science, and engineering—are different from those in an old industrial economy. Friedman says we need a new kind of Great Society and a new kind of government committed to investing in education, new technologies, and the institutions and infrastructure that will make Americans more employable and more secure in an economy that no longer guarantees lifetime employment. Friedman calls this *compassionate flatism.*[29]

Other than the turmoil in the financial markets, nothing symbolizes the profound structural changes at work in the world better than the manufacturing sector. Eight years after Clinton left office, we are losing manufacturing jobs, but the economy is still relatively strong because productivity—net output per employee—continues to improve. Although the economy needs fewer people to produce more goods and services, we need more markets and more customers. In addition to this domestic anomaly, there are numerous political and economic changes taking place internationally. While China is emerging as an economic giant, other industrialized economies are having trouble with high unemployment rates. On top of that, democracy in Russia and several of the former republics is unstable. In Africa, there is widespread poverty, disease, and tribal conflict. In the Balkans and elsewhere, religious and ethnic hatred continue to fester. Obviously, there are numerous political and economic challenges in the new era, just as Clinton predicted.

It is natural—or at least predictable—that people should reexamine the premises of their political and economic systems while the new millennium is still young. Defining the role of government is more than an abstract argument. It is all about defining the country's new mission and the national government's new role in that mission. First and foremost, the national government's job is security at home and abroad. We should use our preeminent economic position—while we can—to serve as a force for peace, freedom, and democracy, but the information age requires a more flexible and more efficient government, as well as a smaller and less bureaucratic one. In short, said Clinton, *"The role of the government should be to change the government."*[30] What a difference from 1981, when Reagan said government is the problem.

New Federalism

In 1987, Reagan spoke at a meeting of the National Governors' Association at the White House. His three top agenda items were welfare reform, education, and competitiveness. At the end of his brief speech Reagan said, "Well, now I've broken my promise of last night at dinner. I've talked too long. Our friends from the press will be leaving now. And when they've cleared the room, I'll just turn to your Chairman, Bill Clinton, so that I can hear some of your ideas."[31] Yes, Bill Clinton, the forty-year-old governor from Arkansas. A few short years later, President Clinton would himself host the annual meeting of the National Governors' Association. The topic of his remarks was, of course, the role of government in the new economy. When it was his turn, he encouraged his colleagues to make government more user-friendly without undermining the public interest; help the private sector open new markets; and not shut ourselves out of any part of the world, particularly China. "Thank you very much," he said. "We'll let the press leave, and we'll go on with the program."[32]

The February 1987 meeting at the White House was the result of an invitation Reagan issued earlier that month. Although welfare reform was one of Reagan's top priorities, his goal was to create a process that allowed states to implement their own reforms based on their own unique circumstances. "Many governors have already broken new ground with creative and unique approaches. I applaud those efforts, and want to begin a process to encourage many more of these state- and community-based reform efforts." With a few exceptions such as national defense and interstate commerce, Reagan wanted to shift as many government services as possible to state and local governments, which epitomized Reagan's approach to federalism.

Early in his presidency, Reagan established a bipartisan advisory committee on federalism to restore the "proper constitutional relationship" among federal, state, and local governments. He established a network of Federal Regional Councils to identify significant problems and reduce the number of federal regulations, and he signed several executive orders on federalism. In 1987, Reagan's executive order on federalism redefined the fundamental principles of conservatism in an attempt to limit the size and scope of the national government. Reagan's order referred to the Bill of Rights, specifically the Tenth Amendment, which reserves all powers to the states neither delegated to nor prohibited by the federal government. Of course, his approach encouraged strict adherence to constitutional principles established by the framers, but there was nothing inherently partisan about it.

It is almost impossible to overstate the value Reagan placed on federalism. In remarks to the Annual Convention of the National Association of Countries in the second year of his first term, he said:

> Our federalism initiatives are not incidental proposals. They lie at the very heart of our philosophy of government—a philosophy I've long held and, I believe, most of you have as well. We are committed to restoring the intended balance between the levels of government, and, although some people may find this cause not as glamorous or as immediate as some others, we're determined to see it through.

Toward the end of his second term, he was more emphatic: "Federalism is more than just a policy; it's a philosophy of government."

We know Reagan's governing philosophy sprang from two sources: his respect for the Constitution and his memories of the Great Depression. We also know Reagan based his opposition to abortion on Constitutional rather than biblical grounds, and he believed the unborn child had a constitutional right to life according to the Fifth and Fourteenth Amendments of the Constitution. We also know the Great Depression left a lasting impression on Reagan, as it did on so many of his generation. Reagan began his political life as a New Deal Democrat and later considered himself a "reformed New Dealer," but he believed Franklin Roosevelt "would today be amazed and appalled at the growth of the Federal Government's power." Reagan thought Johnson's Great Society was a complete failure because it fostered dependence on government subsidies, created huge bureaucracies, and distorted the proper balance among federal, state, and local governments.

The renaissance of federalism under Reagan was the most significant development in American politics since the New Deal, and Reagan was justifiably proud of it.

> I believe that we have started government on a different course, different than anything we've done in the last half century since Roosevelt began with the New Deal. And that is the recognition that there must be a limit to government size and power and that there has been a distortion of the relationship between the various echelons of government—Federal, State, and local. And I think that we have the most to do with yet, because the higher levels of government are reluctant to give up authority once they have it.[33]

Clinton also signed an executive order on federalism in 1998 and then signed a revised version in 1999—using some of the same language as Reagan—to guarantee the division of governmental responsibilities embodied in the Constitution, as intended by the framers. Clinton's orders required strict adherence to constitutional principles and promoted diversity rather than uniformity of public policies among the states, and competition between them.[34] Clinton's goal to reinvent government is the logical corollary of Reagan's goal to renew federalism. Indeed, no American president could consider reinventing government without taking the framers' intent—not to mention Reagan's intent—into consideration.

If the ultimate goal of federalism is to limit the size and scope of the federal government, cut costs, protect diversity, and restore the balance between governments at all levels, how do you measure success? Near the end of his presidency—brace yourself— Reagan said, "Perhaps the greatest test of federalism is how we meet the urgent need for welfare reform—how successful we are in fashioning local and community solutions to problems that would destroy families, or worse, keep families from forming in the first place."[35] In August 1996, seated in the White House rose garden, Clinton signed House Resolution 3734, also known as the Personal Responsibility and Work Opportunity Reconciliation Act of 1996, and thus passed the greatest test of federalism according to the standard set by Ronald Reagan himself.

Clinton did not consider federalism to be a rigid system but an evolving, flexible system. Naturally, he wanted to redefine it for the twenty-first century, which meant addressing a relatively new phrase in the lexicon—"unfunded mandate"—which is a law imposed by the federal government on state or local governments (or private parties) to carry out specific actions without providing any funding for it. Another new development had to do with the post–Cold War era. In America, federalism is the principle guiding and governing relations among authorities at various levels. Elsewhere in the world, federalism is a system of shared governance among people of various racial, ethnic, or religious groups. In the European Union, federalism takes a very different form because the members are sovereign states much more powerful than the federal government.

Clinton said, "We need a government for the twenty-first century that is less bureaucratic and more entrepreneurial and more oriented toward partnerships where more is done at the grassrootslevel."[36] According to Clinton's version of federalism, everything the federal government did should empower people at the grassroots level. Clinton did not use "empowerment" the same way the human potential movement does. For Clinton, empowerment meant encouraging people and communities to play an active role in public life:

> Empowerment means more than giving people a choice. The great French writer Victor Hugo once observed that the rich and poor are equally free to spend the night under the bridge. Empowerment means not only having the choice, but having the capacity to exercise the choice. That's why we're for education and safe streets and a clean environment and a strong economic policy and a strong foreign policy.[37]

Empowerment means giving individuals and their families the power to make the most of their own lives. True empowerment is impossible when the government is too deeply in debt. Debt relief and deficit reduction, the twin pillars of empowerment, were prerequisites for almost everything Clinton hoped to accomplish in terms of healthcare and welfare reform and repositioning the economy to be more competitive in the global arena.

In a democracy such as ours, the government must follow the

direction of the people, and this is possible only if the government stays connected to all the people: their lives, their families, their values. However, Clinton said, "National leadership can point the way. It can move barriers out of the way that have prevented our states, our cities, and our people from solving their own problems." On paper at least, Clinton's highly decentralized approach recognized the government's role is neither to save the economy nor to sit on the sidelines. Instead, the government's role should be to do everything within its capacity to create the right conditions. At the national level, the right conditions mean responsible fiscal policy. At the grassroots level, the right conditions mean education reform, welfare reform, and healthcare reform.

As we know, there are powerful forces at work in the global economy, and the United States' economic infrastructure was inadequate for the sweeping changes taking place. One of Clinton's goals was to recognize the government had a role to play in the economy, and this role was to serve as partner to the private sector. He wanted to create a new role for the government to fit the unique challenges of our time. In June 1997, budget negotiations were taking place between the House and Senate to reconcile their different versions and reach a consensus. Clinton refused to sign the new budget unless it passed his test: It had to stimulate economic growth; be fair to working families; target his top priority of education; and not explode the long-term deficit—what he sometimes called the *generational deficit*.[38] This not only demonstrated Clinton's commitment to fiscal discipline, it also explains the extent to which the social contract depends on the social balance. Why is this important? First, not all government spending is equal. Second, the logic of globalization means greater depth (more systems within systems) and thus more interdependence between economic subsystems:

The realities of the modern world are that the economy is so globalized and change is so institutionalized that no government of any nation can promise to protect people from the changes of the world economy. You can't make the world go away, to use the phrase from the old song. You cannot do that. So if change is inevitable, and if we will never have a single economy anymore—we'll have a local economy in Cleveland and a state economy in Ohio and a regional economy in the Middle West and a national economy in America and a global economy in the whole world—if that is the reality, then what do we have to do?[39]

In January 1999, with two years remaining in his presidency, Clinton said this regarding the role of government: "We believe the role of government is to empower people, to ride the tides of change to greater heights. *We believe in a government for the Information Age* that is progressive, creative, flexible and, yes, smaller." He considered it a fundamental truth that the private sector, not the government, was the engine of economic growth and job creation. In this respect, the federal government had a positive role to play, serving as an honest broker, an agent bringing management and labor to the table together.

Is it wise, as some Republicans propose, to condemn all government and then try to starve it to death through tax cuts? According to Clinton, some of his political adversaries believed the federal government was "absolutely worthless except for national security," and we could easily balance the budget because it didn't matter what else we cut. Promising to cut taxes is the cheapest way to score a political victory. Nothing is more popular than cutting taxes, but cutting taxes while simultaneously increasing the budget makes bad fiscal policy. We must not go back to the failed economic policies of the past, he said, not pass an arbitrary

tax cut that will raise interest rates, increase inflation, and cause
us to lose control of our economic destiny.

Clinton said the belief that low taxes and high spending levels
would stimulate enough economic growth to balance the budget
was overly optimistic and "almost theological." Clinton ridiculed
Reaganomics as "trickle-down" economics and made no distinction between the theory of Reaganomics and the actual policy.
Clinton blamed trickle-down economics for thirty years of accumulated social problems, from crime to gangs to illegal drugs,
claiming trickle-down theory was "tested and abolished." As we
know, the theoretical basis of Reaganomics is that markets are
more efficient than governments for optimum allocation of resources. In theory, cuts in domestic spending combined with sub-
stantial increases in military spending—along with tax cuts—will
stimulate economic growth and create new sources of revenue,
thus offsetting lost revenues. In practice, lost revenues create
huge deficits. Although Reagan's policies appeared to solve stag-
flation—the economic anomaly of high unemployment and inflation—it came with unintended political consequences. Since
Ronald Reagan's 1980 presidential campaign (really, since Barry
Goldwater's 1964 campaign), the modern conservative movement advocated lower taxes and smaller government. However,
what began as an honest and principled effort to limit government became an organized assault on government "by people
who tried to convince us that we should hold our government in
contempt."[40]

Clinton did not believe the government could or should solve
all our problems, nor did he believe the government should neglect our problems. What he advocated was more grassroots activism and a smaller, more effective national government that
worked for the betterment of ordinary people, promoting human
values, strong families, and skilled workers. The best evidence of
this is Clinton's emphasis on fiscal responsibility. Neither he nor

any other public official can repeal the laws of arithmetic. After years of exploding deficits, however, he made it his mission to get the budget under control, cut the federal bureaucracy, reform the American economy, and reposition it to compete in the global economy. This is the role of governments at all levels, and this is the way to help people absorb changes brought on by technology and global economic competition.

Clinton was at his best neither when he complained about the situation he found when he took office nor when he wagged his finger at his predecessors. He was better when he explained what he wanted to do. He was better still when he scolded members of his own party for placing too much faith in the politics of entitlement, what he called "the idea that big bureaucracies and government spending, demanding nothing in return, can produce the results we want." He sounded positively Republican when he said we should "promote work and responsibility over welfare and dependency" and claimed "no one is more eager to end welfare."

LIKE REAGAN BEFORE him, Clinton had a knack for explaining complex political and economic issues. Like Reagan's new federalism, Clinton's third way brought a new (if short-lived) consensus and injected much needed energy, action, and progress into the vital center. This new governing philosophy held that government should play an active role, not to dictate the flow of investment or restrain competition, but to ensure a level playing field. This entailed reducing the size and redefining the role of government, eliminating government regulations and some government programs, and privatizing those government operations that rightly belong in the private sector.

In February 1993, after a mere twenty-six days in office, Clinton delivered a speech to the nation on economic reform.[41] With the Cold War receding in the rearview mirror and the new century fast approaching, the country faced serious economic problems that would require different policies and thus a different philosophy. Back in 1981, Ronald Reagan said, "We cannot be tied to the old ways of solving our economic and racial problems. But it is time we looked to new answers and new ways of thinking that will accomplish the very ends the New Deal and the Great Society anticipated."[42] Indeed, it is time to turn the page, explore new ways of thinking, and shine a light on the theory of constraints, which we will do in Chapter 8.

CHAPTER 8

Theory of Constraints

One definition of an economist is someone who sees something happen in practice and wonders if it would work in theory.[1]

—RONALD REAGAN, 1987

IN CLINTONOMICS, EVERY POLITICAL problem is also an economic problem, and every economic problem requires thinking and acting in terms of political economy. Because Clinton had a definite governing philosophy, he did not want to eviscerate the government and risk rendering the solutions he proposed impossible. The problems that obsessed Clinton were fundamentally political and economic, involving the distribution of power and resources. Clinton *did not* see the country's problems as cultural, personal, or behavioral—although this is what his political rivals would want you to believe. His adversaries, then and now, believe that there is a culture war going on and that most of our national problems are the result of bad behavior. Based on this misconception, there is little good and much harm the government can do by interfering. This is how Clinton framed that side of the debate:

> There are those who see family problems and children's problems as primarily matters of personal and social morality. And they believe that all the government has to do is to encourage good behavior like praying in school or sexual abstinence, or to punish bad behavior like criminal conduct or the unwillingness to move from welfare to work even when a job's available.[2]

It is not as though Clinton wanted to duck a debate about values. He just wanted the debate to be about politics and economics rather than culture and personal misconduct, because he believed most of our problems were the result of the relentless economic difficulties American families faced. Many families with two incomes have a hard time affording day care. They want to take care of their elderly parents but worry about the cost of sending them to a nursing home. They want to send their kids to college some day but cannot save enough for one child, let alone two or three. This is where Clinton's ideas on entitlements, healthcare, welfare, diversity, education, immigration, trade, national security, and the budget merge into a unified governing philosophy.

A constraint is any kind of limitation to consider in planning, budgeting, scheduling, managing, or evaluating. The theory of constraints is not a theory in the abstract sense but a management tool to improve the performance of organizations—businesses in particular, but other kinds of systems, too. Every system has at least one constraint, one factor that limits the system's capacity to realize its goal, whatever that goal is. Some of these limiting factors (or bottlenecks) are internal, while others are external to the system. Increasing the system's capacity requires identifying the system's goal, then identifying the factors constraining the system, and then managing the constraints. The idea is to manage the constraints at the top of the list. Successfully removing one lower down the list will not necessarily improve performance. Removing the constraint at the top of the list will improve performance but also move a new one to the top.[3]

Following this methodology, first, we should identify the system's goal. In order to give Clintonomics a rigorous test, let us say our goal is *to form a more perfect union* according to the principles of conservatism we described in Chapter 3. Now then, what are the internal and external factors that constrain the system's performance? According to Ronald Reagan, government is the problem, meaning taxes are too high, spending is out of control, and the government is too bureaucratic. At the time of Reagan's presidency, the greatest external threat was communism, which affected almost every aspect of his governing philosophy. He considered it the ultimate abuse of power, the ultimate violation of individual autonomy, and the ultimate form of unlimited government. What did Reagan do to manage the constraints? He cut taxes and increased defense spending and in doing so created what Irving Kristol called the conservative deficit.

Here is an excerpt from a speech early in Reagan's first term to a conservative political action committee. Reagan restates his belief that political freedom is inseparable from economic freedom, then elaborates on a few specific items in the conservative agenda, no doubt tailoring his remarks for the audience:

> Because ours is a consistent philosophy of government, we can be very clear: We do not have a social agenda, ... separate economic agenda, and a separate foreign agenda. We have one agenda. Just as surely as we seek to put our financial house in order and rebuild our nation's defenses, so too we seek to protect the unborn, to end

the manipulation of schoolchildren by utopian planners, and permit the acknowledgement of a Supreme Being in our classrooms just as we allow such acknowledgements in other public institutions. Now, obviously we're not going to be able to accomplish all this at once. The American people are patient. I think they realize that the wrongs done over several decades cannot be corrected instantly.[4]

Although putting our finances in order and rebuilding our defenses are clear statements of economic and foreign policy, the way Reagan itemizes his social agenda is more ambiguous. He wants to "protect the unborn" rather than outlaw abortion. He wants to acknowledge "a Supreme Being in our classrooms" rather than legalize prayer in public schools. Finally, he wants "to end the manipulation of schoolchildren by utopian planners." Anyone in attendance at the conservative political action conference where Reagan gave this speech—and anyone reading it now—would agree we should end manipulation of schoolchildren. The phrase "utopian planners" can only mean socialists and communists and perhaps liberals given to impractical theories of social reform. Altogether, this excerpt leaves no doubt that Reagan considered his social policy inseparable from his economic and foreign policies.

Here is another excerpt, this one a preview of Reagan's upcoming State of the Union message in January 1986. Several themes are familiar, particularly the government as a roadblock and the weight of taxes. He also looks forward to new industries; a smarter economy; and a very competitive, technologically advanced global economy:

We know the challenges we must meet. We must make sure that government no longer stands as a roadblock to a stronger and smarter economy—an economy that becomes more sophisticated technologically in both our new and traditional industries, so we can compete successfully with our trading partners. We need to make sure that the weight of taxes and education, health and retirement costs, doesn't crush those who will lead America into the twenty-first century with their risk-taking and hard work. And we need to do all that's required of us to keep America secure.[5]

As you read this excerpt, notice none of the issues have gone away, not taxes, education, healthcare, retirement costs, and certainly not the hope for a technologically advanced, "smarter" economy. In the early years of the twenty-first century, there are as many constraining factors as ever, including international trade, ethnic and religious diversity, terrorism, climate change, immigration, and others. In addition, the process of globalization has blurred the line between foreign and domestic policy, which makes it difficult to categorize constraints as either internal or external. Although the line has been getting blurry since the Great Depression, the phenomenon has become more apparent in the post–Cold War era. Why should we get rid of *yesterday's* government? Globalization renders distinctions between domestic and foreign policy meaningless and requires every aspect of our national policy to recognize our economic, technological, and ecological interdependence.

Budgeting

Anyone who doubts Reagan's political influence on Clinton should read what Reagan and Clinton both said about John Maynard Keynes and the structural deficit. Here is an excerpt from one of Reagan's radio addresses:

> Following the theories of a noted English economist of the period, John Maynard Keynes, economists and politicians used to say that when bad times occur the only way to restore prosperity is to spend our way out of it with massive new government programs paid for by borrowing. "We owe it to ourselves!" they used to chant. . . . And that's why the automatic recourse to government spending sent interest rates and inflation skyrocketing, slowed the economy, caused unemployment, and gave us what they call today a structural deficit.[6]

That seems clear enough. Now, compare it to what Clinton said late in his presidency regarding Reagan's economic policies:

> So the idea of stimulating the economy in the early years—of the Reagan years—even though it was masked in anti-Government rhetoric, was basically traditional Keynesian economics. But the problem is, when we had a recovery, because it was sold as a . . . "tax cuts are good; Government's bad" package, we wound up with a structural deficit that couldn't be overcome without a series of highly difficult and controversial decisions that were embodied in the Budget Act of '93, which required both tax increases and spending restraint. . . . It seems to me that was the problem with the eighties philosophy, that we wound up with a structural deficit that was totally unsustainable.[7]

When Reagan became president in 1981, the Democrats had controlled one or both houses of Congress almost every year for more than fifty years. It is true during that time deficit spending was out of control. Since 1981, however, control of both the House and Senate has changed regularly. Although deficit spending is still out of control, it is less convenient to blame Democrats or defunct economists. As a reminder, during those decades of one-party domination and Keynesian deficit spending, the country faced the Great Depression (1929–1939), World War II (1939–1945), and the Cold War (1947–1989). If future generations benefit from these victories, they should pay their fair share.

Why does Reagan's strategy no longer work? What is the difference? The calendar is the difference. "When I ran for president in 1992, our government was discredited," said Clinton. "In fact, you could hardly run for president unless you had something bad to say about the government. Indeed, part of the political genius of the ascendancy of President Reagan and his associates was to attain power by discrediting the very idea of government." Clinton's acknowledgment of Reagan's political genius is not an act of generosity; it is one master recognizing another. That does not mean what worked for Reagan will work for anyone else today. Even if you agree with Clinton's assessment of Reagan, and even if you supported Reagan's policies back in the day, this does not mean you still should, because the facts we have today were not available back then.

Clinton devoted special attention to the defense budget and argued the need to restructure our post–Cold War military forces and reduce our defense budget in a way that would not threaten our security. However, the two primary goals of his economic policy were to increase investment—by shifting federal spending priorities—and reduce the deficit. This is why the assumption buried in Clinton's argument, that we could "no longer count on the Cold War," deserves consideration.[8] On previous occasions, Clinton ridiculed Reaganomics, supply-side economics, and the trickle-down theory. Regardless of the tone, it remained a disagreement over economic policy. However, if we were in fact counting on the Cold War, then Reagan deserves about as much credit for revitalizing the economy in the 1980s as Roosevelt deserves for revitalizing the economy in the 1940s. Although Roosevelt's New Deal programs provided much needed relief, the United States' entry into World War II finally ended the Depression.

As we know, Reagan made little or no distinction between good and bad deficit spending. All deficit spending was bad because it was inflationary, and he probably would not have considered creating the so-called conservative deficit an act of bold leadership. Why are deficits bad? It is a simple but important question. The way Clinton explained it, the larger the deficit, the more of our taxes goes toward interest on the debt and the less there is to invest in education and training, new technologies, and public infrastructure.

Clinton was usually careful to make a distinction between the deficit (the annual budget shortfall) and the debt (the accumulated balance), but this time he made no distinction. In addition, his down-home metaphor vividly explains the theory of constraints. In his words:

> So that is why we have done what we have done. And I'll say again, as somebody who was a governor in a state with a very tough budgeting system, it was very painful for me to ask anybody to pay any money just to pay down the deficit. But unless we do something about this, we will never—it's like *a bone in our throat* as a nation— unless we deal with this, we can't get on to dealing with our other problems. We'll spend all our time in Washington working around the edges of these other problems because we have not faced the problem of the deficit.[9]

Clinton often remarked on the difference between Arkansas politics and national politics. In Washington, there was "too little partnership and too much partisanship," too little concern about the future and too much preoccupation with the past, too little action and too much talk altogether. Though it was meaningless rhetoric, it was very good rhetoric. The issue was not whether we went left or right, he said, but whether we moved forward. It is okay to be philosophically conservative, never losing sight of our values, but not operationally conservative if it ignores new global economic realities. This, he said, justified his decision to make deficit reduction a high priority. According to Clinton's strategy, deficit reduction is not only the leading economic indicator but also the prerequisite for sustained economic growth, lower inflation, lower unemployment, and a narrower income gap.

This is where Clinton showed his gift for taking an incredibly complex subject and explaining it so anybody can understand. Cutting the deficit is good policy not because experts said so and not because it has intrinsic merit, Clinton said. The rationale for deficit reduction is twofold. First, the more we spend paying interest on the debt, the more the social balance will continue to deteriorate. Second, the more we spend paying interest on the debt, the harder it is for people to borrow money for college loans, for home mortgages, or for new business start-ups. That is why we should cut the deficit; not because budget deficits are immoral or illegal—except in the sense they violate the economic principle of some defunct economist—but because they crowd out other things Americans could be and should be doing with their money. We have to get our economic house in order, cut the deficit, open new markets, create new jobs, and stay ahead of the technology curve.

Debt is a complex issue, particularly the size of the debt. Although Clinton did not specify a dollar amount or a percentage relative to the size of the economy, he did a good job of explaining why we should balance the budget and bring down the deficit. If you run a permanent high deficit in a global economy and keep borrowing money to finance normal government operations, you give away too much control over your economic well-being. That does not mean cutting taxes so low the government has to start borrowing more money. That does not mean cutting taxes so low we undermine our ability to invest in education and training, new technologies, and public infrastructure. According to Clinton, tax increases for the wealthiest Americans and welfare reform for the poorest are two halves of the same puzzle. This is a key difference between Clintonomics and Reaganomics: To compensate for the tax increase for the wealthiest Americans, Clinton promised to reform the welfare system. Balance the budget, yes, but *do no harm.*

An important (if unproven) benefit of balancing the budget and paying down the debt is the moderating effect it has on the highs and lows of the business cycle. Clinton related that his own team of economic advisors said if we kept unemployment below 5 percent for too long it would cause inflation.[10] In theory, that may be true. The laws of economics are still in effect, but the laws governing the global economy are still being written. It is possible new markets and emerging technologies will change the parameters of business cycles, exacerbate the highs and lows, change the dynamic between inflation and full employment, and force us to question our previous assumptions.

Clinton believed fiscal responsibility was the best economic policy over the long term. As we know, however, there is more to Clintonomics than that. His approach also includes tax incentives for small and family-owned businesses, which encourages people to invest and expand, plus other incentives for businesses in designated empowerment zones and enterprise communities located in economically disadvantaged cities and rural communities. When he describes his vision to achieve long-term economic growth through a private-public partnership, he also neatly summarizes the personal philosophy behind his economic policy.

> [Wherever] in America there are people who are underutilized, there is a market opportunity. Because when people are working up to the fullest of their capacity, then they have money to spend and they create jobs for others. So when I look at all these places in America which for too long have been without businesses on their street corners or in their small towns, or in their hamlets, I see enormous opportunity. I see in people whose potential is not fulfilled the opportunity to make free enterprise work again.[11]

Investing in people is good economics. It pays off in higher productivity and gives our companies a competitive edge in the global marketplace. It is a simple but powerful assertion, though I doubt if any economist would ever make such a claim. Most economists (if not all) dismiss the idea of zero unemployment as unrealistic in a market economy, but Clinton, the political economist, says we do not have a single person to waste. Using a nice little rhetorical flourish, Clinton said that one of the things he was trying to do with his economic program was to revitalize the economy and restore "the middle class and the values of the middle class to a central part in American life."[12] Clinton wanted to reposition the economy to be more competitive in the global economy, so that every person, regardless of his or her background had the potential to take advantage of it. As he worked deliberately to lower trade barriers, he also tried to lift people through education, training, and welfare reform to make our workforce as competitive as possible.

Investing in people is good economics. That seems like common sense, especially in the global economy. You can practically hear the conservative talk show host asking rhetorically, "Aren't you better off spending your own money?" It seems like a good argument, so overwhelming there is no honest rebuttal. However, it has not been a good argument for decades, ever since legislators discovered deficit spending. What always happens—always—is the government does not just spend your money. It also spends your children's money and grandchildren's money. Because taxes are so unpopular and borrowing money is so easy, the process of spending money (called appropriations) is completely divorced from raising money (called ways and means). This kind of deficit spending—incurring debt not for long-term investment in infrastructure, but to pay for operational expenses—is confiscatory taxation. It taxes people who have no vote because they have not even been born, which makes it the ultimate form of taxation without representation. When conservatives claim to fight for the rights of the unborn, why does that mean only their right to life but not their property? Even though fiscal responsibility makes good sense economically, doing the opposite makes better sense politically.

As Election Day 1996 neared, Clinton worried people would be bored with his insistence on deficit reduction, especially when the economy was so strong.

> Here's why you shouldn't be bored. If we bring the deficit down and we borrow less money just to pay the government's bills then interest rates go down. For you that means a lower home mortgage payment, a lower car payment, a lower credit card payment. For business it means lower loan rates, which means they can borrow more money, hire more people, grow this economy and take us into the twenty-first century. We have to balance the budget.[13]

Fiscal responsibility is also a global leadership issue. In an interdependent system such as the global economy, chronic deficits rob policy makers of flexibility, especially in developing countries. Excessive debt inhibits growth and, worse, drains resources needed to fulfill the most basic human conditions, such as healthcare, clean water, and education. Simply put, poor countries should not have to choose between feeding their people and paying the interest on their debt.

In a global economy with twenty-four-hour capital markets, a crisis anywhere has consequences everywhere, which means economic stability is just as important as political stability. Stock markets rise and fall because of events halfway around the world. Farmers in the American Midwest have trouble paying their mortgages because of events beyond their control half a world away. Stock markets in Tokyo, Hong Kong, Frankfurt, London, and Paris—even as far away as New York—are susceptible to natural disasters such as global warming and insults such as financial mismanagement. According to Clinton, "[when] the tides of capital first flood emerging markets, and then abruptly recede; when bank failures and bankruptcies grip entire economies; when millions who have worked their way into the middle class are plunged suddenly into poverty—the need for reform of the international financial system is clear."

During a speech in Philadelphia, Clinton said, "The real issue was whether we had the courage to come to grips with the economic problems which have paralyzed this country." It is a stretch to say previous administrations lacked courage. After fighting and eventually winning the Cold War over a period of decades, perhaps the real issue was not courage, but timing. True, the national debt increased dramatically during the Reagan-Bush years (1981–1993) and again during George W. Bush's two terms (2001–2009). If you subscribe to the theory of constraints, however, it is necessary to manage the constraint at the top of the list.

In a speech at the West Point Military Academy, Clinton quoted Dwight Eisenhower ("A strong economy is the physical basis . . . of all our military power") to make an instructive analogy. Our economic superiority was an important factor—if not the decisive factor—in our Cold War victory. However, none of the issues from the Cold War era have completely gone away, not taxes, healthcare, immigration, international trade, or education. We still face intense economic competition, chronic budget deficits, and numerous challenges to our national security. "Just as our security cannot rest upon a hollow Army," Clinton said, "neither can it rest upon a hollow economy."

In May 1993, Clinton gave a speech in New Mexico, home of the Los Alamos and Sandia National Laboratories, the origin of many defense-related technologies over the past fifty years. Clinton credited the two New Mexico–based laboratories, as well as the Lawrence Livermore Laboratory in California, with providing the ideas and the muscle America needed to defeat communism and called them "our crown jewels in technology and science." In this speech, Clinton made an interesting observation about the far-reaching effects of the United States' Cold War policy. "That struggle gave us a focus not just in how we spend our defense dollars, but how we invested in everything from our children's education to the interstate highway system." Alas, we can no longer count on the Cold War—or any other war, for that matter—to guide our investment strategy or fiscal policy.

When we balance the budget on a spreadsheet, we must also balance the budget in terms of our values. The budget declares the things important enough to spend money on and thus is the most truthful statement of any organization's values. That sounds very nice, but what values deserve funding? National security must come first. Social security must come next, which requires caring for the least among us, the most vulnerable members of our society, particularly children, the elderly, and the disabled.

After that, the budget is discretionary, which gives us the opportunity to consider not just future preference, but *future value*, meaning the expected value of an investment at a future date. Which future values deserve funding? "Sustained growth requires investment in human capital, education, healthcare, technology, infrastructure," said Clinton. "Particularly in an economy that runs more and more on brainpower, no investment pays off faster than education."[14]

Entitlements

Before we take another step, we should define another useful, though politically loaded, term: *entitlements.* Clinton often referred to "the politics of entitlement" as a way to criticize his own party. Here is an excerpt, vintage 1993, that might make some members of the party question Clinton's judgment:

> Some, but not all, in the national Democratic Party have placed too much faith in the whole politics of entitlement, the idea that big bureaucracies and Government spending, demanding nothing in return, can produce the results we want. We know that is simply not true. There is a limit to how much Government can do in the absence of an appropriate response by the American people at the grassroots level. And there is a limit to how many decisions can be made properly in Washington. And most of our growth has and always will come from the private sector.[15]

If you asked Reagan his definition of entitlement, he would say it "means the redistribution of your earnings."[16] Although it is politically loaded, an entitlement is in fact nothing more than a legal right established by statute or contract. An entitlement provides benefits to people who have certain characteristics or have met some sort of eligibility test, regardless of the amount previously budgeted for that particular program. For example, Social Security is an entitlement program—a contract between generations—that pays retirement, disability, or survivor benefits to people who qualify. Because it is impossible for Congress to know exactly how many people will quality for social security benefits in a given year, Congress directs the treasury to send a check to everyone who provides all the right documents and can prove his or her eligibility, no matter how many other people qualify.

At the federal level, entitlements give budget analysts headaches, particularly when it comes to balancing the budget. Why is this? The law establishes a set of eligibility criteria and requires the government to pay benefits to anyone who meets the criteria. The budgetary challenge with entitlement programs comes when the government attempts to estimate the number of people who will qualify in a given year and then to calculate the exact amount of their benefits. The entitlement is a legal requirement, a mandate based on the eligibility of beneficiaries, not on the availability of funds. This is exactly why fiscal conservatives object to entitlement programs: because they are automatic spending programs over which neither the legislature nor the administration has any control.

In any given year, slightly more than half of federal government spending goes toward entitlements, about 20 percent goes toward defense, another 20 percent goes toward non-defense-related discretionary programs, and the rest toward interest payments. There are a few other entitlement programs called "special category," such as food stamps, medical care for the poor, and agriculture subsidies, precisely because it is so difficult to know how much to budget from year to year. In any given year, there may also be supplemental or emergency appropriations for a variety of purposes: for example, funding the costs of military operations in Afghanistan or Iraq. Back in 1993, welfare payments amounted to approximately 2 percent of the entitlements budget and about 1 percent of the annual federal budget.

At a 1993 conference on the future of entitlements—at a time when Clinton still had hopes for his doomed healthcare plan —he devoted attention to deficit reduction, budget cuts, and tax increases. One was a relatively modest tax increase on gasoline. Another was an increase on income taxes for the wealthiest one percent, which mostly affected the people whose taxes went down shortly after Reagan took office. Clinton also noted that taxes would be slightly lower for the middle class and significantly lower for poor people. He also talked about how his new budget would cut discretionary spending and reduce entitlements, such as agricultural subsidies, Social Security payments to upper-income residents, Medicare, Medicaid, and veterans' benefits.

Clinton then made a seemingly insignificant observation that made average Americans feel as though Clinton truly cared about their problems: "Now, I think it's important to point out . . . that behind every one of these entitlements there's a person."[17] Recipients are not just interest groups lobbying the government, but people who paid into the system for years and believed they were entitled to receive something back. Clearly, the implications of entitlement programs go beyond budgeting. Social Security literally changed the meaning of old age. Before Social Security, old age was synonymous with poverty. However, our duty to guarantee a decent and dignified retirement for the elderly does not excuse us from fiscal responsibility. "The entitlement programs that make up our safety net for the truly needy have worthy goals and many deserving recipients. We will protect them," Reagan said in 1982. "But there's only one way to see to it that these programs really help those whom they were designed to help. And that is to bring their spiraling costs under control."[18]

With this in mind, Clinton proposed increasing the taxes of those social security recipients who were in the 10- to 12-percent income bracket. He said, "Exposing more of the incomes" to taxation of wealthy recipients was fair because, by definition, they had other sources of income and did not have to live on their monthly Social Security check. From their point of view, it was unfair, of course, precisely because Social Security was a contributory program. This explanation set the stage for what Clinton considered the biggest long-term entitlement problem, the one in which government spending was most out of control: healthcare. "The only responsible way to deal with the entitlements problem over the long run is to keep working to help to solve the healthcare problem."[19] Soon, said Clinton, the government will be spending more on Medicare and Medicaid than on Social Security. Soon, the government will be spending more on healthcare than on education. We will never get the deficit under control unless we get entitlements under control, and we will not get entitlements under control unless we do something about the cost of healthcare.

Healthcare

In his first inaugural address, Clinton briefly mentioned the high cost of healthcare but nothing more on the subject. Five days into his presidency, however, he made good on a campaign promise and announced the formation of a new task force on healthcare reform. First Lady Hillary Clinton would chair the task force and prepare healthcare reform legislation for submission to Congress in one hundred days. This repeated a successful model from Clinton's days as governor of Arkansas, when his wife chaired several major committees (on public education and public health) on his behalf.[20]

For those readers who may not be policy wonks, let us pause briefly to comment on the organization of the remainder of this relatively long chapter. There will be as little discussion of the details of Clinton's healthcare plan as possible because we are interested in big ideas, big bottlenecks, and big roadblocks. In the global era, healthcare certainly seems to qualify as one of the factors limiting economic performance. Based on what we learned about the purpose of politics, the foundation of political economy, Reagan's political influence, globalization, and complexity, the system is not a single organization, but a global network of countries, corporations, markets, goods, services, commodities, and currencies, as well as billions of people. In this system, components are interdependent, power is decentralized, control is loose, and centers of decision are plural. Although there is an accumulation of chaos in the system, the entropy value remains within working parameters—meaning the situation is desperate but not hopeless, at least for now.

Of all the forces of change taking place in the new century (with the exception of terrorism, perhaps), none creates as much insecurity among the American people and none needs reforming more than healthcare. Clinton raised the issue in almost every speech, no matter the audience. The high cost of healthcare, according to Clinton, was not merely a problem for workers and their families but a potential long-term threat to the American economy and thus the global economy. Clinton always said the American system provided the world's best healthcare, so the trick was to keep what worked and fix what did not. People who have health insurance today might not have it tomorrow. Those who can afford it today might not be able to tomorrow.

Clearly, Clinton and Reagan go their separate ways regarding healthcare. Reagan strongly opposed national health insurance, mostly because he was adamant that "there is *no* healthcare crisis in the U.S." Despite his opposition to what he ridiculed as *socialized medicine*, Reagan said, "Of course, we all want to insure that no one is denied needed medical care because of poverty."[21] Well, that says it all, does it not? All Reagan wanted was to make sure people (particularly children) could receive decent healthcare even if they could not afford it. All Clinton wanted was to make sure every American and every American family had "health security" as a way to mitigate the local effects of turmoil in the global economy. In an economy where few people enjoyed job security, Clinton wanted to provide a new kind of security where, for example, workers did not lose their healthcare when they lost their jobs. "We must not ask people to choose between being good parents and good workers. We cannot ask people to risk their children's health to participate in the global economy," Clinton said. "And most importantly, we can't just keep working with a system that is fundamentally flawed that we can fix."

The healthcare problem is in fact a healthcare *finance* problem, which disproportionately hurts the poorest, particularly in rural communities. Healthcare costs are rising faster than inflation, and too many Americans, particularly children and the elderly, are not covered. When people without health insurance get sick, they often (but not always) receive healthcare in emergency rooms, where costs and mortality rates are high. Who pays? Those with health insurance assume the burden in the form of higher insurance premiums and hospital bills.

However, it would be an overstatement to argue healthcare is exclusively an economic problem because healthcare security is a major problem for many families, people between jobs, and those with chronic illnesses. Because healthcare *insecurity* represents an unfulfilled physiological or survival need that tends to dominate the attention and behavior of those affected, the motive behind healthcare reform is that reliable, affordable healthcare is an essential element in creating a climate in which people feel personally secure.[22] For Clinton, the lack of healthcare security was analogous to lack of social security, an issue loaded with far-reaching economic consequences. Globalization did not cause the problem, but it does reveal a structural flaw in the American economy, which, if left unattended, will eventually make managing the federal deficit impossible.

Here Clinton makes a strong case in favor of healthcare reform, arguing there are more than ten million children in the country without health insurance. "Do you know what that means?" Clinton asked rhetorically. He answered his own question:

> That means nearly forty percent of the uninsured children don't get the annual checkups they need and may not find those holes in the heart or lead problems or other problems. It means one in four uninsured children don't even have a regular doctor. It means too many children who have trouble seeing a blackboard don't get the glasses they need to correct their vision; that too many nagging coughs go untreated until they worsen into more serious conditions that may require costly treatments and lengthy hospital stays later; that too many parents actually face the agonizing and impossible choice between buying medicine for a sick child or food for the rest of their family.[23]

Under Clinton's healthcare plan—based on recommendations from the task force chaired by Hillary Clinton—every American would receive a healthcare security card and a comprehensive package of benefits guaranteed for life. His goal was to use public policy to provide universal coverage, while guiding market forces to encourage competition and ensure quality. It was a practical application of his third way approach, which in theory makes use of market-based solutions. Clinton was desperate to rebut his critics who falsely claimed he was attempting a hostile takeover of the nation's healthcare system. What he was trying to do, he said, was keep the private system we have now, with private health insurance, private doctors, and private providers, but make sure everyone was covered. In his words:

> So this is really not about whether we're going to put the government in charge of healthcare. The government is involved in healthcare. That's what the Medicare program is all about, and most of you would hang me from the highest tree if you thought we were going to repeal it, wouldn't you? I mean, right? It's not about that. The government is involved in healthcare. Our plan does not put the government in control of healthcare. What it does is to reduce the control of the insurance companies and give more influence to workers and businesses.[24]

The issue (and really the ultimate solution) is portability. We expect people to change jobs seven times, on average, in a lifetime. What about the entrepreneurs who take the risks and develop the new products and new business models? "How can you be secure enough to change, to take on new challenges, to start new businesses, to take new risks, if you think that you may have to let your family go without basic healthcare?" Clinton asked. It is bad economic policy to force people—especially entrepreneurs so vital to the American economy—to choose between work and family. This is never more true than in homes that need two incomes, so both parents work. Any great society that forces people to choose between freedom and security or between work and family is going to fail in the end. In Clinton's words:

> If you have to fail at home in order to succeed at work,
> we're in trouble. But if the only way you can succeed at
> home is to fail at work, we're in trouble. So when I think
> about the kind of world we're trying to create, I often ask
> myself, how can I create an America so that when I leave
> office every American who is willing to work for it can
> get up every day and do well at home and do well at
> work and do well at school. That is what I want.[25]

Clinton said it well during a speech at an event to promote child care. Workers with children make better workers if they do not have to worry about their children. Bringing the office home with you interferes with good parenting, just as bringing your worries to the office interferes with productivity. In his words:

> One of the reasons the business community is interested
> in this is that enlightened business leaders understand
> that, actually, if you permit people to do the right thing
> by their children, you wind up having a happier, more
> upbeat, more affirmative, more positive business envi-
> ronment, and ultimately the business enterprise will be
> more successful because the workers are also successful
> at home. That's what this whole business is about, taking
> care of their children and not asking their parents to
> choose between being good parents and good workers.
> *It all comes down to that.*[26]

Clinton's goal was to establish an affordable, comprehensive system everyone could depend on, which would cover everything from preventive care to prescription drugs. Clinton stressed the importance of having the freedom to choose your own doctor and your own health plan. With freedom comes responsibility; it is up to parents to make sure their children receive immunizations, and it is up to everyone else—particularly smokers—to practice better health habits. "People who smoke should pay more for a pack of cigarettes," Clinton said. If you look at history, you would learn he was not the first president to attempt health-care reform. "President Roosevelt tried. President Truman tried. President Nixon tried. President Carter tried. Every time the special interests were powerful enough to defeat them," he said. "But not this time."[27] Foreshadowing the embarrassing defeat, Clinton said the people and organizations who profited from the status quo—and their lobbyists—would be especially resistant to change.

Welfare

As governor of Arkansas, Clinton worked on welfare reform with all kinds of people, including Republicans and Democrats, members of Congress, and officials in the Bush and Reagan administrations. "I worked on it with people who were on welfare—lots of them."[28] This is something few governors and even fewer presidents could truthfully say. The idea that Clinton was close to the people is the stuff of legend, and Toni Morrison piled it higher when she called Clinton "our first black President" in the October 1998 New Yorker. The legend had roots in Arkansas:

> When I was governor, people used to make fun of me and say that I was basically a courthouse governor, which meant that I loved to go to the county courthouses in the rural areas of my state and sit for hours and talk to the officials and also visit with the people who would come in. But I know this: I know that one of the things that our government in Washington has suf-

fered from for so many years is being too far from the concerns of ordinary Americans.[29]

Although welfare is not technically an entitlement, it was one of Clinton's favorite public policy issues. Again, we will not go into the details of Clinton's welfare reform plan. His four basic principles on the subject were the system should move people from welfare to work, there should be time limits on welfare, it should provide child care and healthcare so people can go to work without hurting their children, and it should crack down on child support enforcement. We also know that welfare reform was very important to Reagan, and that he too had experience working on it as governor. Like Clinton, Reagan had principles of his own. First, Reagan believed work was the only authentic path to independence and self-respect. Second, any effective welfare system must provide the incentives and tools to get off welfare, not to remain dependent on welfare. Third, the federal government must give states wide latitude as they experiment with new ideas and implement new systems.[30]

When you read Clinton's comments on welfare reform that follow, you can see the new role he wanted the federal government to play. First, do no harm, meaning Washington should not stifle innovation or experimentation in welfare reform. Second, Washington had a constitutional role to keep deadbeat parents from exploiting state jurisdictions.

> Do we need welfare reform legislation? We do. We do because states shouldn't have to get approval every time they want to try an experiment. We do because we need to do more to strengthen child support collection across state lines. If everybody paid the child support they owe we would move 800,000 women and children off welfare tomorrow morning—if everybody paid that.[31]

The new welfare reform law, which Clinton signed in 1996, provided a national guarantee, funded by the federal and state governments, for healthcare, nutrition, and child care for people who moved from welfare to work. Instead of monthly entitlement checks mailed directly to welfare recipients, expenditures would go to the states, which would then work to move able-bodied people off welfare within two years. Benefits would expire for able-bodied people after five years unless there were extenuating circumstances. Although the law was not perfect, Clinton considered it a historic opportunity to change the culture of welfare.

Anyone who thinks the premise of this book is fallacious should read what Milton Friedman said in 1979 about welfare reform. He argued that most welfare programs should never have been set up in the first place, and most of the people dependent on these programs would have been much better off never having become wards of the state. "However, given that the welfare programs exist, they cannot simply be abolished overnight. We need some way to ease the transition from where we are to where we would like to be, of providing assistance to people now dependent on welfare while at the same time encouraging an orderly transfer of people from welfare rolls to payrolls."[32] This quotation reinforces conservative values of individualism, economic freedom, and limited government and highlights two of Clinton's favorite themes, opportunity and responsibility. It should convince you that Clintonomics is the logical corollary to the Reagan revolution.

Midway through his first year in the presidency, Reagan spoke at the NAACP national convention. He commented the American economy was "something of an underground railroad" for many African Americans, spiriting them away from poverty into the middle class and beyond. Far too many African Americans, however, had not found economic freedom. Reagan expanded on two of his favorite themes: that political freedom is inseparable from economic freedom, and that we should measure the success of our policies according to how much we decrease the need for welfare:

> The government can provide subsistence, yes, but it seldom moves people up the economic ladder. And as I've said before, you have to get on the ladder before you can move up on it. I believe many in Washington, over the years, have been more dedicated to making needy people government dependent rather than independent. They've created a new kind of bondage, because regardless of how honest their intention in the beginning, those they set out to help soon became clients essential to the well-being of those who administered the programs.[33]

On numerous occasions, Clinton shared Reagan's concern that welfare created and reinforced a corrosive culture of dependency from which it was nearly impossible to escape. Clinton believed the welfare system undermined families and devalued work. Creating workable incentives to get people out of the welfare system and into paying jobs is an essential part of Clinton's governing philosophy. Clinton believed welfare was "the symbol in America of what is wrong with government."[34] The central premise of welfare reform that Clinton wanted to advance was this: Anyone who can work must do so. Of course, real welfare reform would reduce the number of people on the welfare rolls, require work, impose time limits, crack down on deadbeat parents by enforcing child support, and provide child care. But welfare reform would never be entirely successful without healthcare reform, because if you want to get people off welfare, you have to make sure their children have healthcare.

The Bible says, "The poor you will always have with you, and you can help them any time you want" (Mark 14:7). According to *Webster's*, welfare means providing economic or social benefits to disabled or disadvantaged people, especially aid furnished by the government or private agencies. What is the difference between this definition and George W. Bush's faith-based initiatives? In January 2001, Bush signed two executive orders to establish the White House Office of Faith-Based and Community Initiatives, the purpose of which is to increase participation of faith-based organizations in federal efforts to deliver social services. One of the stated goals is to "enlist, equip, enable, empower, and expand the work of faith-based and other secular organizations to the extent permitted by law" so they can deliver services and respond to a variety of social problems such as crime, poverty, and drug addiction in poor and distressed neighborhoods. Although welfare reform is settled policy—and thus may seem unnecessary to include here—poverty is a chronic problem. Regardless of our approach, and no matter what we call it, we cannot remove welfare from the list of constraints anytime soon.[35]

Diversity

Diversity is a trend that will continue into infinity. We will become more diverse racially, ethnically, and religiously without end, which makes the theory of constraints an especially useful approach. As stated, we use this course of action to identify constraints that limit the system's capacity—and then *manage the constraints*, which reminds us to resist the temptation to search for the once-and-for-all solution. Another reminder: Managing the constraints at the top of the list will improve performance, whereas managing constraints at the bottom will not necessarily improve performance.

What did Clinton mean by diversity? Clinton provided a practical definition based on the demographics at a school in the Virginia school system. He noted there were children from a hundred different ethnic groups, with almost a hundred different native languages. I never found a perfect definition, but I came across an excerpt in which Clinton claims Detroit, Michigan, is the epitome of diversity. After WWII, many Southern whites and blacks could not find jobs in the South, so they migrated north and found jobs in the automobile industry. "That was our definition of diversity."[36]

Late in his presidency, Clinton told this story, which reveals the importance he placed on managing diversity and promoting racial harmony:

> [If] somebody said to me today, well, Mr. President . . . your time is up on this Earth and you're not going to get to finish, but we'll give you one wish, I wouldn't wish for the continued economic expansion; I wouldn't wish for even giving everybody health insurance, or anything. I'd wish to make America one America, because the American people will figure out how to solve everything else, if we can have the right kind of relations toward one another.[37]

Clinton envisioned American cities as incubators for the world's first truly great multiracial, multiethnic, multireligious democracy. He hoped to use the opportunity after the end of the Cold War to initiate a national dialogue on race. Clinton's foreign policy dealt mostly with international trade and a few regional crises. In the absence of a national security threat or other national cataclysm, there was no better time to address "our old, unfinished business." There was no better time to address the "vexing, perplexing, often painful issues surrounding our racial history and our future." Indeed, before that vision ever becomes a reality, first we have to pass an important test. The test is whether or not we live up to the founders' ideals; it is a test of perceptions and reality. We have to visualize our future as a multiracial, multiethnic, multireligious democracy that "runs in a straight line from here all the way back to George Washington."[38] With all the evidence of intolerance and bigotry, violence, church burnings and bombings, we are obviously not there yet.

As the country becomes more diverse racially, ethnically, and religiously, we need to teach children to be not only proud of their own heritage but also proud of other heritages. Religious freedom is a case in point. Because of the Bill of Rights, specifically the First Amendment, Congress is prohibited from passing any law "respecting an establishment of religion, or prohibiting the free exercise thereof." Although the First Amendment protects religious freedom in public schools, public schools should neither advocate nor forbid religious expression. Students should be free to express themselves in their homework, artwork, or class presentations as long as their religious beliefs are relevant to the assignment. Clinton said students should be allowed to say a silent prayer before tests—as he used to do. In his words:

> Religion is too important to our history and our heritage for us to keep it out of our schools. Once again, it shouldn't be demanded, but as long as it is not sponsored by school officials and doesn't interfere with other children's rights, it mustn't be denied. For example, students can pray privately and individually whenever they want. They can say grace themselves before lunch. There are times when they can pray out loud together. Student religious clubs in high schools can and should be treated just like any other extracurricular club. They can advertise their meetings, meet on school grounds, use school

facilities just as other clubs can. When students can choose to read a book to themselves, they have every right to read the Bible or any other religious text they want.[39]

In August 1963, Martin Luther King, Jr., led the March on Washington for Jobs and Freedom in Washington, D.C. This was the occasion of King's inspirational masterpiece, the "I Have a Dream" speech, which he delivered standing on the steps of the Lincoln Memorial to an audience of more than two hundred thousand. In October 1995, Louis Farrakhan, head of the Nation of Islam, led the Million Man March in Washington, D.C., the purpose of which was to register people to vote and increase community service and volunteerism. On the day of the march, Bill Clinton was not in Washington, but in Texas. This is what Clinton had to say:

> Well, today's march is also about pride and dignity and respect. But after a generation of deepening social problems that disproportionately impact black Americans, it is also about black men taking renewed responsibility for themselves, their families, and their communities. It's about saying no to crime and drugs and violence. It's about standing up for atonement and reconciliation. It's about insisting that others do the same, and offering to help them. It's about the frank admission that unless black men shoulder their load, no one else can help them or their brothers, their sisters, and their children escape the hard, bleak lives that too many of them still face.[40]

Clinton did not stop there. Although the message of many people marching that day was atonement and reconciliation, he said, "One million men do not make right one man's message of malice and division." He prayed all those who marched would turn away from hatred and bitterness toward unity, opportunity, and reconciliation. It is always easier to see your own grievances than to recognize somebody else's. It is easier to assign responsibility to somebody else than to accept responsibility. He thought blacks needed to understand it was not racism when parents pulled their children close when walking through a high-crime neighborhood, but he derided those who spoke as if blacks were some sort of protected class in America.

In fact, blacks on average earn much less than whites, and more than half of black children live in poverty. Something is terribly wrong when African American men are much more likely to be victims of homicide than any other group in the country. Something is wrong when there are more African American men in prison than in college, when so many young African American men are either in jail or on parole. Clinton then posed the question: "Now, I would like every white person here and in America to take a moment to think how he or she would feel if one in three white men were in similar circumstances."[41]

One method we use to manage diversity and remedy past injustices is affirmative action. What does affirmative action mean in twenty-first-century America, in the most racially and ethnically diverse country in the global system? In principle, we can trace the roots of affirmative action to emancipation, women's suffrage, civil rights, voting rights, and equal rights. In practice, we can trace it to Executive Order 10925, which John Kennedy signed in March 1961, ordering federal contractors to take "affirmative action" to ensure there is no discrimination toward applicants or employees on the basis of race, creed, color, or national origin.[42] In 1995, Clinton said, "The purpose of affirmative action is to give our nation a way to finally address the systemic exclusion of individuals of talent on the basis of their gender or race from opportunities to develop, perform, achieve and contribute." Clinton defined affirmative action as "an effort to develop a systematic approach to open the doors of education, employment and business development opportunities to qualified individuals who happen to be members of groups that have experienced longstanding and persistent discrimination."[43]

Affirmative action began as part of our never-ending quest for equal opportunity. Affirmative action was designed to change the status quo gradually by ensuring a large pool of qualified applicants for jobs, colleges, and contracts, as a temporary intervention toward the goal of equal opportunity. (Clinton would probably say "equal opportunity with equal responsibility.") While affirmative action has effectively created opportunities for many people who might otherwise have been denied, some people believe it is an end in itself instead of a means toward an end. Like welfare, there are some aspects of affirmative action that work, while others do not. As he did with welfare reform, Clinton wanted people to think about what we should do about affirmative action now. He believed it was time to change affirmative action, not end it, not as long as there was any institutional racism or a pattern of racism in the country.

Opponents of affirmative action, even those who believe strongly in the goal of equal opportunity, argue it is inherently unfair and biased. Opponents acknowledge discrimination, conscious and unconscious, still exists in our society but worry about the stigma of reverse discrimination. Success resulting from affirmative action demeans the beneficiaries because they will never know if their success was the result of merit. For Clinton, however, it all came down to the social contract, the basic bargain between people and their fellow citizens, as well as the basic bargain between people and their government. It came down to offering every American equal opportunity to succeed and demanding every American take personal responsibility for making the most of that opportunity.

As a matter of principle, Clinton liked affirmative action as a way to honor diversity. At the policy level, he liked it as a way to build community out of diversity and to make the country less unequal and less stratified. He supported it "until we have stamped out discrimination," which clearly means it is only a temporary remedy. Clinton wanted to make sure people did not confuse means and ends. "Affirmative action *is simply a tool* in the pursuit of that enduring national interest—equal opportunity." As stated, critics of affirmative action argue it demeans the intended beneficiaries. One of our goals should be that no one in America believes his or her race is an impediment to fulfilling his or her aspirations. Affirmative action undermines this goal precisely when it automatically assumes racial or gender discrimination is the cause of the problem.

Clinton acknowledged affirmative action was an imperfect policy, but he was reluctant to simply do away with it. "When I was confronted with the question [in one presidential debate] of what to do about affirmative action, I said it may not please some of my friends, but I don't think all those programs have worked the way they're supposed to." Affirmative action is not a perfect remedy, nor should it go on forever, he said. "It should be changed now to take care of those things that are wrong, and it should be retired when its job is done." What he really wanted was for people (particularly members of his party) to focus on values and principles rather than specific government programs. Clinton was proud of the fact he "consistently opposed the dismantlement of all affirmative action programs." He committed the government to making a conscious effort to ensure every American got a fair shot but not to guarantee a favorable outcome to any citizen.

Clinton was always skeptical of any quick and easy solution. Although doing away with affirmative action would solve the problem of *reverse* discrimination, it would not change the reality that millions of blacks, women, and others were underemployed or relegated to jobs below their qualifications. Because Clinton knew the difference between affirmative action (the government program) and equal opportunity (the principle), he believed there was a way to be faithful to our democratic values and effective in contemporary American politics.

As long as people respect honest differences, our diversity can be an invaluable asset in the global economy rather than a constraining factor. "I want our diversity to be the crown jewel of our assets in the global society," he said. "I want us to revel in the racial and ethnic and religious diversity of America." We should change affirmative action, he said, but "we shouldn't get rid of it until we get rid of discrimination."[44] At a service commemorating Martin Luther King, Jr., Clinton said it particularly well:

> The job of ending discrimination in this country is not over. That's why I still believe we need the right kind of affirmative action. We can mend it, and some day we can end it. But we can't end it until everybody with a straight face can say there is no more discrimination on the basis of race. We must bring more peace to our public discourse, even when we passionately disagree.[45]

On Martin Luther King Day in 1994, Clinton spoke at Howard University and commented on the speech King gave the day before he died, which is most famous for King's prophesy of his own death. "Like anybody, I would like to live a long life—longevity has its place. But I'm not concerned about that now. I just want to do God's will. And He's allowed me to go up to the mountain," said King. "And I've looked over, and I've seen the Promised Land. I may not get there with you."[46] Clinton recounted when King said if he had the option of living in any age in human history, he would choose to live in the second half of the twentieth century. Despite how messed up the world was in 1968, and how messed up it still is, Clinton imagined King would be gratified to see the leaders of Israel and the Palestinian Liberation Organization shaking hands, to see Nelson Mandela released from prison after twenty-seven years. He thought King would be gratified to see the Berlin Wall fall and the Cold War over and freedom reborn in Europe. He reminded his listeners how fragile democracies are, especially new democracies in regions troubled by ancient ethnic tensions, high unemployment, and slow growth.

The idea that America would try to teach this lesson to democracies emerging in Europe is ironic on Martin Luther King Day, to say the least. However, Clinton was never timid talking about race, and rather than ignore the irony, he chose to confront the issue. How were we doing on democracy, minority and individual rights, and widespread economic progress? In this speech, Clinton drew a round applause just for asking the question, so he asked the same question again, word for word, and drew another round of applause. In Clinton's words:

> If democracy is the involvement of all of our people, and if it is making strength out of our diversity, if we want to say to the people in the troubled areas in Europe—put your ethnic hatreds behind you, take the differences, the religious differences, the racial differences, the ethnic differences of your people and make them a strength in a global economy, surely we must do the same here.[47]

Bound together in a web of mutuality, we will never have racial harmony unless we are willing to forgive our enemies. Clinton continued: "All of you know, I'm having to become quite an expert in this business of asking for forgiveness. It gets a little easier the more you do it. And if you have a family, an administration, a Congress and a whole country to ask, you—you're going to get a lot of practice."[48] Then he said one of the great noble truths of human nature: In order to get forgiveness, you have to be willing to give it. Ken Brown, my colleague from the California State University, Long Beach, once told me, "Bitterness is a pill you swallow in the hope it makes your enemy sick." Begrudging people you believe have wronged you hardens your heart and deadens your spirit. It is the ultimate self-inflicted wound.

Education

Along with healthcare, welfare, and diversity, education is another constraint that will limit our success if we fail to manage it. What is education? Clinton provided a typically concise, insightful definition entirely consistent with his governing philosophy, appropriate for the twenty-first century and equal to the powerful forces of globalization: Education is "what we know and what we can learn." In the past, economic security was synonymous with job security. Now, because of the competitive pressures of the global economy, economic security is synonymous with learning: the capacity to acquire new knowledge and new skills. "Education is about more than making money and mastering technology, even in the twenty-first century," Clinton said. "It's about making connections and mastering the complexities of the world. It's about seeing the world as it is and advancing the cause of human dignity."[49] Thus, an educated workforce is a prerequisite for success in the global economy, and that means creating a public education system that promotes lifelong learning.

Peter Drucker (1909–2005), born in Vienna, was a writer, consultant, and professor like so many other influential thinkers. Richard Nixon and Ronald Reagan both quoted him on numerous occasions, and George W. Bush called him "one of the greatest management experts of our time" upon presenting him with the Presidential Medal of Freedom.[50] Along with Frederick W. Taylor (1856–1915) and W. Edwards Deming (1900–1993), Drucker was one of the pioneers of management consulting. Rather than searching for new ways to make workers more efficient, Drucker focused his attention on developing managers far beyond vocational training for executives and on helping organizations improve their performance within a framework of social responsibility. In the sixties, Drucker coined the term *knowledge worker* to describe the individual whose primary economic asset is his or her ability to collect, create, and communicate knowledge.[51]

Robert Reich had an even better descriptor for knowledge workers. He called them symbolic analysts, people whose job is problem solving, problem identifying, and strategic brokering.[52] Symbolic analysts manipulate symbols, using abstract images to simplify reality and thus make it manageable. They manage intellectual property; they produce it, study it, and, most importantly, add value to it. They trade their services worldwide, working alone or in teams, communicating via the telephone or the Web, solving problems or brokering solutions and, ever increasingly, identifying problems that few people realize even exist.

The educational requirements of the symbolic analyst in a knowledge economy are very different from those in an industrial economy. A standardized education is appropriate for a standardized economy, but knowledge workers must master nonstandard skills like abstract thinking, systems thinking, experimentation, and collaboration. "Consider, first, the capacity for abstraction," says Reich. "The real world is nothing but a vast jumble of noises, shapes, colors, smells, and textures—essentially meaningless until the human mind imposes some order upon them." The capacity for abstract thinking enables an individual to model reality, to simplify it using equations, categories, formulas, and metaphors. Systems thinking (see Chapters 4 and 5) is abstract thinking of a higher order.

The purpose of systems thinking is not to predict the future by drawing false analogies from the past but to enhance our ability to address problems that are systemic rather than symptomatic. Our ability to think systemically is a prerequisite to appreciating the mutuality, connectedness, and interdependence of the global system. This, in turn, is a prerequisite for problem identification, because problems are rarely standardized. Problems in the global system are complex and always connected at many levels to other problems. To master abstract and systems thinking, one must be able to experiment, which means using observation and analysis to explain and manage the world around us. It means observing phenomena, collecting and analyzing data, formulating a hypothesis, testing the hypothesis to prove or disprove it, and then drawing conclusions. It means when the data does not support the theory, you know enough to revise your theory rather than ignore the data. It means, as Deming said, knowing that no number of examples proves a theory, but a single unexplained failure requires you to revise or reject the theory.[53]

Clinton believed the United States has the finest system of higher education in the world, based on the diverse number of graduate schools, the proportion of Nobel Laureates at American universities, the volume of basic research, and the thousands of international students who study in the United States each year. He was justifiably proud of the historic breakthroughs in American education, such as guaranteeing free public education, establishing the system of land grant colleges, and enacting the GI Bill, all of which expanded educational opportunities for millions of people. Despite our strengths in higher education, he believed our government would never fulfill its educational mission until we could say two things. First, we are proud of our university system and everyone who is eligible can afford to go. Second, we are also proud of our elementary and secondary education system (kindergarten through twelfth grade, or K–12). *Until our system of elementary and secondary education is as highly respected around the world as our system of higher education, the country will never live up to its potential.*

In his 1994 annual message, Clinton outlined his educational philosophy. He advocated setting national academic standards while ensuring school administration was subject to local control. He wanted to "empower" school districts and encourage them to experiment with ideas such as permitting schools "to be run by private corporations" as long as all schools are measured by the same high standards. Clinton's position exemplifies why setting education policy at the federal level can be difficult and highlights the inherent contradiction between grassroots reforms and top-down reforms mandated by the federal government.[54]

Like Clinton, Reagan advocated local control of schools, with as little federal interference as possible. Reagan practically equated federal intervention with the erosion of quality of public schools and the poor academic performance of students.[55] Although the states, not the federal government, must have the primary responsibility for public education, local school districts simply cannot accept federal aid without inviting federal oversight. Clinton certainly did not want the federal government taking over the schools, but he did want more and better-trained teachers, smaller class sizes, and national standards.[56] He wanted to both limit the federal government's role in public education and encourage states and local school districts to experiment with charter schools and public school choice.

In March 1994, Clinton signed Goals 2000, a framework of outcomes-based education mandating national standards for school readiness (free of drugs, violence, guns, and alcohol), student achievement, parental participation, and professional development for teachers. Clinton's education policy set national education goals to improve our world ranking in math and science, prepare students for responsible citizenship and productive employment in the global economy, increase graduation rates from high school, and increase adult literacy. Goals 2000 was part of a trend in education reform based on national standards for assessment of student learning outcomes, the predecessor to George W. Bush's No Child Left Behind.

It is difficult to pinpoint exactly when this trend began, but it really took off in 1983, when the National Commission on Excellence in Education published its report, "A Nation at Risk: The Imperative for Educational Reform." Shortly after taking office in 1981, Reagan assembled a bipartisan commission and asked members to assess the quality of teaching and learning in America compared to other industrialized nations and relative to our own expectations. In April 1983, the commission bluntly concluded our nation was at risk. Our educational institutions were not setting adequate academic standards, not challenging students, and not using resources effectively. Furthermore, our competitors were gaining on us, matching or surpassing our educational accomplishments and thus threatening our economic, scientific, and technological preeminence. This famous passage sums up the commission's findings pretty well: "If an unfriendly foreign power had attempted to impose on America the mediocre educational performance that exists today, we might well have viewed it as an act of war. As it stands, we have allowed this to happen to ourselves. . . . We have, in effect, been committing an act of unthinking, unilateral educational disarmament."

Although the remark about the act of war captured headlines in 1983, this paragraph on the learning society is what captures the imagination twenty-five years later:

In a world of ever-accelerating competition and change in the conditions of the workplace, of ever-greater danger, and of ever-larger opportunities for those prepared to meet them, educational reform should focus on the goal of creating a Learning Society. At the heart of such a society is the commitment to a set of values and to a system of education that affords all members the opportunity to stretch their minds to full capacity, from early childhood through adulthood, learning more as the world itself changes. Such a society has as a basic foundation the idea that education is important not only because of what it contributes to one's career goals but also because of the value it adds to the general quality of one's life. Also at the heart of the Learning Society are educational opportunities extending far beyond the traditional institutions of learning, our schools and colleges. They extend into homes and workplaces; into libraries, art galleries, museums, and science centers; indeed, into every place where the individual can develop and mature in work and life.[57]

Modern democracies require good citizens educated in the liberal arts, logic, and critical thinking who are exposed to different cultures. "If you're going to have democracies make good decisions in difficult times—not just when everything is going well—the importance of universal education, and not narrowly defined education, is greater than at any time in all of human history," said Clinton.[58] Just as public schools are vehicles for upward mobility, providing the kind of lifelong educational opportunities essential for success in the global economy, establishing national education goals ensures portability from state to state—an important consideration in an economy that rewards geographic mobility.

Indeed, as governor, Clinton was a driving force behind the bipartisan effort to establish national education goals. Back in 1989, the elder Bush and the National Governors Association gathered for an education summit at the University of Virginia. On the last day of the summit, Bush thanked Clinton, "who looks a little tired, but took on an extra responsibility for hammering out a statement upon which there is strong agreement."[59] The ambitious young governor of Arkansas stayed up all night writing and rewriting a framework for national performance goals. The framework included items such as readiness for children to start school; better performance in math and science achievement tests; reducing the dropout rate for at-risk children; increasing the functional literacy of adults; increasing the pool of well-qualified teachers; and making sure schools are safe, disciplined, and drug free. President Bush and the governors also agreed on the need for flexibility, accountability, and decentralized authority when implementing the new mandate.

Clinton's successor, George W. Bush, set some of his own national goals for education. The fundamental goal of Bush's No Child Left Behind policy is to improve the performance of our publicly funded primary and secondary schools; restore accountability; and, as Bush said many times, end the soft bigotry of low expectations. Goals include making sure every child in America receives a first-class education, no matter where the child lives, how he or she is raised, or how much his or her parents earn, thus ensuring that every child can read by the third grade and that every public school "is a place of high expectations and a place of achievement."[60]

In 2001, when Bush signed No Child Left Behind into law, he thanked the several people responsible for the new legislation and singled out Ted Kennedy. Bush called Kennedy a good and able man and a "fabulous" senator and joked how shocked the folks back home at the Crawford coffee shop would be if they knew how much he liked Kennedy. "This bill would not have happened had he decided not to work to make it happen. He put his mind to it. I learned this: You want him on your side in a legislative battle," said Bush. "When he's against you, it's tough; when he's with you, it is a great experience."[61] If you visit Kennedy's official Web site, you'll see he also touts the bipartisan commitment to public education, but he criticizes the Bush administration for neglecting to provide adequate resources to states and school districts to implement No Child Left Behind.[62] Nonetheless, if there is one issue that can and should transcend politics, it is education.

Perhaps because of Clinton's impoverished childhood, he knew he would never have become president if not for his education. For Clinton, education policy was the new foreign policy. During the Cold War, foreign policy was mostly bipartisan because of the communist threat. "If the President of one party went abroad on a mission of world peace, he was never criticized back home by members of the other party because politics stopped at the water's edge," he said. "I think we understand today intuitively that education holds the key to our future in the twenty-first century. And I believe politics must stop at the schoolhouse door."[63] If the No Child Left Behind program is any indication, it appears Clinton's drive to establish national, bipartisan education goals has been mostly successful.

Immigration

How do we begin to understand immigration? I thought of my late father, Robert Godwin, who emigrated from England after serving a brief stint with the British Army in Palestine. In 1948, twenty-two-year-old Robert sailed from Southampton on the *Marine Tiger*, a troop transport ship built in 1945 at the Kaiser

Vancouver Shipyard and converted to accommodate 850 tourist-class passengers, chartered to the United States Lines. He arrived in New York just like millions of other immigrants from Europe who crossed the Atlantic as steamship passengers. For many of those, the Statue of Liberty was their first glimpse of the New World and Ellis Island their first stop. Since 1886, Liberty has stood vigil in New York Harbor, and from 1892 to 1954, Ellis Island was the country's main immigration station.

According to my research, the term *boat people* first entered the presidential lexicon during the Carter administration.[64] The term refers to refugees from Southeast Asia, Cuba, and Haiti—anyone who has to cross a body of water or risk his or her life to find refuge in America. The original boat people were the Polynesians who sailed double-hulled canoes from the Marquesas or Society Islands to the Hawaiian Islands, the northern apex of the Polynesian triangle and the most remote island chain in the world. Navigating without instruments, Polynesian explorers crossed thousands of miles of open ocean and colonized the previously uninhabited Hawaiian Islands hundreds of years before British sailors led by James Cook discovered them (meaning charted their geographic coordinates) in 1778. I guess the first *European* boat people were the Pilgrims, fleeing religious persecution in England, who sailed over on the *Mayflower* and founded Plymouth Colony in 1620. The first African boat people made the long Atlantic voyage as cargo, in miserable, unsanitary, horrifying conditions. Over a span of almost four hundred years, until the end of the Civil War in 1865, traders captured millions of African slaves and shipped them to the United States and other locations in the New World.

When we listen to our political leaders talk about the principles of the founding fathers, we should remember not to take them literally. We should recall that during the Constitutional Convention in 1787, the founding fathers agreed to a compromise, which postponed banning the international slave trade. According to Article I, Section 9, "The migration or importation of such persons as any of the states now existing shall think proper to admit, shall not be prohibited by the Congress prior to the year 1808." This compromise took away the U.S. Government's power to outlaw the international slave trade for twenty years. Thomas Jefferson eventually signed a bill outlawing the international slave trade in 1807, which took effect on the earliest date constitutionally possible: January 1, 1808. In 1820, Congress enacted a law that made buying and selling slaves internationally an act of piracy that carried the death penalty, but even that did not put a stop to the inhuman practice for many years.

I was never able to decide whether the term *boat people* was condescending or whether it epitomized a very special kind of American immigrant, the kind George Bush the elder called "liberty-loving risk takers in search of an ideal."[65] That is, until I stumbled across a story Reagan retold in his legendary Farewell Address. As Reagan said, it is a short story about a big ship, a refugee, and a sailor:

> It was back in the early eighties, at the height of the boat people. And the sailor was hard at work on the carrier Midway, which was patrolling the South China Sea. The sailor, like most American servicemen, was young, smart, and fiercely observant. The crew spied on the horizon a leaky little boat. And crammed inside were refugees from Indochina hoping to get to America. The Midway sent a small launch to bring them to the ship and safety. As the refugees made their way through the choppy seas, one spied the sailor on deck, and stood up, and called out to him. He yelled, "Hello, American sailor. Hello, freedom man."[66]

Perhaps the most famous of all the boat people was six-year-old Elian Gonzalez. In November 1999, Elian and his mother fled Cuba in a small boat, but Elian's mother and almost everyone else on board died during the crossing. Elian and the other survivors made it as far as the Florida Straits, where the U.S. Coast Guard took charge. They in turn handed Elian over to members of his extended family in Miami. Some local Cuban-American activists and family members demanded Elian stay in the United States, contrary to the wishes of his father, Juan Miguel Gonzalez, back in Cuba. After several months of intense media coverage, Attorney General Janet Reno enforced a federal court order affirming Juan Miguel Gonzalez had legal custody of his child. In April 2000, Elian and his father were reunited, and in June, father and son returned together to Cuba. When we say there is a blurry line between foreign and domestic policy, particularly immigration policy, the Elian Gonzalez story exemplifies why.

By the time Clinton came into office, the ink was hardly dry on the immigration reforms Reagan and then Bush implemented. The Immigration Reform Act of 1986, which Reagan signed, and the Immigration Act of 1990, which Bush signed, were the most comprehensive reforms of immigration policy in many decades. The 1990 legislation was, as Bush said, an effort to open the front door on legal immigration and close the back door on illegal immigration. Then as now, however, the federal government lacked the means (or will) to enforce good laws already on the books. At that time, enforcement had more to do with securing our borders against drug traffickers than terrorists. The approach then is reminiscent of the war on drugs, which presumed any drug policy that focused exclusively on domestic drug use (demand) but not drug trafficking (supply) would fail. Likewise, the approach presumed any immigration policy that focused exclusively on border control (supply) but not the motivation for illegal immigration (demand) would also fail.

Clinton made exactly the same argument to promote the North American Free Trade Agreement (NAFTA). One of NAFTA's alleged benefits was that it would create jobs south of the border, so the United States would not be the only place where there were economic opportunities. As the benefits of economic growth spread to working people in Mexico, said Clinton, "They'll have more disposable income to buy more American products, and there will be less illegal immigration because more Mexicans will be able to support their children by staying home." Perhaps the biggest disappointment of NAFTA is that it failed to stem the tide of illegal immigration between Mexico and the United States. Despite that, immigration—through the front door—remains one of our fundamental principles and a policy issue integral to our ability to grow the economy, create jobs, and safeguard national security.

Despite all our technological advances and educational achievements, Clinton worried the epidemic of illegal immigration in places such as California would lead to an epidemic of hostility toward all kinds of diversity. Why is this? It goes back tens of thousands of years to prehistoric times, to when people split into tribes based on facial features and skin pigmentation. Our biggest problem is also our oldest problem, which is the tendency to fear and dehumanize people different from ourselves. When you are afraid of somebody, it is a short step to disliking them, and if you dislike them, it is a short step to hating them, then another short step to dehumanizing them, and then a final step to killing them.[67] Look at the world, said Clinton:

> Look at the world. Look at how the world is convulsed by the—how children, innocent children are still being killed on the brink of the twenty-first century because of tribal, ethnic, racial, and religious differences around the world. Consider the Holy Land, the home of the three

great religions of the world who all believe we are all created in the image of one God, our Creator, our Judge. How shall He judge us for keeping on killing each other into the twenty-first century because we're different from somebody else?[68]

As the country moves from a national economy to a global economy—and to a global society dominated by technology—we cannot afford to ignore our racial, regional, gender, and income differences. Nor can we afford to ignore what a tremendous advantage it is to have kids in our schools from every country, culture, and religious faith on earth. Clinton said diversity was "our meal ticket to the future."[69] He considered it a godsend economically, politically, and in terms of our quality of life—but only if we never take it for granted. Clinton understood ethnic diversity was an asset in the global economy and urged Americans whose ancestors immigrated long ago not to lock the door behind them. New immigrants had a responsibility to obey the law and learn our language, history, and culture and a responsibility to work and contribute to the country. For the rest of us, we had a responsibility to welcome new immigrants and to overcome our anxieties, ignorance, and personal insecurities. Said Clinton:

> Americans whose parents were denied the rights of citizenship simply because of the color of their skin must not deny those rights to others because of the country of their birth or the nature of their faith. We should treat new immigrants as we would have wanted our own grandparents to be treated. We should share our country with them, not shun them or shut them out.[70]

The best summary of Clinton's approach is *we are a nation of immigrants and we are a nation of laws.* "Let me be clear," said Clinton. "I also think it's wrong to condone illegal immigration that flouts our laws, strains our tolerance, taxes our resources. Even a nation of immigrants must have rules and conditions and limits, and when they are disregarded, public support for immigration erodes in ways that are destructive to those who are newly arrived and those who are still waiting patiently to come."[71] Each new generation of immigrants gives a new target to old prejudices, no matter how well concealed it is by the language of religious belief or political conviction. Racial prejudice is an old affliction, one that nearly destroyed our country in the mid-nineteenth century, and continues to tear other nations apart well into the twenty-first century.

Trade

NAFTA was Clinton's first big test on international trade. In August 1990, less than a year after the fall of the Berlin Wall, Carlos Salinas, president of Mexico, sent a letter to George Bush proposing negotiations on a free trade agreement. The following month, American and Mexican government officials held a meeting to explore the possibility. Early the following year, Bush announced to Tom Foley (then speaker of the House of Representatives) that Bush, Salinas, and Brian Mulroney of Canada had entered into trade negotiations, which was a necessary step for the president to obtain "fast-track" negotiating authority. While the Constitution gives the president power to conduct foreign diplomacy, it vests in Congress the power to conduct foreign commerce. Fast-track authority allows the president to negotiate a commercial treaty and present it to Congress as a package, which Congress must accept or reject as is without alteration or extraneous amendments.

In August 1992, negotiators from the United States, Canada,

and Mexico reached an accord. In November, after some intense debate, Congress voted to pass the trade agreement. On New Year's Day 1994, NAFTA became law. The official purpose of NAFTA is to stimulate economic growth; create jobs; increase incomes; promote competition; increase investment; and enforce intellectual property rights, patents, copyrights, trademarks, and other proprietary materials. The agreement recognized most-favored-nation status for each member, lowering and then gradually eliminating tariffs for most products. The agreement restricted foreign ownership of Mexican oil reserves and foreign ownership of financial services and insurance companies. There was an environmental side agreement, which established a commission to arbitrate environmental disputes, and another establishing rules for child labor, minimum wage, work hours, and standards for worker health and safety. Finally, the agreement also established dispute resolution procedures through consultation, review by a trilateral trade commission, or arbitration by a panel of trade experts. Although trade has increased significantly since passage of NAFTA, and it remains the world's largest trading bloc, it has not fulfilled all of its stated objectives.

During an event to generate support for NAFTA, Clinton provided numerous reasons why lower trade barriers would create jobs and be good for the economy. Clinton said it would give more security to American investors in Mexico; it would give American companies better access to the Mexican market and give Mexican companies freer access to the enormous buying power of American consumers. In response to critics who said NAFTA would increase unemployment by inducing American companies to relocate, Clinton predicted it would create jobs that would pay better than those not involved in international trade.

The basic premise of Clinton's support for NAFTA, and free trade in general, is that the only way for a wealthy country to grow wealthier is to increase the number of customers beyond its borders. If this premise is true, then it is true for every wealthy country. America would be sending the wrong message if it rejected free trade with Mexico and Canada. Clinton acknowledged there were legitimate objections to NAFTA, especially among workers who exerted little control over their jobs and lives. The challenge, he said, was to keep Americans looking outward, committed to free trade and open markets. At the same time, we owed working people something. If not job security, we owed them the opportunity to acquire marketable skills, to be employable, and to have access to basic healthcare for themselves and their families.

The psychological aspect of the debate over NAFTA fascinated Clinton. Although he saw NAFTA as a real test for the country, he acknowledged the debate acquired a symbolic significance out of proportion to NAFTA's relatively narrow economic impact. In the anti-NAFTA arguments, he saw mostly irrational fears driven by isolationist tendencies rather than legitimate grievances. Despite priding himself on being "a fairly good reader of the political tea leaves," he found it difficult to understand why there was so much opposition to free trade, why NAFTA in particular was the flypaper catching all the emotion. He thought it was too simplistic to suggest all the resistance was the result of the labor movement or Ross Perot's opposition. The strength of the opposition was perhaps symptomatic of the deep ambivalence Americans felt about the future. According to Clinton, NAFTA became "the receptacle of their resentment" and a vessel "for the accumulated resentments of the past, the anxieties about the future and the frustrations of the present."

As the date for the vote to ratify NAFTA approached, he sought to elevate the level of debate. The American people, he said, would decide the issue based on their personal interests, but members of Congress needed to realize what was at stake for the country. In other words, rejecting NAFTA would be unstatesmanlike. It would send the message that America intended to retreat into isolation rather than go charging into the twenty-first century. To make his point, Clinton rounded up every statesman and stateswoman he could find, including every living former president; secretary of state, defense, and commerce; and national security advisor to garner their support for NAFTA. Whatever political disagreements divided them in the past, now it was time for leadership that transcended partisan politics. He jokingly pulled out a phony "extraterrestrial" telegram from Otto von Bismarck, the Prussian statesman and first Chancellor of the German Empire, declaring, "I, too, am for NAFTA."

Clinton presented the rationale for NAFTA within the larger context of his economic goals: creating more jobs and higher growth rates, lowering the deficit, and keeping interest rates and inflation down. NAFTA could lead to new partnerships, he said, with any number of other countries in the region. He said NAFTA was a building block within a much larger framework in Latin America, perhaps someday resulting in a Free Trade Area of the Americas. Passing NAFTA would set a new precedent and inevitably lead to other trade agreements, which would create a hemisphere-wide trading bloc with more than seven hundred million consumers.

Clinton *did not* suggest the benefits of free trade would solve all our problems. He believed industrialized and developing nations alike needed to strengthen financial regulation and bank supervision and pay attention to social safety nets.[72] Incomes and employment rates were still too low in many wealthy countries, even though their economies were growing. Many nations with high per capita incomes, not just poor countries, were struggling to keep up with the forces of globalization. The United States' economic infrastructure was inadequate for the sweeping economic changes taking place around the world. Regarding entitlements, people who worked hard and played by the rules were perhaps unaware the rules had changed, because ultimately opportunity is the best entitlement Clintonomics has to offer.

At the bill-signing ceremony in December 1993, Clinton predicted NAFTA would help create a new economic order in the world that would promote growth and equality, help preserve the environment, and contribute to world peace. Overestimating the significance of NAFTA, but careful to soothe one of his core constituencies, Clinton said the side agreement on labor would make NAFTA "a force for social progress" and protect the rights of workers to organize. Ultimately, he touted NAFTA as a symbol of America's leadership. In Clinton's words:

> Today, we have the chance to do what our parents did before us. We have the opportunity to remake the world. For this new era, our national security we now know will be determined as much by our ability to pull down foreign trade barriers as by our ability to breach distant ramparts. Once again, we are leading. And in so doing, we are rediscovering a fundamental truth about ourselves. When we lead, we build security; we build prosperity for our own people.[73]

Clinton promoted NAFTA as one part of a "national export strategy." He also pitched it as an economic development agreement and predicted—wrongly, as it turned out—that it would check illegal immigration from Mexico.[74] David Gergen, who served in the White House under four presidents, including both Clinton and Reagan, says even though Clinton oversold the benefits, his successful fight on behalf of NAFTA disproved critics who claimed he had no backbone, principles, or core beliefs.[75] In retrospect, the economic arguments for and against NAFTA were overstated. As of this writing, the size of the Mexican economy remains a fraction of the American economy. As long as this continues to be the case, the huge disproportion will moderate the economic effects of NAFTA and mitigate the advantages and disadvantages.

What was Reagan's position on international trade? We need only return to the Great Depression—the inexhaustible source for so much of Reagan's governing philosophy—for an answer. In 1930, Herbert Hoover signed into law the Smoot-Hawley Tariff Act, legislation that significantly raised American tariffs on thousands of imported goods. Reed Smoot was a Republican senator from Utah, and Willis Hawley was a Republican member of Congress from Oregon. Hoover signed the bill, denounced Roosevelt's opposition to it, defended it while he was running for reelection, and even campaigned on behalf of Smoot's reelection in Utah. Coming so soon after the stock market crash of 1929, the Smoot-Hawley Act triggered a trade war, which in turn expanded and extended the Depression. The new legislation provoked retaliation by major trading nations, causing American exports and imports to fall more than 50 percent. It may be the worst American economic policy in the history of the twentieth century.

Reagan mentioned Smoot-Hawley many times to explain his position in favor of free trade and his strong opposition to protectionism. Here is one of many examples:

> Well now, some of us remember the 1930s, when the most destructive trade bill in history, the Smoot-Hawley Tariff Act, helped plunge this nation and the world into a decade of depression and despair. From now on, if the ghost of Smoot-Hawley rears its ugly head in Congress, if Congress crafts a depression-making bill, I'll fight it. And whether it's tax, trade, or farm legislation that comes across my desk, my primary consideration will be whether it is in the long-run economic interest of the

United States. And any tax hike or spending bill or pro-
tectionist legislation that doesn't meet the test of whether
it advances America's prosperity must and will be opposed.[76]

In the course of my research, I was never able to find an occasion where Clinton even mentioned Smoot-Hawley. (Clinton
often said there were only two kinds of protectionism he liked.
One was consumer protection and the other was environmental
protection.) However, during the 1993 NAFTA debate on *Larry
King Live* between Vice President Al Gore and Texas billionaire
Ross Perot, Gore presented Perot with a framed picture of Smoot
and Hawley shaking hands. Perot made his opposition to NAFTA
a major campaign issue when he ran for president the year before. He said the massive loss of American jobs going south to
Mexico would create a *giant sucking sound.* During the signing ceremony for the Uruguay Round Agreements a few months later
(the World Trade Organization [WTO] calls its negotiations
"rounds"), Clinton responded to Perot's colorful metaphor and
acknowledged Al Gore's contribution. "As usual, you did a generous and magnificent job of recognizing the contributions of all
these people who made this day possible. You did, however, leave
one very important person out. If you hadn't gone on television
in that national debate on NAFTA and refuted the theory of the
giant sucking sound—I'm not sure we would be here today."

The foundation of Clinton's confidence in NAFTA was based
on some vague economic theory. As Clinton stated it, the only
way a wealthy country could create jobs and raise incomes was
by increasing the number of its customers for goods and services.
On his way to a meeting of the Asia-Pacific Economic Cooperation (APEC) group in November 1993, Clinton said his threefold
economic strategy was simple and direct: Put the United States'
economic house in order, enable the American people to com-

pete and win in the global economy, and find more markets for our products and services. "As the world becomes smaller, the ties between Asia and the United States—the political ties, the family ties, the trade ties, the security ties—they will only become stronger."

Though the United States runs large bilateral trade deficits with several countries (particularly China, Japan, Germany, and several oil-producing countries), it is still a leading exporter. NAFTA, the GATT (General Agreement on Tariffs and Trade) negotiations, and the APEC meetings are all part of an ongoing and mostly bipartisan effort to increase exports and make the American economy more competitive. Here is a nice turn of phrase from Clinton's speech at the 2000 World Economic Forum (in Davos, Switzerland), so well written it makes international trade almost poetic: "Trade broadens the frontiers of possibility for all of those who have access to its benefits and the tools to claim them." Open markets are more competitive. Competition keeps prices down and thus decreases the risk of inflation. In the global society of the twenty-first century, governments cannot guarantee outcomes for everyone. However, they can create the right conditions—by investing in cities, investing in education and research, reforming the way the government delivers services, and reducing the size of government—and thus increase the odds of success in the global economy.

The end of the Cold War presented an opportunity "to create a new Pacific community." Mutual security would always be the most fundamental issue in the community, but Clinton believed lowering barriers to free trade would reduce regional tensions. Clinton said his effort to bring China into the WTO was a good example of his "constructive engagement" strategy, which relied on economic integration as a way to spread democracy and promote human rights. He argued China's membership in the WTO would promote competition in China's capital markets and strengthen the private sector at the expense of the communist-controlled national government. Beyond the obvious economic benefits, he hoped and believed putting trade relations on a permanent footing would strengthen the rule of law and foster positive change across Chinese society.

What is the best way for us to encourage China to take the right course? Though China remains a one-party state and restricts many of the rights Americans take for granted, what is the best way to make the world more peaceful and more prosperous? "I do not believe we can hope to bring change to China if we isolate China from the forces of change. Of course, we have our differences, and we must press them," Clinton said. "But we can do that and expand our cooperation through principled and purposeful engagement with China, its government, and its people."[77]

Along with NAFTA and APEC, Clinton predicted the next round of GATT talks would help create hundreds of thousands of jobs in the United States and millions worldwide. Beyond GATT, Clinton said there were some problems he needed to take up with our European friends. Clinton said we could learn a lot from Europe, particularly about its workforce training and retraining programs. The Europeans had a lot to learn from us too, such as how to create a flexible and mobile workforce and an entrepreneurial environment, which might help lower their chronic unemployment problems. Clinton said economic development was impractical without private investment and urged people to take a good look at emerging markets in Central and Eastern Europe. The new Partnership for Peace (see below) would create important political and military ties, but economic development and economic integration would determine the future of Europe.

In January 1994, shortly after NAFTA went into effect, the North Atlantic Treaty Organization (NATO) adopted the Partnership for Peace, an outreach project for several European countries in Central and Eastern Europe, which paved the way for their full membership to NATO. At a meeting with business leaders in Brussels, Clinton noted all the new partners were former members of the Soviet bloc, and some had even been part of the Soviet Union itself.[78] In 2004, several members of the partnership would become members of the European Union (Estonia, Czech Republic, Hungary, Latvia, Lithuania, Poland, Slovakia, and Slovenia), and two more (Romania and Bulgaria) in 2007.

These developments were hardly imaginable in 1987, when Reagan made his famous speech at the Brandenburg Gate in West Berlin and politely suggested that Mikhail Gorbachev tear down the Berlin Wall. It should remind us not to overlook the psychological aspects of globalization as we debate the political and economic aspects of international trade. It should remind us change is unsettling. In times of profound change like the tumultuous years following the Cold War, people not only lost their balance, but their sense of direction, too. Clinton said it was as if you woke up every day and checked the scale inside your body. One side of the scale measured hope, and the other side measured fear, and every day the scales were different, always a little out of balance.

At the 1999 WTO Ministerial Conference in Seattle, Clinton spoke at a luncheon as tens of thousands of people—some of them violent—protested in the streets outside the Seattle Convention Center. Said Clinton:

> Some of them, I think, have a short memory—or maybe no memory—of what life was like in most of your countries not so very long ago. So let me say again, I condemn the small number who were violent, and who tried to prevent you from meeting. But I'm glad the others showed up, because they represent millions of people who are now asking questions about whether this enter-

prise in fact will take us all where we want to go. And we ought to welcome their questions, and be prepared to give an answer, because if we cannot create an inter-connected global economy that is increasing prosperity and genuine opportunity for people everywhere, then all of our political initiatives are going to be less successful.[79]

Less than charitable critics might suggest Clinton was splitting the difference, as was his custom. His thesis—if our economic policies do not increase prosperity and opportunity, then our po-litical objectives will fail—is quintessential Clinton. Meanwhile, thousands of protesters outside rallied and marched and eventu-ally overwhelmed the police. The protests were large, disruptive, and completely unexpected. The extent of the property destruc-tion and vandalism makes it impossible to dismiss the anti-globalization movement in industrialized or developing coun-tries. Subsequent rounds of trade negotiations took place in Doha, Qatar, on schedule and without incident. When it comes to the theory of constraints, however, the Battle of Seattle ex-plains why managing international trade belongs at or near the top of the list.

Defense

Here is a fascinating excerpt from the 2000 Republican Party plat-form:

Republicans endorse the four principles of U.S. counter-terrorism policy that were laid down originally by Vice President George Bush's Commission on Combating Ter-rorism in 1985. First, we will make no concessions to terrorists. Giving in simply encourages future terrorist

actions and debases America's power and moral authority. Second, we will isolate, pressure, and punish the state
sponsors of terrorism. Third, we will bring individual terrorists to justice. Past and potential terrorists will know
that America will never stop hunting them. Fourth, we
will provide assistance to other governments combating
terrorism. Fighting international terrorism requires international collaboration. Once again, allies matter.[80]

The Republican platform refers to a task force on combating
terrorism that Ronald Reagan announced in June 1985, in response to a terrorist attack in El Salvador that killed several off-
duty marines and American business executives. Reagan also announced Vice President George Bush would chair the task force
and develop recommendations for combating terrorism.[81] In February 1986, the task force issued its public report. As Vice President Bush noted in the cover letter, terrorism is a dangerous
threat "for which there is no quick or easy solution." Admittedly,
the task force report is more than twenty years old. However, the
Republicans reendorsed it in July 2000, a little over one year before the 9/11 attacks. The recommendations epitomize the law
enforcement approach to combating terrorism prevalent at the
time, analogous to the way we fight organized crime or big drug
cartels. Also noteworthy is the complete absence of any ideological bias, conservative or otherwise.

The report gives terrorism a curious definition: "Terrorism is
political theater designed to undermine or alter governmental authority or behavior." The report notes terrorists take advantage
of our free press, as they machine-gun their way through airports,
bomb our embassies and military facilities, and hijack planes and
ships as if performing for a global audience. "These international
criminals have seized not only innocent victims but also the at-

tention of viewers who sit helplessly before televisions around the world."[82]

The report lists four principles of counterterrorism policy, including recommendations for national policy, international cooperation, intelligence, and legislative action. Although some of the task force's recommendations remain classified, the report includes public recommendations such as establishing guidelines to decide "when, if and how to use force to preempt, react and retaliate." It recommends creating a full-time antiterrorism position on the National Security Council, increasing international cooperation (particularly the exchange of intelligence), closing extradition loopholes, and strengthening port and airport security. Finally, the report issues several legislative recommendations, such as making murder of American citizens outside the country a federal crime, establishing the death penalty for terrorists, outlawing terrorist organizations, and prohibiting terrorist (or mercenary) training camps, among other items.

During the 2000 presidential campaign, the subject of national security came up in the debates between Al Gore and George W. Bush. In response to the moderator's question of how, as president, Bush would decide when it was in the national interest to use military force, Bush first defined our vital national interest to mean whether our people, territory, or allies, particularly our allies in the Middle East, were under threat. Then Bush specified the mission must be clear; our forces must be well equipped, well trained, and prepared to win; and finally, we must have an exit strategy. The future president went on to highlight a point of disagreement between himself and Gore. "He believes in nation building," said Bush. "I would be very careful about using our troops as nation builders. I believe the role of the military is to fight and win war [sic] and therefore prevent war from happening in the first place."[83]

The first part of Bush's response is a restatement of the Weinberger Doctrine, courtesy of Caspar Weinberger, Reagan's defense secretary from 1981 to 1987. The Weinberger Doctrine is a useful template to decide when to use combat forces abroad. The doctrine is not for cases of self-defense when America is under direct attack. It is discretionary, for those cases in the gray area between the extremes of aggressive and defensive use of force.

- We should not commit combat forces unless it is vital to our (or our allies') national interest.
- If we commit combat forces, we must do so without reservation, with the clear intention of winning.
- If we commit forces, we must define our political and military objectives clearly.
- We must continuously assess and reassess the composition and disposition of our forces, and adjust them as conditions change.
- Before we commit combat forces overseas, we should have the support of the American people and their elected representatives.
- Finally, we should commit U.S. forces only as a last resort.[84]

The idea is to maintain an effective military deterrent, respond to the situation appropriately, and avoid another Vietnam. (Weinberger might also use this template to avoid another Iraq, but I would hesitate to put words in his mouth.) The doctrine recognizes the mutual interdependence of the international system and acknowledges our enemies will take advantage of our open society. If our enemies divide our national will at home, Weinberger said, they would not have to defeat our forces abroad, a useful reminder in our present circumstances. The Weinberger Doctrine is one element of Reagan's governing philosophy not rendered obsolete by changes in the global system since the Cold War ended.

While Clinton was in office—meaning after the disintegration of the Soviet Union and before 9/11—terrorism belonged to the same "growing web of threats" as drug trafficking, organized crime, and proliferation of weapons of mass destruction. During the interwar years, the government's top priorities were securing stockpiles of nuclear weapons, strengthening control over transfer of weapons technologies, and preserving the Middle East peace process. In the global era, terrorism is part of the chaos we have to deter and contain, but that does not make it any easier to gauge the extent to which terrorism acts as a constraint on the system. Other than the immediate loss of life and the theatrical or psychological aspect, it is unclear how much terrorism undermines or alters governmental authority or behavior. That is, unless we overact and give the terrorists exactly what they want: the attention of a large television audience.

The Weinberger Doctrine has lost none of its utility as a template to guide decision makers in the post–Cold War, post-9/11 era if decision makers would only abide by it. American history is replete with doctrines, and it falls on presidents to execute policies that uphold, overturn, or redefine precedents set by their predecessors. In George Washington's 1796 Farewell Address, he laid the foundation for his successors when he recommended, whenever possible, to avoid foreign entanglements, avoid making permanent allies as well as permanent enemies, and always establish foreign relations on mutually beneficial commercial relationships.

In 1823, James Monroe (with the advice of his able secretary of state John Quincy Adams) declared the Western Hemisphere off limits to future European colonization and thus established the geographic boundaries of the American sphere of influence. By 1901, the United States was a major naval power, and Theodore Roosevelt revised and expanded the Monroe Doctrine such that America's sphere of influence included the whole world. In 1918, near the end of WWI, Woodrow Wilson proposed reforming the international system based on the universal principle of self-determination, meaning the right of all people to self-government without external interference.

Beginning in 1945, Harry Truman set several precedents. The first was his order to attack the Japanese cities of Hiroshima and Nagasaki with atomic weapons. Following World War II, the Truman administration created the national security framework that eventually won the Cold War. This included the European Recovery Program (or Marshall Plan) to rebuild Europe's political and economic infrastructure devastated by the war. During Truman's eventful presidency, the creation of the Central Intelligence Agency, Department of Defense, Joint Chiefs of Staff, National Security Council, and North Atlantic Treaty Organization also took place.

In 2002, George W. Bush set the precedent for preemptive action, which declares the United States may lawfully defend itself whether or not enemy forces are openly mobilizing or preparing for an attack. (Bush established this, in theory, with the September 2002 National Security Strategy and then established it in practice with the March 2003 invasion of Iraq.) Preemptive action is part of the Bush Doctrine, which essentially makes no distinction between terrorist organizations and those countries that harbor or sponsor them. The link between terrorism and high technology has created new threats, which make it possible for rogue states and terrorist networks to attack America's civilian population with weapons of mass destruction without warning. Because of the difficulty of defending against such attacks, the United States may now lawfully take preemptive action whether or not a threat is imminent.

Regardless of any future assessment of George W. Bush's presidency or his leadership and management of the Iraq War, pre-emptive action sets an important precedent. Bush likes to compare himself to Harry Truman and compare the war on terror to the Cold War.[85] In this instance, the comparison is appropriate. Truman was the first and only president or chief executive of any country to launch a nuclear attack. As a national security strat-egy, nuclear deterrence threatens massive retaliation in response to an attack. The threat forces potential aggressors to weigh prob-able gains against the risk of total destruction. While none of Truman's successors launched a nuclear attack, none of them ever took nuclear warfare off the table. Accordingly, now that Bush has put preemptive action on the table, his successors should never take it off the table, either.

Before we turn the page, do you remember "the Rumble in the Jungle"? It was a classic boxing match in 1974 between George Foreman and Muhammad Ali that took place in Kinshasa, Zaire (now the Democratic Republic of Congo). In that match, Ali exe-cuted the "rope-a-dope" strategy, meaning he took a defensive position against the ropes and allowed Foreman to punch him, which Foreman did mercilessly. The more Ali taunted him, the harder Foreman punched. Fortunately, Ali could take a punch, and Foreman began to tire after a few rounds in the stifling heat. Ali knocked him out in the eighth.

The rope-a-dope strategy highlights a few principles of politi-cal economy, which may come in handy. Remember, the objec-tive of public policy (including defense policy) is to produce the maximum positive outcome while optimizing the allocation of scarce resources and minimizing waste. Power is a decisive factor only in short conflicts. This means the longer a conflict lasts, the more important endurance becomes. It is important, therefore, not to underestimate our adversary's endurance and not to over-estimate our own power. It is important to know when it is in our best interest to engage in a prolonged conflict and when it is not. When we have an absolute advantage of power, it is imperative to incapacitate our adversary as quickly as possible using as little force as possible. Otherwise, we should conserve energy, encourage our adversaries to dissipate theirs, and bide our time.

CHAPTER 9

Bridge to the Future

When I met Hillary in 1971, we started a conversation about this stuff that was going on at 1:30 a.m. last night, twenty-eight years later. . . . I said, you know, I hope you're not tired of this after all these years. She said, no, it's very interesting to me. She said, you may be a lot of things, but you're not boring.[1]

—BILL CLINTON, 1999

IN GEORGE W. BUSH'S 2005 inaugural address, he said, "After the shipwreck of communism came years of relative quiet, years of repose, years of sabbatical, and then there came a day of fire."[2] Reading this excerpt now, the phrase "years of sabbatical" is conspicuous. The word *sabbatical* has etymological roots in Hebrew and Greek, which gives it a double meaning. The sabbatical is the seventh day of the week: Friday for Muslims, Saturday for Jews, and Sunday for Christians. In Mosaic Law, farmers leave their fields and vineyards fallow every seventh year. In institutions of higher education, professors take a sabbatical to study or travel

248

typically every seven years. Bush seems to equate sabbatical with *hiatus*, which means a gap or interruption of something that should be continuous. According to the Bush narrative, the hiatus began December 3, 1989—the last day of the Cold War—and ended September 11, 2001, the day of fire.

When the Cold War ended, the world exited one era and entered another. To suggest that era ended in September 2001 indicates a severe case of tunnel vision—not merely the lack of peripheral vision, but a failure to recognize that globalization, not terrorism or any specific act of terrorism, is the central reality of our time. Globalization is a political phenomenon capable of sustaining numerous and distinctive cultures, subcultures, and countercultures with an almost infinite range of preferences, values, and norms—including perverse forms of fundamentalism and ostentatious displays of violence. It is an economic phenomenon that multiplies trade and communication across borders and every continent. It is a spatial and temporal phenomenon driven by advances in transportation and communication technology that reduces the constraints of geography.

The design Clinton chose for his presidential library—a metal and glass cantilever bridge that floats above the south bank of the Arkansas River—symbolizes his presidency, which coincided not just with the end of the Cold War but also the beginning of a new millennium. He began using the bridge metaphor in his speeches in spring 1996 and then introduced it to a national audience for the first time at the 1996 Democratic National Convention. "We have to build a bridge to the twenty-first century that enables every person in this country, every family, every community to make the most of their God-given potential. We have to build that bridge to the future strong and wide enough for all of us to walk across." The bridge metaphor is simple enough to appeal to a diverse constituency while offering guidance about the past (water under the bridge), the present (bridge over troubled water), or the future (we will cross that bridge when we come to it), but not burning bridges—or venturing past the point of no return.[3]

Although the world exited one era and entered another, Clinton's metaphorical bridge keeps us connected to the past and the future. If there is one idea that should convince us to keep moving forward, it is future preference, the belief that the future can be better than the past and that each of us has a personal responsibility to plan for it, work for it, and make it so. We cannot make it so without the social contract, based on both Rousseau's contract between fellow citizens and Clinton's New Covenant between citizens and their government. People must cede some of their natural rights to the government so it has the power it needs to function. Dostoyevsky wrestled with this fundamental issue in his fictional account of the Grand Inquisition, though all he could do was estimate the level of security most people needed.

As we know, Alexander Hamilton, James Madison, and John Jay did not agree on everything, but they did agree that no government would be necessary if only angels were to govern us. According to the founders, the greatest problem with self-government is enabling the government to control the governed and then expecting the government to control itself. Without these two functions of the social contract, there is no freedom and there is no security; there are no civil rights, no property rights, and no reasonable expectation the future will be better than the past. Thus, explicit legal guarantees of freedom of speech, press, and religion; the right to self-defense; protection against unlawful search and seizure; the right to a speedy trial and a trial by jury; and protection against cruel or unusual punishment are indispensable, particularly in the global era.

The idea that people must cede some of their rights to the government deserves more attention. Along with national security, the federal government's primary responsibilities are to protect individuals and their property and build a public infrastructure to facilitate commerce, education, and other basic services. Performing these functions requires the power to levy taxes, a strong (but not too strong) central government, and an energetic executive branch. According to the founders, money is the vital element of the body politic. Without money, the government cannot perform its primary functions and inevitably loses respect at home and abroad.

Governance in the global era requires the right tools to produce the maximum positive outcome while optimizing allocation of scarce resources and minimizing waste. This requires expanding political economy beyond the social sciences and drawing ideas from complexity and management with practical applications in the new era. The premise of the theory of constraints is that every organization and every system has one or more factors that constrain the organization's capacity to produce the maximum positive outcome.

Our first step is to ascertain the goal, because we must know the destination before we go in any direction. The second step is to identify the internal and external factors, which can be more difficult than it seems. Most internal constraints are the result of our own flawed strategy, and many external constraints are intrinsic obstacles on the path we have chosen. Either way, identifying the factors that limit performance is largely a process of introspection. The third step is to rank the constraints in terms of their disservice to our goal. The fourth step is to manage as many constraints at the top of the list as resources will allow and watch for new constraints moving up the list as older constraints respond to managerial intervention.

In the global era, there are many constraining factors requiring intervention, but two deserve special reference here: education and national defense. Clinton's concise definition of education (what we know and what we can learn) reminded me of Harold Lasswell's definition of politics—who gets what, when, and how—so I created my own mash-up the way people integrate music from different tracks to create an entirely new track. Here's what I came up with: *What we know and what we can learn determines who gets what, when, and how.* This means there is a positive correlation between education and income, or, in nonpolicy-wonk terms, the more you learn the more you earn.

This summarizes the economic rationale for education, as if our only goal was to plug people into the economy, so they could sell their services in the labor market. This economic rationale reflects an economic bias, which may or may not be an accurate representation of human nature. As we know from Chapter 2, Karl Marx had a fundamentally different understanding of human nature than several of his predecessors, particularly John Locke and Adam Smith. Marx questioned whether labor was simply a commodity to be bought and sold, and he believed the pursuit of self-interest was a response to our capitalist economic system and not necessarily innate. This is a valid point, consistent with the findings of the National Commission on Excellence in Education and its 1983 report "A Nation at Risk," which said the goal of our educational reform efforts should be to create a "learning society," because education should increase your standard of living as well as your quality of life.

The other constraining factor worthy of an additional reference is national defense. In the global era, there is still no better template for deciding when to use combat forces abroad than the Weinberger Doctrine. We should not commit combat forces unless it is in our vital national interest to do so. Before we commit forces abroad, we should clearly define our political and military objectives and make sure we have the support of the American people. When we commit combat forces abroad, we should do so without reservation, with the clear intention of winning. Finally, we should commit U.S. forces abroad only as a last resort—and leave all our options on the table.

ACCORDING TO DAVID GERGEN, presidents must be able to say in a single sentence—or two at the most—what their presidencies are all about. Lincoln's purpose, for example, was to save the Union. FDR's was to end the Great Depression and later win WWII. Reagan's was "to reduce taxes, reduce spending, cut regulations, reduce the deficit, and increase the defense budget." Clinton on the other hand, according to Gergen, never articulated a central, compelling purpose for his presidency.[4] Although I would not suggest Clinton used good judgment in every case or always demonstrated responsible and effective leadership, I respectfully disagree with Gergen on this particular issue and think *Clintonomics* disproves his assessment.

In 1991, a year before his first presidential campaign, Clinton outlined his political philosophy in a three-part lecture series at Georgetown University. Throughout his presidency, as we have seen, Clinton articulated core values that clearly drew inspiration from the founders and other political figures he admired. He articulated a governing philosophy whose overarching agenda was to privatize the economy; support international trade and investment; limit government intervention in the labor market; reform the welfare system; and, of course, balance the budget and cut the deficit. His cornerstone ideals: (1) equal opportunity for all and special privilege for none; (2) mutual responsibility, meaning rejection of the politics of entitlement and the politics of social abandonment; and (3) encouraging citizens and communities to play an active role in public life. His central faith: Free market policies will promote shared economic growth across society in a way neither arbitrary nor inequitable.

One could argue, as conservative columnist Charles Krauthammer has argued, that Clinton's presidency was not historically consequential because he never faced a great crisis. "What is the legacy of the Clinton presidency?" Krauthammer asked. "Consolidator of the Reagan Revolution."[5] However, if you reject the false premise that the years following the Cold War but before 9/11 were some kind of holiday from history, there is a more plausible conclusion: Clinton succeeded where Reagan failed by transcending the simplistic debate between liberals who want to expand government and conservatives who want to starve it to death. No doubt, some of Reagan's admirers will disagree. No disrespect intended.

Back in 1980, when Reagan accepted the Republican Party's nomination, he said more than anything he hoped his presidency would unify the country. He invited all Americans, regardless of their party affiliation, to join him as he sought to redefine the role of government and regain control over the cost of government. Then he told a story about a group of families who crossed the Atlantic Ocean a long time ago and founded a new colony at Plymouth, Massachusetts. There they formed a compact—a social contract—to bind themselves together, build a community together, and voluntarily abide by its laws. That singular act almost four hundred years ago set the pattern for things to come. Isn't it time to renew the compact, he asked, isn't it time to recapture our destiny and rededicate ourselves to the unfinished work so nobly begun?[6]

Back in 1937, Franklin Roosevelt observed that as the complexity of human relationships increased, so must the power to govern those relationships increase, in equal proportion. Maintaining our political and economic systems will require "a vast amount of patience in dealing with differing methods, a vast amount of humility. But out of the confusion of many voices rises an understanding of dominant public need. Then political leadership can voice common ideals, and aid in their realization."[7] Political leadership is what Reagan and Clinton had in common. Reagan was the storyteller, the prophet who interpreted American nationality and inspired people to reach across the line that separates the practical from the ideal. Clinton was the fixer, the policy wonk who reengineered the Reagan Revolution, effectively solved problems such as welfare and the budget, and offered a coherent governing philosophy equal to the global era.

Selected Bibliography

I am indebted to the William J. Clinton Presidential Center online library archives, which is part of the presidential library system administered by the National Archives and Records Administration. I am also indebted to the American Presidency Project at the University of California, Santa Barbara, which has collected and cataloged thousands of documents pertaining to every American president. The American Presidency Project Web site also has links to presidential libraries and the national archives. The search engine at the American Presidency Project, a collaborative project with the Harry S. Truman Library, has been invaluable.

I would also like to acknowledge my debt to Richard Chadwick, my mentor at the University of Hawai'i, who first introduced me to systems thinking and gave me the idea of using the eight basic trigrams in the *Book of Change* to model change in complex systems. I have wonderful memories of the countless hours I spent in Chadwick's book-lined office learning how to think, trying to ignore the spectacular view out the window.

Books and Articles

Bailey, Kenneth D. *Sociology and the New Systems Theory: Toward a Theoretical Synthesis.* Albany: State University of New York Press, 1994.

Barber, Benjamin R. *The Truth of Power: Intellectual Affairs in the Clinton White House*. New York: Norton, 2001.

Buckley, William F. and Charles R. Kesler, eds. *Keeping the Tablets: Modern American Conservative Thought*. Revised edition of *American Conservative Thought in the Twentieth Century*. New York: Harper & Row, 1988.

Burke, Edmund. *Reflections on the Revolution in France*. New York: Liberal Arts Press, 1955.

Carey, Henry C. *The Harmony of Interests: Agricultural, Manufacturing & Commercial* (1851). New York: Augustus M. Kelley, 1967.

Champy, James. *Reengineering Management: The Mandate for New Leadership*. New York: HarperBusiness, 1995.

Cleary, Thomas. *Classics of Strategy and Counsel, Collected Translations, Vols. 1–3*. Boston: Shambhala, 2000.

Cleary, Thomas. *The Essential Confucius: The Heart of Confucius' Teachings in Authentic I Ching Order*. New York: HarperCollins, 1992.

Cleary, Thomas. *The Taoist Classics, Vol. 4: The Taoist I Ching and the I Ching Mandalas*. Boston: Shambhala, 2000.

Cleveland, Harlan. *The Future Executive: A Guide for Tomorrow's Managers*. New York: Harper & Row, 1972.

Clinton, Bill. *My Life: The Presidential Years*. New York: Vintage Books, 2004.

Deming, W. Edwards. *The New Economics, for Industry, Government, Education*. Cambridge: MIT Center for Advanced Engineering Study, 1993.

Drucker, Peter F. *The Age of Discontinuity: Guidelines to Our Changing Society*. New York: Harper & Row, 1969.

Drucker, Peter F. *The Effective Executive*. New York: Harper & Row, 1967.

Drucker, Peter F. *Managing in a Time of Great Change*. New York: Truman Talley Books/Dutton, 1995.

Friedman, Milton. *Why Government Is the Problem*. Stanford: Hoover Institution, 1993.

Friedman, Milton and Rose D. Friedman. *Free to Choose: A Personal Statement*. New York: Harcourt Brace Jovanovich, 1980.

Friedman, Milton with Rose D. Friedman. *Capitalism and Freedom*. Chicago: University of Chicago Press, 1982.

Friedman, Thomas L. *The World Is Flat: A Brief History of the Twenty-First Century*. New York: Picador/Farrar, Straus, and Giroux, 2007.

Fukuyama, Francis. *The End of History and the Last Man.* New York: Free Press, 1992.

Galbraith, John Kenneth. *The Affluent Society,* 4th ed. Boston: Houghton Mifflin, 1984.

Galbraith, John Kenneth. *The New Industrial State.* Boston: Houghton Mifflin, 1967.

Gergen, David. *Eyewitness to Power: The Essence of Leadership, Nixon to Clinton.* New York: Simon & Schuster, 2000.

Giddens, Anthony. *Beyond Left and Right: The Future of Radical Politics.* Stanford, CA: Stanford University Press, 1994.

Giddens, Anthony. *The Third Way: The Renewal of Social Democracy.* Malden, MA: Blackwell Publishers, 2000.

Goldratt, Eliyahu M. and Jeff Cox. *The Goal: A Process of Ongoing Improvement,* 2nd revised ed. Great Barrington, MA: North River Press, 1992.

Green, Joshua. "Reagan's Liberal Legacy," *Washington Monthly,* January/February 2003, http://www.washingtonmonthly.com/

Hammer, Michael. *Beyond Reengineering: How Process-Centered Organization is Changing Our Work and Our Lives.* New York: HarperBusiness, 1996.

Hammer, Michael and James Champy. *Reengineering the Corporation: A Manifesto for Business Revolution.* New York: HarperBusiness, 1993.

Hayek, F.A. *The Constitution of Liberty.* Chicago: University of Chicago Press, 1960.

Hayek, F.A. *The Fatal Conceit: The Errors of Socialism* in *Collected Works,* W.W. Bartley III, ed. Chicago: University of Chicago Press, 1988.

Huang, Alfred. *The Complete I Ching: The Definitive Translation.* Rochester, VT: Inner Traditions, 1998.

Jefferson, Thomas. Letter to John Trumbull, February 15, 1789. *Jefferson: Autobiography, Notes on the State of Virginia, Public and Private Papers, Address, Letters.* Merrill D. Peterson, ed. New York: Library of America, 1984.

Jervis, Robert. *System Effects: Complexity in Political and Social Life.* Princeton, NJ: Princeton University Press, 1997.

Keynes, John Maynard. *General Theory of Employment, Interest and Money* in *Collected Writings VII.* London: St. Martin's Press, 1973.

Kristol, Irving. *Neo-Conservatism: The Autobiography of an Idea, Selected Essays, 1949–1995*. New York: Free Press, 1995.

Kristol, Irving. *Reflection of a Neoconservative: Looking Back, Looking Forward.* New York: Basic Books, 1983.

Lasswell, Harold. *Politics: Who Gets What, When, How.* New York: Meridian Books, 1958.

Lewin, Roger. *Complexity: Life at the Edge of Chaos*, 2nd ed. Chicago: University of Chicago Press, 1999.

Limbaugh, Rush. *The Way Things Ought to Be.* New York: Simon & Schuster, 1992.

List, Friedrich. *The National System of Political Economy*, trans. by Sampson S. Lloyd. New York: Augustus M. Kelley, 1966.

Locke, John. *Two Treatises of Government: A Critical Edition,* 2nd ed., Peter Laslett, ed. Cambridge: Cambridge University Press, 1967.

Marx, Karl. *Capital: A Critique of Political Economy, Volume II: The Process of Circulation of Capital,* Frederick Engels, ed. New York: International Publishers, 1967.

Maslow, Abraham. *Toward a Psychology of Being.* Princeton, NJ: Van Nostrand, 1968.

Mill, John Stuart. *Essays on Economics and Society* in *Collected Works IV.* London, Ontario: University of Toronto Press, 1967.

Mill, John Stuart. *The Principles of Political Economy.* New York: D. Appleton and Company, 1864.

Moynihan, Daniel P. "The Negro Family: The Case for National Action," Office of Policy Planning and Research, United States Department of Labor, March 1965.

O'Neill, Thomas P., Jr., with William Novak. *Man of the House: The Life and Political Memoirs of Speaker Tip O'Neill.* New York: Random House, 1987.

Osborne, David and Peter Plastrik. *Banishing Bureaucracy: The Five Strategies for Reinventing Government.* Reading, MA: Addison-Wesley, 1997.

Osborne, David and Ted Gaebler. *Reinventing Government: How the Entrepreneurial Spirit Is Transforming the Public Sector.* Reading, MA: Addison-Wesley, 1992.

Prigogine, Ilya and Isabelle Stengers. *Order Out of Chaos: Man's New Dialogue with Nature.* New York: Bantam, 1984.

Reagan, Ronald. *Reagan: In His Own Hand,* Kiron K. Skinner, Annelise Anderson, and Martin Anderson, eds. Foreword by George P. Shultz. New York: Free Press, 2001.

Reagan, Ronald. *Reagan's Path to Victory: The Shaping of Ronald Reagan's Vision: Selected Writings,* Kiron K. Skinner, Annelise Anderson, and Martin Anderson, eds. Foreword by George P. Shultz. New York: Free Press, 2004.

Reich, Robert B. "We Are All Third Wayers Now." *The American Prospect* 43 (March–April 1999):46–51.

Reich, Robert B. *The Work of Nations: Preparing Ourselves for 21st Century Capitalism.* New York: Alfred A. Knopf, 1991.

Ricardo, David. *On the Principles of Political Economy and Taxation* in *Works of David Ricardo,* J.R. McCulloch, ed. London: John Murray, 1888.

Rousseau, Jean-Jacques. *The Social Contract and Discourses,* trans. by G.D.H. Cole. New York: E.P. Dutton, 1950.

Schmidtke, Oliver, ed. *The Third Way Transformation of Social Democracy: Normative Claims and Policy Initiatives in the 21st Century.* Hampshire, UK: Ashgate, 2002.

Senge, Peter M. *The Fifth Discipline: The Art & Practice of the Learning Organization.* New York: Doubleday/Currency, 1990.

Smith, Adam. *An Inquiry into the Nature and Causes of the Wealth of Nations,* Edwin Cannan, ed. New York: Modern Library, 1994.

Thatcher, Margaret. *The Downing Street Years: 1979–1990.* New York: HarperCollins, 1995.

Waldman, Michael. *Potus Speaks: Finding the Words That Defined the Clinton Presidency.* New York: Simon & Schuster, 2000.

Waters, Malcolm. *Globalization.* New York: Routledge, 1995.

Wilhelm, Richard (1924). *The I Ching or Book of Changes,* trans. by Cary F. Baynes. Foreword by Carl Jung. Princeton, NJ: Princeton University Press, 1997.

Wilhelm, Richard. *Lectures on the I Ching,* trans. by Irene Eber. Princeton, NJ: Princeton University Press, 1979.

Web Sites

Abraham Lincoln Association, 1 Old State Capitol Plaza, Springfield, IL 62701 • http://www.abrahamlincolnassociation.org/

American Presidency Project, John Woolley and Gerhard Peters, Department of Political Science, University of California, Santa Barbara, CA 93106 • http://www.presidency.ucsb.edu/

Avalon Project at Yale University, 127 Wall Street, New Haven CT 06520 • http://www.yale.edu/lawweb/avalon/avalon.htm

Democratic Leadership Council and the Progressive Policy Institute, 600 Pennsylvania Avenue, SE, Suite 400, Washington, DC 20003 • http://www.dlc.org/ • http://www.ppionline.org/

Fund for Peace, 1701 K Street, NW, Washington, DC 20006 • http://www.fundforpeace.org/

Hoover Institution on War, Revolution and Peace, Stanford University, 434 Galvez Mall, Stanford, CA 94305 • http://www.hoover.org/

Log Cabin Republicans, 1901 Pennsylvania Avenue, NW, Suite 902, Washington, DC 20006 • http://online.logcabin.org/

Martin Luther King, Jr., Papers Project at Stanford University, Cypress Hall D-Wing, Stanford, CA 94305-4146 • http://www.stanford.edu/group/King/

Policy Network, Third Floor, 11 Tufton Street, London SW1P 3OB, United Kingdom • http://www.policy-network.net/

Project Gutenberg Literary Archive Foundation, 809 North 1500 West, Salt Lake City, UT 84116 • http://www.gutenberg.org/

Ronald Reagan Presidential Library and Museum, 40 Presidential Drive, Simi Valley, CA 93065 • http://www.reaganlibrary.net/ • http://www.reaganlibrary.com/

United States National Archives and Records Administration, 700 Pennsylvania Avenue, NW, Washington, DC 20408 • http://www.archives.gov/

Washington Monthly, 1319 F Street, NW, Suite 710, Washington, DC 20004 • http://www.washingtonmonthly.com/

William J. Clinton Presidential Center, 1200 President Clinton Avenue, Little Rock, AR 72201 • http://www.clintonlibrary.gov/

Notes

Introduction

1. Ronald Reagan, *Farewell Address to the Nation*, January 11, 1989.
2. John Solomon and Matthew Mosk, "For Clinton, New Wealth in Speeches," *Washington Post*, February 23, 2007: A01.
3. Bill Clinton, *Speech by President on Patients' Bill in Louisville*, August 10, 1998.
4. Bill Clinton, *Speech by President via Satellite to La Raza Convention*, July 19, 1995.
5. Thanks to Steve Winn of the *San Francisco Chronicle* for that nice turn of phrase.
6. David Osborne and Peter Plastrik, *Banishing Bureaucracy: The Five Strategies for Reinventing Government*. Reading, MA: Addison-Wesley, 1997: 13–14.
7. Bill Clinton, *Remarks by President and VP at Reinventing Government Anniversary*, September 14, 1994.
8. Bill Clinton, *Speech by President at Democratic Governors Association Dinner*, February 1, 1993.
9. Michael Hammer and James Champy, *Reengineering the Corporation: A Manifesto for Business Revolution*. New York: HarperBusiness, 1993: 32.
10. Bill Clinton, *Farewell Address to the Nation*, January 18, 2001.
11. United States Department of Justice, Office of the Pardon Attorney. http://www.usdoj.gov/pardon/clintonpardon_grants.htm#january 202001

Chapter 1

1. Bill Clinton, *Speech by President to Mayors Conference,* January 27, 1995.
2. Harold Lasswell, *Politics: Who Gets What, When, How.* Meridian Books: Cleveland: 1958.
3. Bill Clinton, *Speech by President to DNC Gala,* December 11, 1997; Clinton, *Speech by President on Business Social Responsibility,* October 21, 1993; Clinton, *Speech by President to DNC Gala.*
4. Bill Clinton, *Speech by President to DNC Dinner in New York City,* March 30, 2000.
5. Bill Clinton, *Speech by President at Unity Dinner,* August 5, 1998.
6. Bill Clinton, *Speech by President at City Year Convention in Ohio,* June 3, 1998.
7. Bill Clinton, *Speech by President at Unity Dinner in Boston,* September 17, 1998.
8. Bill Clinton, *Remarks at a Democratic National Committee Dinner,* October 7, 1998; Clinton, *Speech by President to DNC Dinner,* October 7, 1998; Clinton, *Speech by President at DNC Lunch in West Palm Beach,* February 29, 2000; Clinton, *Speech by President at Dinner for Barbara Boxer,* February 28, 1998; Clinton, *My Life: The Presidential Years.* New York: Vintage Books, 2004: 134; Clinton, *Speech by President to the People of Warwick Rhode Island,* May 9, 1994; Clinton, *Remarks by the President to the American Society of Association Executives,* March 8, 1994; Clinton, *Speech by President at Florida President Dinner,* March 21, 1994.
9. Bill Clinton, *Speech by President at DNC Dinner,* September 26, 1997; Clinton, *Speech by President at DNC Dinner in New York,* February 2, 1999.
10. Bill Clinton, *Speech by President at Florida President Dinner,* March 21, 1994.
11. Bill Clinton, *Speech by President at New Democrat Network Dinner,* June 28, 2000.
12. Bill Clinton, *Speech by President to National Baptist Convention,* September 9, 1994.
13. Bill Clinton, *Speech by President in Presentation of Budget,* February 7, 2000; Clinton, *Speech by President at Health Care Rally Minneapolis,* April 8, 1994.

14. Bill Clinton, *Speech by President at DNC Dinner*, June 18, 1997.

15. Bill Clinton, *Speech by President at DNC Lunch*, September 29, 2000.

16. Bill Clinton, *State of the Union* (as delivered), February 17, 1993. Technically, this was an address on administration goals.

17. Bill Clinton, *Speech by President at DNC Gala*, May 2, 1997.

18. Bill Clinton, *Speech by President to Harley Davidson Employees*, November 10, 1999; Clinton, *Speech by President at DLC Gala*, December 6, 1994.

Chapter 2

1. Jean-Jacques Rousseau, *The Social Contract and Discourses*, trans. by G.D.H. Cole. New York: E.P. Dutton, 1950: 54.

2. John Maynard Keynes, *General Theory of Employment, Interest and Money* in *Collected Writings VII*. London: St. Martin's Press, 1973: 383.

3. Thomas Jefferson, Letter to John Trumbull, February 15, 1789. *Jefferson: Autobiography, Notes on the State of Virginia, Public and Private Papers, Address, Letters*. Merrill D. Peterson, ed. Library of America: New York, 1984: 939; John Locke, *Two Treatises of Government; A Critical Edition*, 2nd ed., Peter Laslett, ed. Cambridge: Cambridge University Press, 1967: 317.

4. Jean-Jacques Rousseau, *The Social Contract and Discourses*, 13; Cf. Ronald Reagan, *Farewell Address to the Nation*, January 11, 1989. The original source of the shining city metaphor is the Bible (Matthew 5:14–16) and a sermon by John Winthrop, governor of the Massachusetts Bay Colony.

5. Michael Hammer and James Champy. *Reengineering the Corporation: A Manifesto for Business Revolution*. New York: HarperBusiness, 1993: 49.

6. Bill Clinton, *Speech by President at Tom Harkin Reception in Des Moines*, July 16, 1999; Cf. Clinton, *Speech by President on Business Social Responsibility*, October 21, 1993; Clinton, *Speech by President at DCCC Reception*, February 25, 1998.

7. David Ricardo, *On the Principles of Political Economy and Taxation* in *Works of David Ricardo*, J.R. McCulloch, ed., London: John Murray 1888: 75–76.

8. Friedrich List, *The National System of Political Economy*, trans. by Sampson S. Lloyd. New York: Augustus M. Kelley, 1966: 11, 368.

9. Henry C. Carey, *The Harmony of Interests: Agricultural, Manufacturing &* *Commercial* (1851). New York: Augustus M. Kelley, 1967: 229.

10. Ibid., 77.

11. John Stuart Mill, *The Principles of Political Economy*. New York: D. Appleton and Company, 1864: 479, 487; John Stuart Mill, *Essays on Economics and Society* in *Collected Works IV*. London: University of Toronto Press, 1967: 157; Bill Clinton, *Remarks to Business and Labor Leaders and an Exchange with Reporters on the Economic Program*, February 25, 1993.

12. Karl Marx, *Capital: A Critique of Political Economy, Volume II: The Process of Circulation of Capital*, Frederick Engels, ed. New York: International Publishers, 1967: 186.

13. Keynes, *General Theory of Employment, Interest and Money*, 129.

14. Keynes, *General Theory of Employment, Interest and Money*, 372; Bill Clinton, *Speech by President to AFSCME Convention*, June 21, 1996.

15. Joseph A. Schumpeter, *Capitalism, Socialism and Democracy*, with a new introduction by Tom Bottomore. New York: Harper & Row, 1976: 132.

16. Schumpeter, *Capitalism, Socialism and Democracy*, 82–83; David Osborne and Ted Gaebler, *Reinventing Government: How the Entrepreneurial Spirit Is Transforming the Public Sector*. Reading, MA: Addison-Wesley, 1992: 22; Bill Clinton, *Remarks Announcing the National Performance Review*, March 3, 1993.

17. F.A. Hayek, *The Constitution of Liberty*. Chicago: University of Chicago Press, 1960: 260.

18. F.A. Hayek, *The Fatal Conceit: The Errors of Socialism* in *Collected Works*, W.W. Bartley III, ed. Chicago: University of Chicago Press, 1988: 34 (italics original), 87; John Ranelagh, *Thatcher's People: An Insider's Account of the Politics, the Power, and the Personalities*. London: HarperCollins, 1991: ix; Cf. Anthony Giddens, *The Third Way: The Renewal of Social Democracy*. Malden, MA: Blackwell, 2000: 2.

19. Cf. John Kenneth Galbraith, *The New Industrial State*. Boston: Houghton Mifflin, 1967: 310.

20. Robert B. Reich, *The Work of Nations: Preparing Ourselves for 21st Century Capitalism*. New York: Alfred A. Knopf, 1991: 259.

21. Robert Reich, personal correspondence (e-mail) with the author, September 11, 2007. Although Reich exerted a strong intellectual influence on Clinton, fortunately he does not qualify as a defunct economist as of this writing.

Chapter 3

1. Bill Clinton, *Speech by President at New York Democratic Victory Dinner,* August 28, 1999.
2. Cf. foreword by George P. Shultz in Ronald Reagan, *Reagan: In His Own Hand.* New York: Free Press, 2001.
3. Adapted from the mission statement of the Hoover Institution on War, Revolution and Peace: http://www.hoover.org/about/mission
4. Adapted from the mission statement of the Heritage Foundation: http://www.heritage.org/about/
5. Rush Limbaugh, *The Way Things Ought to Be.* New York: Simon & Schuster, 1992: 283.
6. Limbaugh, *The Way Things Ought to Be,* 2–3.
7. Log Cabin Republicans, http://online.logcabin.org/
8. Margaret Thatcher, *The Downing Street Years: 1979–1990.* New York: HarperCollins, 1995: 6–13.
9. Ronald Reagan and Margaret Thatcher, *Toasts of the President and Prime Minister Margaret Thatcher of the United Kingdom at the State Dinner,* February 26, 1981.
10. F.A. Hayek, *The Constitution of Liberty.* Chicago: University of Chicago Press, 1960: 397.
11. Cf. Edmund Burke, *Reflections on the Revolution in France* (1790). New York: Liberal Arts Press, 1955: 70.
12. Burke, *Reflections on the Revolution in France* (1790), 178–79.
13. Ibid., 122.
14. Milton Friedman with Rose D. Friedman, *Capitalism and Freedom.* Chicago: University of Chicago Press, 1982: 13; Milton Friedman and Rose D. Friedman, *Free to Choose: A Personal Statement.* New York: Harcourt Brace Jovanovich, 1980: 69; Milton Friedman with Rose D. Friedman, *Capitalism and Freedom,* 2, 176.

15. Ronald Reagan, *Address to the Nation on Tax Reform*, May 28, 1985; Reagan, *Remarks to Participants in the President's Inaugural Bands Parade at Walt Disney's EPCOT Center Near Orlando, Florida*, May 27, 1985.

16. Ronald Reagan, *Reagan's Path to Victory: The Shaping of Ronald Reagan's Vision: Selected Writings*. New York: Free Press, 2004: 90 (italics original).

17. Ronald Reagan, *Televised Campaign Address for Goldwater Presidential Campaign*, October 27, 1964.

18. Ronald Reagan, *Remarks at a Cuban Independence Day Celebration in Miami, Florida*, May 20, 1983; Reagan, *Remarks at the National Conference of the National Federation of Independent Business*, June 22, 1983.

19. Cf. Ronald Reagan, *Remarks at a Fund-Raising Luncheon for Senator Jeremiah Denton in Birmingham, Alabama*, June 6, 1985.

20. Cf. Abraham Maslow, *Toward a Psychology of Being*. Princeton, NJ: Van Nostrand, 1968.

21. Ronald Reagan, *Remarks to Polish Americans in Chicago, Illinois*, June 23, 1983; Reagan, *Remarks to the American Enterprise Institute for Public Policy Research*, December 7, 1988.

22. Reagan, *Reagan: In His Own Hand*, 143, 266.

23. Ronald Reagan, *Remarks in Denver, Colorado, at the Annual Convention of the National Association for the Advancement of Colored People*, June 29, 1981.

24. Ronald Reagan, *Address Before a Joint Session of Congress on the State of the Union*, February 4, 1986.

25. Cf. Ronald Reagan, *Interview with Managing Editors on Domestic Issues*, December 3, 1981. Cf. Thomas P. O'Neill, Jr., *Man of the House: The Life and Political Memoirs of Speaker Tip O'Neill*. New York: Random House, 1987: 349.

26. O'Neill, Jr., *Man of the House*, 336; Ronald Reagan, *Remarks at a Dinner Honoring Speaker of the House of Representatives Thomas P. O'Neill, Jr.*, March 17, 1986.

27. Ronald Reagan, *Presidential Debate with Walter Mondale (Domestic Issues)*, October 7, 1984.

28. Reagan, *Reagan: In His Own Hand*, 50.

29. "Reagan Urges Johnson to Tell Vietnam Facts," *Los Angeles Times*,

October 21, 1965; Ronald Reagan, *Radio Address to the Nation on Civil Rights*, June 15, 1985; Reagan, *The President's News Conference*, January 19, 1982.

30. Ronald Reagan, *Address to the Nation Announcing Reagan's Candidacy for Reelection*, January 29, 1984; Reagan, *The President's News Conference*, December 17, 1981; Reagan, *The President's News Conference*, January 29, 1981.

31. Irving Kristol, *Reflections of a Neoconservative: Looking Back, Looking Forward*. New York: Basic Books, 1983: 255.

32. Ronald Reagan, *Address to the Nation on the Economy*, February 5, 1981.

33. Ronald Reagan, *Reagan's Path to Victory: The Shaping of Ronald Reagan's Vision: Selected Writings*. New York: Free Press, 2004: 426; Reagan, *Remarks at a White House Reception for Members of the American Retail Federation*, May 20, 1982; Reagan, *Radio Address to the Nation on the Deficit*, November 29, 1986; Reagan, *Reagan's Path to Victory*, 164, 187, 426.

34. Reagan, *Reagan: In His Own Hand*, 274 (emphasis original); Reagan, *Reagan's Path to Victory*, 93.

35. Ronald Reagan, *Radio Address to the Nation on the Economic Recovery Program*, February 5, 1983.

36. Ronald Reagan, *Question-and-Answer Session with Students at St. Peter's Catholic Elementary School in Geneva, Illinois*, April 15, 1982.

37. Ronald Reagan, *State of the Union Address*, February 4, 1986; Reagan, *Remarks at a Conservative Political Action Conference Dinner*, February 26, 1982; Cf. Reagan, *Remarks at a White House Briefing for Supporters of Welfare Reform*, February 9, 1987; Reagan, *Reagan's Path to Victory*, 354.

38. Ronald Reagan, *Remarks and a Question-and-Answer Session at a Working Luncheon with Out-of-Town Editors*, October 16, 1981; Reagan, *Address to the Nation on Federal Tax and Budget Reconciliation Legislation*, August 16, 1982.

39. Ronald Reagan, *Remarks at a Rally Supporting the Proposed Constitutional Amendment for a Balanced Federal Budget*, July 19, 1982.

40. Ronald Reagan, *Annual Message*, February 4, 1986.

41. Bill Clinton, *Annual Message*, January 24, 1995.

42. George H.W. Bush, *Remarks of the President and Soviet Chairman Gorba-*

chev and a Question-and-Answer Session with Reporters in Malta, December 3, 1989.

43. Francis Fukuyama, *The End of History and the Last Man.* New York: Free Press, 1992.

Chapter 4

1. Thomas Cleary, *The Essential Confucius: The Heart of Confucius' Teachings in Authentic I Ching Order.* New York: HarperCollins, 1992: 115.

2. Frank White coined this phrase. See *The Overview Effect: Space Exploration and Human Evolution,* 2nd ed. Reston, VA: American Institute of Aeronautics and Astronautics, 1998.

3. Ronald Reagan, *Remarks to the People of Berlin,* June 11, 1982.

4. Bill Clinton, *Remarks to the American Society of Newspaper Editors in Annapolis,* April 1, 1993; Clinton, *Speech by President at Opening of Africa Summit,* February 17, 2000.

5. Malcolm Waters, *Globalization.* London: Routledge, 1995: 3 (italics original); Cf. Anthony Giddens, *The Third Way: The Renewal of Social Democracy.* Malden, MA: Blackwell, 2000: 31.

6. Waters, *Globalization,* 1995: 3.

7. Anthony Giddens, *Beyond Left and Right: The Future of Radical Politics.* Stanford, CA: Stanford University Press, 1994: 3–4.

8. Bill Clinton, *Speech by President on Foreign Policy,* April 7, 1999.

9. See the *2007 Failed States Index* at The Fund for Peace, http://www .fundforpeace.org

10. Sections of this chapter appeared in my doctoral dissertation: *The Peristatal System and the Deep Structure of Political Economy* (PhD dissertation, University of Hawai'i, 1995).

11. Harlan Cleveland, *The Future Executive: A Guide for Tomorrow's Managers.* New York: Harper & Row, 1972: 13; W. Edwards Deming, *The New Economics, for Industry, Government, Education.* Cambridge, MA: MIT Center for Advanced Engineering Study, 1993: 50; Kenneth D. Bailey, *Sociology and the New Systems Theory: Toward a Theoretical Synthesis.* Albany: State University of New York Press, 1994: 44; Robert Jervis, *System Effects: Complexity in Political and Social Life.* Princeton, NJ: Princeton University Press, 1997: 6. Jervis drew this definition from

the works of Herbert Simon, Anatol Rapoport, and Ludwig von Bertalanffy, among others.

12. Jervis, *System Effects*, 60.

13. Cf. Roger Lewin, *Complexity: Life at the Edge of Chaos*, 2nd ed. Chicago: University of Chicago Press, 1999: x. Lewin credits the editors of the scientific journal *Science*.

14. Ilya Prigogine coined the term and received the 1977 Nobel Prize in chemistry for his contributions to nonequilibrium thermodynamics. Cf. Ilya Prigogine and Isabelle Stengers, *Order Out of Chaos: Man's New Dialogue with Nature*. New York: Bantam, 1984.

15. Bill Clinton, *Speech by President on Foreign Policy*, February 26, 1999.

16. Bill Clinton, *Speech by President on Global Climate Change*, October 22, 1997.

17. Bill Clinton, *Interview of the President by Joe Klein of the New Yorker*, July 5, 2000.

18. Al Gore, *An Inconvenient Truth: The Planetary Emergency of Global Warming and What We Can Do About It*. New York: Rodale, 2006.

19. Cf. George W. Bush, *Remarks on the War on Terror in Annapolis, Maryland*, November 30, 2005.

20. Cf. Robert Jervis and Birute Regine in Jervis, *System Effects*, 198.

21. Bill Clinton, *Address to the Nation by the President*, August 20, 1998.

22. Bill Clinton, *Speech by President to the United Nations General Assembly*, September 21, 1998.

23. George W. Bush, *Remarks on Arrival at the White House and an Exchange with Reporters*, September 16, 2001; Bush, *President's News Conference*, October 11, 2001.

24. Bill Clinton, *Speech by President to Council on Foreign Relations*, September 14, 1998.

25. Bill Clinton, *Remarks of the President in Commemoration of the 35th Anniversary of the March on Washington*, August 28, 1998. King wrote, "We are caught in an inescapable network of mutuality, tied in a single garment of destiny. Whatever affects one directly, affects all indirectly." Martin Luther King, Jr., *Letter from Birmingham Jail*, April 16, 1963.

26. Bill Clinton, *Speech by President on Funding for Debt Relief*, November 6, 2000.

27. Bill Clinton, *Speech by President to World Bank IMF*, October 6, 1998.

28. Bill Clinton, *Inaugural Address*, January 20, 1993.

29. Cleary, *The Essential Confucius*, 67.

Chapter 5

1. Bill Clinton, *Remarks at the National Italian-American Foundation Dinner*, October 29, 1994. This passage comes from *The Prince*, Chapter 6.

2. W. Edwards Deming, *The New Economics, for Industry, Government, Education*. Cambridge, MA: MIT Center for Advanced Engineering Study, 1993:106.

3. Ibid., 1993: 55.

4. Bill Clinton, *Remarks at the Edmund A. Walsh School of Foreign Service at Georgetown University*, November 10, 1994; Cf. Clinton, *Remarks at Georgetown University*, February 9, 1998; Clinton, *Remarks on Legislative Priorities for the Budget Surplus*, February 17, 1999; Clinton, *Remarks to the Presidential Scholars*, June 25, 1999.

5. Bill Clinton, *Speech by President to DNC Luncheon*, September 20, 1997.

6. Cf. Bill Clinton, *Remarks at a National Coalition of Minority Business Award Dinner*, November 10, 1999.

7. Bill Clinton, *Remarks to the Seattle APEC Host Committee*, November 19, 1993.

8. Bill Clinton, *Speech by President to UCLA 75th Anniversary Convocation*, May 20, 1994; Cf. Clinton, *Speech by President at Naval Academy Commencement*, May 25, 1994; Clinton, *Speech by President at Coast Guard Academy Commencement*, May 22, 1996.

9. Bill Clinton, *Remarks to the International Monetary Fund and the World Bank*, October 11, 1995.

10. Bill Clinton, *Speech by President at Dinner for Garry Mauro*, June 23, 1998; Cf. Clinton, *Remarks and a Question-and-Answer Session at the Cleveland City Club*, October 24, 1994.

Chapter 6

1. Bill Clinton, *Speech by President at DNC Reception in Philadelphia*, September 25, 1996.

2. Cf. George Will in William F. Buckley and Charles R. Kesler, *Keeping the Tablets: Modern American Conservative Thought.* New York: Harper & Row, 1988: 232–33.

3. Ronald Reagan, *Inaugural Address,* January 20, 1981. Late in Clinton's first term, he gave a little ground on this issue when he said, "I accept the fact that in times past Government has been a problem." See Bill Clinton, *Remarks to Harman International Industries Employees in Northridge, California,* March 8, 1996.

4. Bill Clinton, *Annual Message,* January 25, 1994.

5. Bill Clinton, *Speech by President at Georgetown,* November 10, 1994.

6. Cf. Lou Cannon, *Remembering Reagan,* LiveOnline, *Washington Post,* June 8, 2004.

7. http://www.house.gov/house/Contract/CONTRACT.html

8. Bill Clinton, *Speech by President to Citizens of Bridgeport, CT,* October 15, 1994.

9. Bill Clinton, *My Life: The Presidential Years.* New York: Vintage Books, 2004: 222.

10. Bill Clinton, *Speech by President at DSCC Dinner in Miami,* October 16, 1994; Clinton, *My Life,* 205.

11. Bill Clinton, *Speech by President at DNC Luncheon in Sacramento,* November 15, 1997; Clinton, *Speech by President at DLC Gala,* December 6, 1994; Clinton, *Speech by President to National Jewish Democratic Council,* November 2, 1995 (italics added); Clinton, *Speech by President to National Democratic Club,* January 9, 1996.

12. Ronald Reagan, *Remarks at a Senate Campaign Rally for Christopher S. Bond in Springfield, Missouri,* October 23, 1986; Reagan, *Remarks at a Senate Campaign Fundraiser for Representative Ken Kramer in Denver, Colorado,* September 8, 1986; Reagan, *Remarks at the Annual Convention of the National Association of Broadcasters in Las Vegas, Nevada,* April 10, 1988.

13. Bill Clinton, *Speech by President SOTU Address,* January 23, 1996.

14. Bill Clinton, *Speech by President at Hispanic Dinner,* January 26, 1996.

15. "How George W. Bush Squares the Fiscally Expansive/Conservative Circle," *Wall Street Journal,* August 15, 2003.

16. George W. Bush, *Remarks on the Aftermath of Hurricane Katrina in Mobile, Alabama,* September 2, 2005.

17. Irving Kristol, *Neo-Conservatism: The Autobiography of an Idea, Selected Essays, 1949–1995.* New York: Free Press, 1995: 355.

18. Bill Clinton, *Speech by President at St. Cecilias Social Hall,* Manchester, NH, February 3, 1996.

19. Bill Clinton, *Speech by President at Reception,* July 26, 1998.

20. Benjamin R. Barber, *The Truth of Power: Intellectual Affairs in the Clinton White House.* New York: Norton, 2001: 74; Bill Clinton, *Remarks to a Democratic National Committee Meeting,* January 21, 1997; Clinton, *Speech by President in Manchester, New Hampshire,* February 17, 1996; Clinton, *Speech by President at DNC Gala at Stamford, CT,* May 22, 1996 (italics added).

21. Bill Clinton, *Speech by President to Citizens of Fort Worth, Texas,* September 27, 1996.

22. Bill Clinton, *Speech by President, Address to Nation—Inaugural,* January 20, 1997; Clinton, *Speech by President to Galesburg High School Students,* January 10, 1995.

23. Clinton credits Georgetown professor Carroll Quigley for teaching him "future preference." Benjamin Barber credits Bill Galston for the New Covenant concept. Barber, *The Truth of Power,* 25.

24. Bill Clinton, *The New Covenant: Responsibility and Rebuilding the American Community,* October 23, 1991.

25. Bill Clinton, *New Covenant for Economic Change,* November 20, 1991; Clinton, *A New Covenant for American Security, Remarks to Students at Georgetown University,* December 12, 1991 (italics added).

26. Bill Clinton, *Speech by President to the Democratic Leadership Council,* October 27, 1997; Clinton, *Speech by President at Reinventing Government Event,* March 27, 1995; Clinton, *Speech by President to the Democratic Leadership Council,* October 27, 1997; Clinton, *Speech by President at DNC Dinner in Washington, D.C.,* October 9, 1997.

27. Bill Clinton, *Speech by President to National Governors Association,* January 30, 1995; Clinton, *Speech by President, SOTU Address,* January 24, 1995; Clinton, *Speech by President to FL Legislature Joint Session,* March 30, 1995; Clinton, *Annual Message,* January 25, 1994.

28. Bill Clinton, *Speech by President to National League of Cities,* March 13, 1995. Regarding my frequent usage of the phrase "In his words"

throughout this book, see Michael Waldman, *POTUS Speaks: Finding the Words That Defined the Clinton Presidency*. New York: Simon & Schuster, 2000. According to Waldman (p. 4), although Clinton had many speechwriters, he rewrote and improvised regularly and thus gave his own speeches.

29. Bill Clinton, *Speech by President to National Association of Counties*, March 7, 1995.

30. Clinton, *The New Covenant*.

Chapter 7

1. Bill Clinton, *Speech by President at Hispanic Caucus Institute Dinner*, September 25, 1996.

2. Fyodor Dostoyevsky, *The Grand Inquisitor: With Related Chapters from The Brothers Karamazov*, ed. with an introduction by Charles B. Guignon, trans. by Constance Garnett. Indianapolis, IN: Hackett, 1993.

3. Cf. Anthony Giddens, *The Third Way: The Renewal of Social Democracy*. Malden, MA: Blackwell, 2000: 13–14, 47–48, 99.

4. The list of first-generation third way political leaders includes Jean Chrétien (Canada), Lionel Jospin (France), Wim Kok (Netherlands), Göran Persson (Sweden), Gerhard Schroeder (Germany), and Massimo D'Alema (Italy), as well as Clinton and Blair.

5. Variations of these definitions are posted on the Democratic Leadership Council's Web site: http://www.dlc.org/ and the Progressive Policy Institute's Web site: http://www.ppionline.org. See also, *The New Progressive Declaration: A Political Philosophy for the Information Age*, July 10, 1996.

6. Bill Clinton, *Speech by President at Senator Robb Victory Dinner*, October 3, 1994.

7. Bill Clinton, *My Life: The Presidential Years*. New York: Vintage Books, 2004: 256.

8. Bill Clinton, *Speech by President at Realtors Conference*, November 5, 1994.

9. Robert B. Reich, "We Are All Third Wayers Now," *The American Prospect* 43 (March–April 1999): 46–51.

10. Bill Clinton, *Speech by President at Wright Junior College in Chicago*, February 28, 1994; Clinton, *Speech by President to the University of Warwick*, December 14, 2000.

11. Bill Clinton, *Speech by President to Iowa State Legislature*, April 25, 1995; Clinton, *Speech by President at Roosevelt Commemorative Services*, April 12, 1995; Clinton, *Speech by President at DNC Dinner in Washington, D.C.*, October 9, 1997; Clinton, *Speech by President to National Governors Association*, July 28, 1997; Clinton, *Speech by President to Democratic Leadership Council*, December 11, 1996.

12. Bill Clinton, *Speech by President at New England Dinner*, March 14, 1994; Clinton, *Speech by President to Democratic National Committee (DNC) Breakfast*, October 8, 1993.

13. Daniel P. Moynihan, "The Negro Family: The Case for National Action," Office of Policy Planning and Research, United States Department of Labor, March 1965.

14. Bill Clinton, *Speech by President to the Joint Democratic Caucus*, February 12, 1998.

15. Ronald Reagan, *Remarks at a White House Reception for New Republicans*, June 10, 1985.

16. "Meditation on the Divine Will," *Collected Works of Abraham Lincoln*, *Volume 5*, Roy P. Basler, ed. Abraham Lincoln Association, 1953: 404. Online at http://www.abrahamlincolnassociation.org/

17. Bill Clinton, *Speech by President at Roosevelt Commemorative Services*, April 12, 1995.

18. Bill Clinton, *Speech by President to Iowa State Legislature*, April 25, 1995.

19. Lyndon Johnson, *Remarks at the University of Michigan*, May 22, 1964; Johnson, *Annual Message*, January 8, 1964.

20. Cf. Milton Friedman and Rose D. Friedman, *Free to Choose: A Personal Statement*. New York: Harcourt Brace Jovanovich, 1980: 70–71.

21. Cf. Milton Friedman with Rose D. Friedman, *Capitalism and Freedom*. Chicago: University of Chicago Press, 1982: 197.

22. Bill Clinton, *Speech by President to House Democrats*, July 20, 1993; Clinton, *Speech by President at Kathleen Brown Fundraiser*, October 3, 1994.

23. Bill Clinton, *Speech by President at DNC Dinner*, October 8, 1997.

24. Bill Clinton, *Speech by President at Reception for Marty Chavez*, July 27, 1998.

25. Bill Clinton, *Speech by President at the University of North Carolina as Delivered*, October 12, 1993.

26. *Democratic Party Platform of 2000*, August 14, 2000.

27. *Republican Party Platform of 2000*, July 31, 2000.

28. George W. Bush, *Memorandum on Implementing Government Reform*, July 11, 2001; *Memorandum on Electronic Government's Role in Implementing the President's Management Agenda*, July 9, 2002.

29. Thomas L. Friedman, *The World Is Flat: A Brief History of the Twenty-first Century*. New York: Picador/Farrar, Straus, and Giroux, 2007: 375–76.

30. Bill Clinton, *Speech by President upon Arrival at McClellan AFB CA*, April 7, 1995 (italics added).

31. Ronald Reagan, *Remarks to Members of the National Governors' Association*, February 23, 1987.

32. Bill Clinton, *Remarks in a Roundtable Discussion with the National Governors' Association*, February 28, 2000.

33. Ronald Reagan, *Letter to the Nation's Governors on Welfare Reform*, February 6, 1987; Reagan, *Statement on Signing the Executive Order Establishing the Presidential Advisory Committee on Federalism*, April 8, 1981; Reagan, *Executive Order 12612—Federalism*, October 26, 1987; Reagan, *Remarks at the Annual Convention of the National Association of Counties in Baltimore, Maryland*, July 13, 1982; Reagan, *Remarks at the Republican Governors Club Dinner*, October 4, 1988; Reagan, *Remarks in Atlanta, Georgia, at the Annual Convention of the National Conference of State Legislatures*, July 30, 1981; Reagan, *Interview with Reporters from the* Los Angeles Times, January 20, 1982.

34. Bill Clinton, *Executive Order 13083—Federalism*, May 14, 1998, superseded by *Executive Order 13132—Federalism*, August 4, 1999.

35. Ronald Reagan, *Remarks to Members of the National Governors' Association*, February 22, 1988.

36. Bill Clinton, *Speech by President to Conference of Mayors*, June 20, 1995.

37. Bill Clinton, *Speech by President at Democratic Dinner Miami, Florida*, April 29, 1996.

38. Bill Clinton, *Speech by President to Maryland State Legislature*, February 10, 1997; Clinton, *Speech by President at Cleveland City Club*, October 24, 1994; Clinton, *Speech by President at Business Roundtable*, June 12, 1997.

39. Clinton, *Speech by President at Cleveland City Club*.

40. Bill Clinton, *Speech by President to the Economic Club of Detroit*, January 8, 1999 (italics added); Clinton, *Speech by President at NJ President Gala*, June 22, 1995; Clinton, *My Life*, 94; Clinton, *Speech by President at Democratic Business Council*, January 28, 1997; Clinton, *Speech by President at Cuomo Dinner in NYC*, October 19, 1994.

41. Bill Clinton, *Speech by President, SOTU Address*, January 24, 1995; Clinton, *Speech by President to the People of Macon, GA*, October 25, 1996; Cf. Clinton, *Speech by President to People of Denver, CO*, October 30, 1996; Cf. Clinton, *Speech by President at DNC Dinner in New Orleans*, July 20, 1998; Clinton, *Address to Nation on Economic Reform*, February 15, 1993.

42. Ronald Reagan, *Remarks in Denver, Colorado, at the Annual Convention of the National Association for the Advancement of Colored People*, June 29, 1981.

Chapter 8

1. Ronald Reagan, *Remarks to Business Leaders During a White House Briefing on Budget Reform*, March 13, 1987.

2. Bill Clinton, *Speech by President to American Federation of Teachers*, July 28, 1995.

3. Business consultant and author Eli Goldratt popularized the theory of constraints. Cf. Eliyahu M. Goldratt and Jeff Cox, *The Goal: A Process of Ongoing Improvement*, 2nd rev. ed. Great Barrington, MA: North River Press, 1992.

4. Ronald Reagan, *Remarks at the Conservative Political Action Conference Dinner*, March 20, 1981.

5. Ronald Reagan, *Radio Address to the Nation on the State of the Union*, January 25, 1986.

6. Ronald Reagan, *Radio Address to the Nation on the Deficit*, November 29, 1986.

7. Bill Clinton, *Interview with the* Chicago Tribune, the Los Angeles Times, *and* USA Today, February 10, 2000.

8. Bill Clinton, *Speech by President to Conference on Political Tradition*, Octo-

ber 5, 2000; Clinton, *Speech by President in San Francisco*, October 4, 1993.

9. Bill Clinton, *Remarks by the President to the National Federation of Independent Businesses*, June 29, 1993 (italics added).

10. Bill Clinton, *Speech by President to Greater Houston Partnership*, February 7, 1994; Clinton, *Speech by President at DNC Dinner in California*, October 1, 1999.

11. Bill Clinton, *Speech by President to Small Business Leaders*, May 11, 1993.

12. Cf. Bill Clinton, *Speech by President to Business Roundtable*, June 21, 1994; Clinton, *Speech by President to the Citizens of Cleveland*, May 10, 1993.

13. Bill Clinton, *Speech by President to the People of Longview, WA*, September 19, 1996.

14. Bill Clinton, *Speech by President to IMF and World Bank*, September 29, 1999; Clinton, *Speech by President on Foreign Policy*, February 26, 1999; Clinton, *Remarks by the President to the People of Philadelphia*, May 28, 1993; Clinton, *Speech by President at West Point*, May 29, 1993; Clinton, *Speech by President to the Los Alamos Community*, May 17, 1993; Clinton, *Speech by President to World Economic Forum in Switzerland*, January 29, 2000.

15. Bill Clinton, *Remarks to the Community in Milwaukee, Wisconsin*, June 1, 1993.

16. Ronald Reagan, *Remarks in Chicago, Illinois, at the Annual Convention and Centennial Observance of the United Brotherhood of Carpenters and Joiners*, September 3, 1981.

17. Bill Clinton, *Remarks by President in Addressing the Future of Entitlements Conference*, December 13, 1993.

18. Ronald Reagan, *Annual Message*, January 26, 1982.

19. Bill Clinton, *Speech by President to Business Council Dinner*, February 22, 1995.

20. Bill Clinton, *Remarks and an Exchange with Reporters on Health Care Reform*, January 25, 1993.

21. Ronald Reagan, *Reagan: In His Own Hand*. New York: Free Press, 2001: 365–67 (italics original).

22. Bill Clinton, *Remarks to the Business Roundtable*, June 21, 1994; Clinton,

Speech by President, Address to Joint Session of Congress as Delivered, September 22, 1993; Cf. Abraham Maslow, *Toward a Psychology of Being*. Princeton, NJ: Van Nostrand, 1968.

23. Bill Clinton, *Speech by President on Health Care for Children*, June 23, 1997.

24. Bill Clinton, *Speech by President to General Motors Workers Shreveport, Louisiana*, February 8, 1994.

25. Bill Clinton, *Speech by President at Glendale Community College*, June 11, 1996.

26. Bill Clinton, *Speech by President at Child Care Event*, April 23, 1998 (italics added).

27. Bill Clinton, *Address Before a Joint Session of the Congress on the State of the Union*, January 25, 1994.

28. Bill Clinton, *Annual Message*, January 25, 1994.

29. Bill Clinton, *Speech by President to National Association of Counties*, March 7, 1995.

30. Ronald Reagan, *Remarks and a Panel Discussion with Community Leaders on Welfare Reform*, February 11, 1987.

31. Bill Clinton, *Speech by President at Weave Center Sacramento, CA*, July 23, 1996.

32. Cf. Milton Friedman and Rose D. Friedman, *Free to Choose: A Personal Statement*. New York: Harcourt Brace Jovanovich, 1980: 119.

33. Ronald Reagan, *Remarks in Denver, Colorado, at the Annual Convention of the National Association for the Advancement of Colored People*, June 29, 1981.

34. Bill Clinton, *Speech by President to Louisiana Legislature*, May 30, 1996.

35. George W. Bush, *Executive Orders 13198 and 13199*, January 29, 2001.

36. Bill Clinton, *Speech by President at DNC Dinner in Austin, Texas*, May 7, 1999; Clinton, *Speech by President to Majority in Massachusetts*, April 16, 1999.

37. Bill Clinton, *Speech by President at Mayors Conference Breakfast*, January 28, 2000.

38. Bill Clinton, *Speech by President to National Association of Black Journalists*, July 17, 1997; Clinton, *Speech by President at American University*, September 9, 1997.

39. Bill Clinton, *Speech by President on Religious Liberties*, July 12, 1995.

40. Bill Clinton, *Speech by President at University of Texas at Austin*, October 16, 1995.

41. Ibid.

42. John Kennedy, *Executive Order 10925*, March 6, 1961. Lyndon Johnson signed a similar one, *Executive Order 11246*, on September 24, 1965.

43. Bill Clinton, *Speech by President on Affirmative Action*, July 19, 1995; ibid.

44. Bill Clinton, *Speech by President via Satellite to La Raza Convention*, July 19, 1995 (italics added); Clinton, *Speech by President to the United Michigan Clergy*, October 21, 1996; Clinton, *Speech by President on Affirmative Action*; Clinton, *Speech by President at Democratic Senatorial Reception*, May 21, 1997; Clinton, *Speech by President to the U.S. Conference of Mayors, Cleveland*, June 22, 1996; Clinton, *Speech by President at DNC Gala at Stamford, CT*, May 22, 1996.

45. Bill Clinton, *Speech by President at King Commemorative Service*, January 15, 1996.

46. Martin Luther King, Jr., "I've Been to the Mountaintop," April 3, 1968. Martin Luther King, Jr. Papers Project at Stanford University, http://www.stanford.edu/group/King/

47. Bill Clinton, *Speech by President Address at Howard University*, January 17, 1994.

48. Bill Clinton, *Speech by President in Commemoration of MLK March*, August 28, 1998.

49. Bill Clinton, *Speech by President at Dartmouth College Commencement*, June 11, 1995.

50. George W. Bush, *Remarks on Presenting the Presidential Medal of Freedom*, July 9, 2002.

51. Peter Drucker, *The Age of Discontinuity: Guidelines to Our Changing Society*. New York: Harper & Row, 1969. See also Peter Drucker, *The Effective Executive*. New York: Harper & Row, 1967.

52. Robert B. Reich, *The Work of Nations: Preparing Ourselves for 21st Century Capitalism*. New York: Alfred A. Knopf, 1991: 177, 229.

53. W. Edwards Deming, *The New Economics for Industry, Government, Edu-*

cation. Cambridge, MA: MIT Center for Advanced Engineering Study, 1993: 107.

54. Bill Clinton, *Annual Message*, January 25, 1994.

55. Reagan, *Reagan: In His Own Hand*, 350.

56. Bill Clinton, *Speech by President to National School Board Association*, February 1, 1999.

57. "A Nation at Risk: The Imperative for Educational Reform," *Report to the Nation and the Secretary of Education by the National Commission on Excellence in Education*, April 1983.

58. Bill Clinton, *Speech by President in Session Two of Third Way Conference*, November 21, 1999.

59. George H.W. Bush, *Remarks at the Education Summit Farewell Ceremony at the University of Virginia in Charlottesville*, September 28, 1989. George Bush singled out Clinton again during his *Annual Message*, January 31, 1990.

60. George W. Bush, *Remarks on the Anniversary of the No Child Left Behind Act*, January 8, 2003.

61. George W. Bush, *Remarks on Signing the No Child Left Behind Act of 2001 in Hamilton, Ohio*, January 8, 2002; *Remarks on Implementation of the No Child Left Behind Act of 2001*, January 9, 2002.

62. See "Issues & Agenda," http://kennedy.senate.gov/index.cfm

63. Bill Clinton, *Speech by President to North Carolina Legislature*, March 13, 1997.

64. Jimmy Carter, *Remarks and a Question-and-Answer Session at the National Convention of the Order of the Sons of Italy in America*, August 7, 1979.

65. George H.W. Bush, *Remarks on Signing the Immigration Act of 1990*, November 29, 1990.

66. Ronald Reagan, *Farewell Address to the Nation*, January 11, 1989.

67. Bill Clinton, *Remarks at the Signing Ceremony for the Supplemental Agreements to the North American Free Trade Agreement*, September 14, 1993; Clinton, *Speech by President to DNC Luncheon in San Diego*, May 16, 1999; Clinton, *Remarks to American Troops at Camp Bondsteel, Kosovo*, November 23, 1999.

68. Bill Clinton, *Speech by President to the United Michigan Clergy*, October 21, 1996.

69. Bill Clinton, *Speech by President at State Democratic 100 Club Dinner*, February 18, 1999.

70. Bill Clinton, *Speech by President at Portland State University Commencement*, June 13, 1998.

71. Bill Clinton, *Commencement Address at Portland State University in Portland, Oregon*, June 13, 1998; Clinton, *Remarks to the Congressional Hispanic Caucus Institute*, September 16, 1993.

72. Bill Clinton, *Speech by President at NAFTA Product Day*, October 20, 1993; Clinton, *Remarks by the President to the* Wall Street Journal, Second Annual Conference on the Americas, October 28, 1993; Clinton, *Speech by President to NAFTA Opinion Leaders*, November 9, 1993; Clinton, *Speech by President at NAFTA Event*, November 2, 1993; Clinton, *Speech by President to NAFTA Opinion Leaders*, November 9, 1993; Clinton, *Speech by President on the Economy*, April 20, 1999.

73. Bill Clinton, *Speech by President at NAFTA Bill Signing Ceremony*, December 8, 1993.

74. Bill Clinton, *Speech by President on the California Economy with Business and Political Leaders*, December 4, 1993; Clinton, *Speech by President at NAFTA Product Day*.

75. David Gergen, *Eyewitness to Power: The Essence of Leadership, Nixon to Clinton*. New York: Simon & Schuster, 2000: 281–84.

76. Ronald Reagan, *Radio Address to the Nation on Free and Fair Trade*, August 31, 1985.

77. Bill Clinton, *Remarks on Signing the Uruguay Round Agreements Act*, December 8, 1994; Clinton, *Speech by President at Baldridge Awards*, December 14, 1993; Clinton, *Remarks by the President upon Arrival, Boeing Field, Seattle, Washington*, November 18, 1993; Clinton, *Speech by President to Hong Kong Chamber of Commerce*, July 3, 1998; Clinton, *Speech by President to World Economic Forum in Switzerland*, January 29, 2000; Clinton, *Speech by President to Korean National Assembly*, July 10, 1993; Clinton, *Remarks on United States Foreign Policy in San Francisco*, February 26, 1999.

78. Bill Clinton, *Remarks by the President with the American Business Community*, January 11, 1994. The ten members were Bulgaria, Czech Republic, Estonia, Hungary, Latvia, Lithuania, Poland, Romania,

Slovakia, and Slovenia. On May 1, 2004, eight of these became members of the European Union. The other two, Romania and Bulgaria, became members in 2007.

79. Bill Clinton, *Speech by President to WTO Ministers at Luncheon in Seattle*, December 1, 1999.

80. *Republican Party Platform of 2000*, July 31, 2000.

81. Ronald Reagan, *Statement Announcing Actions Against Terrorism*, June 20, 1985.

82. U.S. Government Printing Office, *Public Report of the Vice President's Task Force on Combating Terrorism*, February 1986.

83. *Presidential Debate in Boston*, October 3, 2000.

84. "The Uses of Military Power," *Remarks Prepared for Delivery by the Hon. Caspar Weinberger, Secretary of Defense to the National Press Club*, November 28, 1984.

85. George W. Bush, *Address to a Joint Session of Congress and the American People*, September 20, 2001; *President Commemorates 60th Anniversary of V-J Day*, August 30, 2005; *President Discusses War on Terror at National Endowment for Democracy*, October 6, 2005.

Chapter 9

1. Bill Clinton, *Remarks at a Victory 2000 Dinner in East Hampton, New York*, August 28, 1999.

2. George W. Bush, *Inaugural Address*, January 20, 2005.

3. Bill Clinton, *Speech by President at Green Bay, WI, Labor Day Picnic*, September 2, 1996.

4. David Gergen, *Eyewitness to Power: The Essence of Leadership, Nixon to Clinton*. New York: Simon & Schuster, 2000: 347–48.

5. Charles Krauthammer, "Clawing for a Legacy," *Washington Post*, February 1, 2008: A21.

6. Ronald Reagan, *Republican National Convention Acceptance Speech*, July 17, 1980.

7. Franklin Roosevelt, *Inaugural Address*, January 20, 1937.

Index